How N(
a B.

Also by C.J. Williams
and from McFarland

Sentencing Advocacy: Principles and Strategy
(McFarland, 2022)

How Not to Rob a Bank

And Other Stories from 20 Years as a Federal Prosecutor

C.J. Williams

Jefferson, North Carolina

ISBN (print) 978-1-4766-9021-6
ISBN (ebook) 978-1-4766-4836-1

Library of Congress and British Library
cataloguing data are available

Library of Congress Control Number 2022049774

Printed in the United States of America

Exposit is an imprint of McFarland & Company, Inc., Publishers

Exposit
Box 611, Jefferson, North Carolina 28640
www.expositbooks.com

Table of Contents

Introduction

I became an Assistant United States Attorney in July 1997 and served in that capacity in the Northern District of Iowa until I became a federal judge in 2016. In that nearly two-decade period I had the privilege of representing the United States in almost 1,000 cases, some of which resulted in trials, many of which were fascinating, all of which were important at least to the offender I was prosecuting. I was very fortunate to be assigned to most of the significant cases in our district during that time, and to serve on a detail in Washington, D.C., that allowed me to work on cases in a half-dozen other districts across the United States.

During most of my service Sali VanWeelden was my right hand, serving first as a legal assistant and then as a paralegal. She was instrumental assisting me in my most important cases. When I became a judge, she joined my staff as my judicial assistant. She continues to be my right hand.

I have been on the bench now for seven years. During that time, I have occasionally regaled my law clerks with stories of my years prosecuting federal criminal cases. Sali often accompanies me on these trips down memory lane, occasionally tactfully correcting my errant memory. I suppose my faulty memory has altered some of the facts, perhaps embellished some details, and conveniently erased my many errors. Nevertheless, my law clerks seem to find the stories interesting, however divorced from factual accuracy they may be.

Thus, it occurred to me that perhaps I should write down my memories now, while they are still relatively fresh and only moderately altered by my cognitive dissonance. What follows is, in rough chronological order, a series of stories about cases I prosecuted while serving as a federal prosecutor. The label "stories" is intentional; I don't here purport to recite all the facts of the cases or even guarantee that the recitations are completely factually accurate. Rather, these are my memories of the cases. I have changed the names of all defendants for that reason, referring to them by nickname or descriptive label only. As for the outstanding prosecutors, law enforcement officers, and others I worked with over the years, I would love to mention them by name if only because they deserve praise for their work. But they also deserve their privacy and may not wish to have their names associated with this book. So, alas, I haven't used their names either.

The value of these stories lay not in their role as a history of criminal cases but in their role as a study of the human drama involved in criminal cases and, in some instances and to some degree, in their role of teaching others what to do and more often what not to do as a prosecutor. I have attempted to make each of these chapters as short as possible, relating only highlights and the salient facts and events, rather than recount every twist and turn in the cases. I have, as much as possible, refrained from delving into legal details, procedures, or issues. For some stories, this wasn't difficult as their value lay in a single episode or simple event and the rest of the case and prosecution was routine and un-noteworthy. For others, however, condensing the stories was extremely difficult. Several could easily, and perhaps should someday, justify and support full-length books. For these longer chapters I apologize for their length; both that they are too short and that they are too long. I likely omitted that which I should have included, and included that which I should have omitted.

Some of these stories are funny, too many others are tragic. Some, the reader must be forewarned, involve graphic descriptions of violence and vulgar language. No matter what the tone, I mean no disrespect to anyone mentioned in this book, including criminal defendants and certainly not victims. It has been my experience that the vast majority of criminal offenders are good people at their core who have made grievous errors in judgment. I can count on one hand the number of criminal defendants I prosecuted whom I considered truly evil. Crime victims can encompass a broad group including not only the direct victims of a crime but also the indirect victims. This category, in my mind, rightfully includes the offenders' families, friends and loved ones.

I haven't attempted to recount every case I worked. Nor, unfortunately, have I tried to reference every co-worker or law enforcement agent who taught, aided, supported, and made me a better prosecutor and person. To those I failed to reference in this book, I'm sorry. I remember you all and the failure to reference your contribution wasn't intended as a slight in any way.

In any event, here are my stories. My hope is that the reader finds them entertaining, somewhat informative, and perhaps thought-provoking.

Chapter 1

Don't Make a Federal Case Out of It!

When I began at the United States Attorney's Office I was immediately assigned several cases. We'll call them what they were: dogs. They were the rejects other prosecutors wanted to dump for various reasons. As is often the case, the rookie in the office gets the reject cases to take over. I was also assigned two areas of specialty I was expected to develop, also considered dogs: bankruptcy fraud and environmental crimes. As it turned out, several of the so-called dog cases ended up being quite captivating, and I enjoyed the bankruptcy fraud and environmental crimes duties.

One of the first of such cases assigned to me came from the criminal chief and resulted in my first trial in the district. The Criminal Chief was a legend in the United States Attorney's Office even then. He went on to serve another twenty-five years and retire as the longest-serving prosecutor in the history of the Northern District of Iowa. He was known then and to this day as a dogged prosecutor who worked tirelessly, and pursued every angle possible, to ensure that cases were properly and full prosecuted.

Before I started at the office, the Criminal Chief had initiated the prosecution of suspects involved in a hate crime in Dubuque, Iowa. A group of young, white men harbored racial animus toward blacks. When the former girlfriend of one of these guys began dating a black coworker at the daycare center where they both worked, the white men began a campaign of harassment and intimidation against the couple. This included vandalism and graffiti containing racial slurs and symbols, along with threatening notes and packages. The conduct culminated in the detonation of an improvised explosive device, a pipe bomb, outside the daycare center, causing substantial damage, but fortunately no injuries.

The criminal chief approached the case in his typical fashion: by working with the Federal Bureau of Investigation (FBI) and other law enforcement agencies to thoroughly investigate the case, identify suspects, and look for weak links in the group. This is a common prosecutorial strategy I learned from the criminal chief. It involves trying to determine if any member of a criminal group or organization, or their supporters, committed any federal crime, even if it isn't the primary crime then under investigation. If a prosecutor can uncover another crime, it can be used to put pressure on the person to cooperate against others in the group. It can also sometimes serve as a means of arresting and incarcerating a dangerous person even if there is never enough evidence to prosecute the target for the crime that led to the investigation in the first place.

In this particular case, the criminal chief learned that this group of white men were also involved in other somewhat petty crimes, such as thefts. Among other crimes, he discovered that members of this group stole motorcycles. The theft of a motorcycle isn't a federal offense. That is, it isn't a federal offense unless one takes the stolen motorcycle across a state line.

Dubuque is an old river town hugging the western shore of the Mississippi River. Directly across the river is East Dubuque, Illinois. A bridge allows for quick and easy access over the river. On one occasion, some of the men in this group stole a motorcycle valued at $85 from East Dubuque and brought it back to Iowa. It is a federal offense for anyone to transport a motor vehicle across state lines knowing that it is stolen, regardless of the vehicle's value.

Thus, the criminal chief began an investigation into the stolen motorcycle and developed evidence identifying the member of the group who stole the motorcycle. The criminal chief sent a rather new FBI agent out to talk to the suspect.

The raw FBI agent turned out to be one of the finest FBI agents I worked with. He was dedicated and focused, thorough and thoughtful. Most of all, he was as honest as the day is long. Incidentally, he didn't look like what I think of the typical FBI agent. He was somewhat thin, short, spoke quietly, and was mild-mannered.

The FBI agent went to the suspect's house and spoke with the suspect outside his house. The agent questioned the suspect who made some incriminating statements about the motorcycle theft and also about the pipe bombing. When the suspect said he wanted to speak to an attorney, the FBI agent ended the conversation and left.

A few days later the criminal chief sent the FBI agent back to the suspect a second time not to question him but to tell the suspect he would be charged, should get a lawyer, and have that lawyer contact the criminal chief. The FBI agent dutifully went back to visit the suspect and delivered the message as instructed. The suspect immediately informed the FBI agent that he was already represented by counsel and didn't want to talk to the agent. The agent thanked the suspect and turned to leave without asking any questions. But as the FBI agent was leaving, the suspect made an incriminating statement even though the agent hadn't asked him any questions. The agent knew it would violate the suspect's constitutional rights to ask him questions once the suspect informed the agent he was represented by counsel, so the FBI agent left without responding. When he got back to the office, though, the agent wrote a report about the incriminating statement the suspect had volunteered.

A grand jury shortly thereafter returned an indictment against the suspect, charging him with aiding and abetting the interstate transportation of the motorcycle, conspiracy to commit that crime, and obstruction of justice. Contrary to the criminal chief's hope, the suspect didn't feel compelled to cooperate and assist the criminal chief in his quest to solve the bombing case. The criminal chief doggedly followed other leads and other avenues, though, and ultimately convicted the men responsible for the bombing. This suspect wasn't among them. Meanwhile, the suspect's case proceeded toward trial.

This is when I came in. By the time I started in the office in the summer of 1997, the criminal chief already had plea agreements signed by the bombers and the bombing investigation was wrapped up while this tangential case remained on the docket and headed to trial over a stolen $85 motorcycle. The criminal chief assigned the case to me, the rookie, so that he could turn to more important and interesting cases.

Within the first month I was in the office there was a hearing on a motion to suppress evidence in the case. Because I wasn't yet up to speed on the case, the criminal chief said he'd handle the hearing, but had me watch because it would help me learn the case. The motion to suppress evidence turned on an allegation that the FBI agent had violated the suspect's constitutional right by questioning him during the second visit. The hearing was before a judge who was known to have a temper and a predisposition against the government and law enforcement officers. Nevertheless, that hearing went smoothly. The FBI agent testified that he delivered the message from the criminal chief, asked no questions and that the suspect had volunteered the incriminating statement as the FBI agent was leaving and not in response to any question the agent had asked. The judge credited the FBI agent's testimony, found that the agent hadn't violated the suspect's constitutional rights, and denied the motion to suppress the incriminating statement.

About a month later, the case came on for a jury trial. I was trying the case alone; my first solo flight. We were somewhere in the middle of the trial when I called the FBI agent to testify. After some preliminary questions I turned toward the topic of the defendant's incriminating statements. I intended to ask about them in chronological order; first the statements the suspect made during the first visit when the FBI agent questioned the suspect, and then the unsolicited incriminating statements the suspect made when the agent went to deliver the criminal chief's message during the second visit.

I was halfway through questioning the FBI agent about the first visit when, in answering my questions, the agent began to relate the questions he asked the suspect and the answers the suspect provided. From the corner of my eye I caught growing agitation in the judge's demeanor as the agent continued to testify, but I was at a loss about why the judge was getting upset.

"Stop," the judge suddenly yelled. "No more questions. Ladies and gentlemen of the jury, I have a matter I need to take up with the parties so I'm sending you out for a brief recess."

As the jury filed out of the courtroom I looked at the judge and could see him turning red. He was clearly very angry about something and my mind was reeling trying to figure out what it was that he could possibly be upset about. The FBI agent, too, was aware that the judge was very angry. We, both rookies, had heard many stories about this judge's anger and how he had it out for law enforcement officers. If a judge finds a law enforcement officer lied, especially while under oath, it essentially ends the officer's career. Under the law, the government must disclose that fact to the defense in every case that officer testifies in the future. That is so damaging to an officer's credibility that the officer is virtually worthless as a witness henceforward and if the officer doesn't resign, the officer is often put out to pasture, assigned to be in charge of the evidence room or some other duty that would never require the officer to testify.

All of this was going through the agent's mind, and mine, as we sat there waiting for the jury to leave, and yet neither of us knew what was coming.

As soon as the jury was out of the room, the judge exploded. I don't recall today the exact words he used, but it was something along the line of: "Agent, you have lied! You have betrayed your oath! You committed perjury in front of me and by God you will pay! You testified not a month ago in the suppression hearing that when you visited the suspect, you just passed on the criminal chief's message and didn't ask a single question. You swore under oath you didn't ask the defendant anything. And now all I've heard for the past fifteen minutes is about all the questions you asked him! You lied!"

The agent was in shock. His eyes were wide open, his mouth agape, and he began sweating profusely. Several times he tried to start saying something but the judge just kept yelling at him.

By now I was on my feet. Indeed, I had been on my feet since about the third word out of the judge's mouth. It had dawned on me that the judge was somehow unaware that there were two conversations with the suspect; the first one before the suspect had an attorney and the second one after he had an attorney. During the first interview, the agent asked questions and could do so without violating the suspect's constitutional rights. But the judge was confused and thought that the agent was talking about the second visit when the agent couldn't, and didn't, ask the suspect any questions.

As the judge continued to yell at the agent the judge saw me from the corner of his eye and realized that I had something to say. As unhinged as this judge could be at times, he was also very smart and so it suddenly clicked in his head that he could be mistaken and there perhaps could be more than one time the agent talked to the suspect.

"You lied to me under oath!" the judge said, and then hesitated as he glanced at me. "That is, … that is unless.… Did you talk to the suspect more than once?"

"Yes, your honor," came the FBI agent's shaky response.

In less than a minute of explanation I had satisfied the judge that he had made an honest mistake, there were two interactions with the suspect, that the FBI agent hadn't violated the suspect's rights, that the agent hadn't lied in the prior hearing, and that all was well in the world. The judge simply said something like "fine," called the jury back into the room, and we continued with the trial as if nothing had happened.

We won the trial.

The judge never apologized to the agent for accusing him of committing perjury. I strongly suspect the agent suffered from post-traumatic judge disorder or some such thing. Years later the agent could laugh about it, but he had seen his career flash before his eyes that day.

Chapter 2

Bungling Burglars

Another case I tried early in my career was an attempted bank robbery. I was excited to try a bank robbery case. Somehow it seemed like the quintessential federal crime with fascinating facts involving guns, violence, getaway cars and all the other stuff of which crime shows and old westerns are made. So, I was happy when my criminal chief assigned the case to me. It was also a great experience because I got to work with another outstanding FBI agent and an all-around quality guy. I ended up working with this particular agent in many more cases over the next two decades.

One of the two defendants involved in the attempted holdup, the getaway driver, pled guilty, cooperated with us, and ultimately testified against the other robber who went to trial and was convicted. The interesting part of this story isn't the trial and has nothing to do with me. The interesting part is the story of this duncey duo who attempted the bank robbery. I will call them Mutt and Jeff, with Jeff being the getaway driver. Much of the story came from Jeff after he chose to cooperate. He sat down to talk with the FBI agent and me. His defense attorney brought donuts to the debrief, as I recall. Jeff turned out to be a nice, if not too bright, man. I recall that he particularly liked jelly donuts which he ate while handcuffed, sitting in one of the conference rooms in the courthouse as he recounted what occurred. Here's the story according to Jeff.

Mutt and Jeff met while in prison in Georgia. As it turned out, they were both to be released from prison within a week of each other. I don't recall the crimes for which they were in prison at the time, but after they became buddies they decided that whatever they had been before they would now become bank robbers. Mutt was the brains of the duo, though that is a very generous description. Mutt was a short, pudgy man in his mid–30s with a prematurely receding hairline and an ugly mug. Jeff was tall and lanky, whose natural facial façade included an open mouth and a lost expression.

When they got out of prison, the first thing they decided to do was to get out of Georgia. Mutt was from that state, had been in trouble with the law since childhood, and was convinced that every law enforcement officer in the state knew him on a first-name basis. When they were released from prison, they met in a small town northwest of Atlanta where they were supposed to check into a halfway house. On their way there, they came across a church and in the church parking lot was a large passenger van with the church's logo on the side. Trusting in God, the pastor had left the keys in the van. Mutt and Jeff considered this as manna from heaven. It was actually a Dodge from Detroit.

Mutt and Jeff stole the van and hit the road. Their road trip took them from Georgia to Arkansas. In Arkansas, they dumped the church van and stole another car when they found the keys inside. They put the church van's license plates on the stolen car. Jeff, who had found God in prison, decided that he should retain the Bible he found in the van, figuring that God would forgive him this trespass. The retention of the Bible, it later turned out, was the only link law enforcement had to Mutt and Jeff stealing the church van for which they were later held accountable. After their arrest, officers found the Bible in the back seat of the stolen car. Perhaps God forgave Jeff, but the government didn't.

In any event, they drove the stolen car north and into Missouri. While driving the back roads of Missouri, Mutt exercised his considerable intellect to develop a plan for committing bank robberies. He figured the key was to find a small-town bank because they had plenty of money, but little in the way of technology like cameras and other security measures. Mutt and Jeff didn't have a gun, but Mutt said he'd hold his hand in his coat pocket and claim he had a gun. He was confident that a hick, small-town teller would believe him. Mutt also reasoned that if the town was small enough it wouldn't even have its own police force. That would mean, in Mutt's estimation, that the bank would rely on the understaffed county sheriff's office. Mutt figured that by the time the law enforcement officers learned about the bank robbery Mutt and Jeff would be long gone.

As they drove the back roads north through Missouri they came to what Mutt decided was the ideal town. It was a one-stoplight town of about a thousand quiet citizens, no police department, and a very small bank. Mutt had Jeff drive through the town several times so Mutt could case out the bank and an escape route out of town. It was better than Mutt could dream of, he said. In all the times they drove by the bank they didn't see a single customer go into or come out of the bank. Mutt concluded this was such a sleepy little town that the bank robbery would be a cinch. Eventually Mutt told Jeff to park the car around the corner from the bank. Mutt pulled out a bandana and tied it around his face like in an old western, got out of the car and struck forth toward the bank with deliberate and confident strides. In a second he turned the corner and Jeff lost sight of him.

Jeff, who had never robbed a bank before, was very nervous. He kept the car running, his hands on the wheel, sweating and looking nervously all around him sure that they would soon be caught. In less than a couple minutes, though, what he saw wasn't flashing lights but Mutt slowly come around the corner of the bank, his bandana pulled down around his neck, a dejected look on his face. Jeff was totally perplexed as Mutt opened the car door, flopped down in the seat, and slammed the door.

"What the hell?"

"The fuckin bank's closed!" Mutt exclaimed.

It turned out that it happened to be President's Day, a bank holiday. Mutt and Jeff saw no one going in and out of the bank because the bank wasn't open.

Frustrated in Missouri, Mutt and Jeff continued north, crossed the border into Iowa, and ultimately arrived in Waterloo where Jeff's great aunt lived. Mutt and Jeff crashed on her couches for a couple days, enjoying home cooked meals, while Mutt continued to plot the ideal bank robbery. Among other things, Mutt found a ski mask and an old BB gun in the garage. After searching around a bit, they found a hacksaw and sawed off the barrel of the BB gun to make it look more like a real firearm. Mutt also identified some small towns on an Iowa map he believed would be ideal for their next heist. He settled on a small town in north central Iowa, an hour's drive north of the state capital in Des Moines and only about twelve miles east of Interstate 35. Mutt figured that the proximity of the interstate would make for a quick getaway after the heist. He also checked the calendar this time for bank holidays.

A couple days later Mutt and Jeff bid farewell to Jeff's great aunt, thanking her for her hospitality and for the home-baked cookies she sent along with them. They drove directly to the small town in their stolen car. They arrived mid-morning on a quiet Tuesday in early March. As in Missouri, this was a one-stoplight town of about a thousand people. The business district was two blocks long with a barbershop, a hardware store, a convenience store, a small café, and several empty storefronts. And a bank. A very small bank that occupied one corner of the business district, such as it was. The bank was in a one-story brick building built in the late 1800s. The entrance to the bank was built into the corner of the building. Inside was a small lobby with a single teller station, a small office off to the side, and behind the teller the bank vault. Only a few months before the robbery the bank installed a single security camera above and behind the teller's station that captured the back of the teller's station and the entire lobby, including the front door of the bank. Fortunately for our entertainment value, it also included audio recording capability, an unusual feature for bank security cameras.

Mutt and Jeff drove around the small town for close to an hour checking out the roads out of town toward the interstate, making sure the town didn't have a police station, and searching for any sign of a law enforcement presence. Finding none and satisfied with the escape route, Mutt had Jeff park the car about a block from the bank with a view of the front door so that they could watch the bank for a while. This time Mutt was determined to make sure at least someone entered or left the bank before he attempted to rob it. Before long they saw a woman enter the bank and a short time later walk out and drive away. Satisfied that the bank was indeed open, Mutt instructed Jeff to drive around the block and park the car on the side road next to the bank, and out of view of the windows on the side of the bank.

Once again Mutt prepared to rob the bank. He donned the ski mask and pulled it down over his face, adjusting it to make sure he could see out of the eye holes. Then he grabbed the sawed-off BB gun, held it inside his unzipped coat, and jumped out of the car, reminding Jeff to keep the car running and in gear.

The rest of the bank robbery was caught on tape from the bank's lone security camera. At the beginning of the video it shows the teller, a kind woman in her late 40s standing at her teller station, leaning on the counter. She is engaged in a conversation with the lone customer, a man in his 30s. They know each other well and aren't talking about banking business. The conversation went something like this as I recall: "It's worth the effort to prime first," the customer advised. "The paint will go on smoother and will last longer. But make sure you buy the right primer. I'd buy drywall primer if I were you."

"Is there more than one kind?"

"Oh, ya. There's bunches. But they make a primer just for drywall. You can get it at Menards in Mason City."

It's at about this time in the video that the viewer can see Mutt approaching the front door of the bank, looking rather menacing in his ski mask. As Mutt enters the bank he pushes open the door with one hand, pulls the sawed-off BB gun out of his jacket with his other hand, … and then promptly trips on the threshold and falls flat on his face. The customer turns to the sound of the commotion. Mutt jumps to his feet, brandishes the sawed-off BB gun and announces the purpose of his visit.

"This is a hold-up!" Mutt declares.

The response wasn't what Mutt was expecting.

"That's not funny," says the teller.

"You shouldn't do things like that," the customer advises Mutt. "It could scare someone and you could get in trouble."

Turning back to the teller, the customer continues the conversation he was having with her before they were so rudely interrupted. "Anyway, the drywall primer costs a little more, but it is worth it."

In frustration, Mutt stomps his foot down on the floor and reiterates, "I said, this is a hold-up!"

The customer turns slightly, gestures dismissively with his hand toward Mutt, and continues on. "I think a typical gallon of primer costs about $20, but drywall primer will run you more like $28 or $29."

Mutt stands there for a moment. One can almost see the gears in his mind slowly grinding, utterly perplexed at the conundrum in which he has found himself.

"Well, okay," Mutt mutters, "have a good day."

With that Mutt saunters out of the bank, turns the corner, and one can see him passing by the side window in the bank, his head down, walking dejectedly along.

At this point the conversation shifts to a new topic.

"Do you know who that was?" asks the teller.

"No. Didn't you?"

"No. I've never seen the guy before. I thought you knew him!"

There was a pause.

"I think he was serious," the teller suddenly concludes.

"Oh shit," the customer exclaims, and rushes to the side window.

The teller runs out from behind her teller station and joins the customer peering out the window. Together they see Jeff speed past the bank, blow through a stop sign, and head down main street and out of town.

The teller rushed to the phone and called 911 to report the attempted bank robbery. She gave the operator a description of Mutt and the car; together the teller and the customer managed to make out part of the license plate number. The 911 operator quickly called dispatch and put out an all-points bulletin reporting the attempted robbery and the description of the would-be robbers.

Mutt and Jeff's bad luck hadn't yet run out.

By chance, the Iowa State Patrol had a training program that morning in Des Moines. State Patrol troopers from around the state were in attendance. When it let out at 10:00 a.m., scores of State Patrol troopers took to the road in their squad cars to head back to their home offices. Thus, when the all-points bulletin was called out over the radio, Mutt and Jeff were headed toward Interstate 35 and four State Troopers were driving north on Interstate 35 and, as it happened, were approaching the same interchange that was on Mutt and Jeff's escape route.

All four state troopers took the exit and headed toward the scene of the attempted bank robbery. Only three miles down the road the troopers saw a car approaching that matched the description of the getaway car. The lead trooper activated his overhead emergency lights. Jeff was at the wheel. He told us later that he when he saw all the troopers his heart sank and he knew that God had brought retribution upon him for all his sins. His instinct was to stop and give up. That wasn't Mutt's response, though. Mutt yelled at Jeff to turn quickly down a country road, just before their car met up with the line of troopers approaching from the other direction. Jeff did as he was ordered and screeched around the corner and started down the gravel road.

Iowa farm roads are often topped with gravel, but sometimes the gravel gives way to dirt when the road serves only as means of transport for farm equipment in the more sparsely populated portions of Iowa. Within a couple of miles down the road on which Jeff was speeding, trying to escape capture, the gravel gave out.

In Iowa, March weather can be unpredictable. Sometimes it is cold and dry, but other years there is early thaws and rain. This March, the ground was thawing and the rain falling.

So, when the gravel gave out, the mud came in. When Jeff hit the mud road he immediately lost control and crashed into the ditch on the right. The troopers were close behind and came to a stop within seconds of Jeff's crash. Mutt still wanted to make a run for it, but their car had come to a stop with the right side of the car jammed up against the side of the ditch such that Mutt couldn't get his door open more than a few inches. Cursing, he then looked up and down the barrel of several guns the troopers had pointing at him. Even Mutt then knew he was defeated.

It's odd, but I have little recollection of the trial, or what possible defense Mutt thought he had. I have a vague memory that he was a career offender, meaning that his prior convictions would have called for a very harsh sentence under the then-mandatory sentencing guidelines. In that case, perhaps he had nothing to lose by going to trial because the guidelines sentence was greater than the statutory maximum sentence. In any event, a jury convicted Mutt, Jeff got a reduction in his sentence for cooperating, and a teller in a small town in north central Iowa learned not to be quite so trusting. The great aunt's cookies went to waste.

Chapter 3

Dr. Feelgood

One of the purported dog cases I was handed when I started at the United States Attorney's Office involved a local psychiatrist. He was well-connected with some important people in the city and had a reputation as a generous philanthropist. But he also had a reputation on the street for prescribing controlled substances to nearly anyone who wanted them. On the street, the doctor was known as "Dr. Feelgood." He had been under investigation by the Drug Enforcement Administration over the quantity and purpose of his prescription of controlled substances to patients, and by the Department of Health and Human Services for possible fraudulent billing practices. Before the case was assigned to me, it had been through three other prosecutors, each of whom worked on the case for a while before punting it to the next prosecutor. So, when I first reviewed the file and saw its history, I didn't have much hope. The criminal chief told me that we just needed to make a decision about the case and if I didn't think there was enough there to just decline prosecution, "kill it," is how he worded it.

The one constant on the case was our office's paralegal who kept pushing the case with the prosecutors, convinced there was a gem hidden within. She made the same pitch with me and I promised to look long and hard at it. I also proposed a meeting with the two lead case agents working on the case, a DEA diversion agent (agents focused on the diversion of prescription-controlled substances from legal use to illegal use) and an FBI agent.

As I slogged through the reams of paper comprising the case file, I became more confused and befuddled the more I sought clarity. There were hundreds of pages of billing records and supporting documents. I could faintly discern a pattern of improper billing that, perhaps with further investigation, could form a basis of a fraudulent billing case. But poor or mistaken billing practices don't constitute a crime; it has to be an intentional act and here evidence of criminal intent seemed to be lacking. As for the distribution of the controlled substances, the diversion agent's focus also seemed to be on whether the doctor was wrongfully prescribing controlled substances to somehow reap profits, but there was a disconnect because the doctor didn't directly profit from the sale of the controlled substances. Patients (or more accurately, their insurance companies) paid pharmacies for the controlled substances, not the doctor.

In any event, I met with the paralegal and the agents and let them talk to me for a couple hours about the case in an effort to convince me that there was something there to prosecute. I remained unconvinced that we had any real case of billing fraud; the meeting convinced me all the more that what we had here was very sloppy and inept record-keeping and billing practices. When we changed the subject to talk about the drug distribution angle, however, I began to become more interested. The diversion agent mentioned that at least two of the psychiatrist's patients had died from overdosing on controlled substances he prescribed. The agent educated me on the practice by some drug addicts of doctor shopping until they find a doctor who will prescribe them drugs to feed their drug addiction habit even when there is no medical justification for the prescription. If they cannot fool a doctor, sometimes they will bribe the doctor or provide sexual favors or other compensation to the doctor. The agent told me that the word among drug addicts was that Doctor Feelgood prescribed drugs regardless of a medical need, and that he had been doing it for decades. The rumor was that some females used to trade sexual favors for the drugs, but the agent was unable to confirm that rumor. The agent had attempted an undercover operation by sending in a female agent to pretend to be a drug addict, but Dr. Feelgood sniffed out the subterfuge and refused to prescribe any drugs.

After mulling it over for a while, I started asking some questions. How may opiates is he prescribing per year? How does this compare to how many other doctors with similarly-sized practices are prescribing per year? Can we identify the top 25 or 50 patients receiving the most opiate prescriptions? Can we look at the medical files for those patients to see if there is any possible basis for prescribing opiates at all, let alone the number of opiates he is prescribing? And so on.

As we talked, the plan developed in my mind that the way to approach this case was with both a macro and micro look. First, we'd look at his overall prescribing practice compared to similar doctors and see if he was within the ballpark or way off in left field. Second, we'd look at individual cases, but only a small manageable number of them, so as to develop examples of cases where perhaps we could show that there was no medical justification for the prescription of the controlled substances or at least not in the numbers he prescribed.

Over the course of the following two years I worked with the agents to develop the case. We subpoenaed thousands of documents from multiple sources, collected data, ran statistical analyses on prescription numbers, and interviewed and questioned scores of current and former patients before the grand jury. Ultimately, we executed a search warrant at Dr. Feelgood's office to seize his medical records, particularly for the patients on which we had focused our investigation.

In the end, we developed evidence that Dr. Feelgood had a pattern of prescribing controlled substances, particularly pain opiates, at an astronomical rate, far beyond what other psychiatrists with similarly-sized practices and with similar patient populations, prescribed. Indeed, his prescriptions of controlled substances were off the chart. We also developed evidence on about 60 patients where we found almost no records or medical conditions that would justify the prescription of controlled substances or at least the amount he prescribed. Some individual cases in particular were egregious. For example, one patient had no records in Dr. Feelgood's files showing she was suffering from a medical condition calling for the prescription of pain opiates, she had only visited him a few times in the course of several years, and yet Dr. Feelgood kept prescribing her enough pain opiates each month to sedate an elephant. I also found an expert to assist in our case. Rather than seek a nationally-known expert or someone from an academic or government setting, I found a psychiatrist from an Iowa city of roughly the same size as Cedar Rapids who had a practice that was very similar to Dr. Feelgood's practice both in terms of size and patient population.

We finally reached the point that I believed it was time to charge

Dr. Feelgood. This wasn't necessarily an easy sell to my superiors in the office, including the United States Attorney. Dr. Feelgood had no criminal history; not even a speeding ticket. He was somewhat aged; 67 by the time we charged him. And he was a medical doctor. If we charged and lost this case, it wouldn't go over well. There were many nervous people in the office about this case, but the criminal chief backed me all the way.

The grand jury ultimately returned an indictment against Dr. Feelgood charging him with 26 counts of illegal distribution (through prescriptions) of controlled substances. Three counts alleged that the distribution led to the deaths of patients. One of the patients who died from an overdose on drugs prescribed by Dr. Feelgood was five months pregnant. Dr. Feelgood, who was wealthy, hired multiple defense attorneys who presented a strenuous defense. After some pretrial litigation, the case came on for trial.

This was the largest case I had handled up to this point, both from the number of witnesses and exhibits and also in its importance. Months earlier I had talked to the criminal chief about the need for another prosecutor to help me on the case. He agreed and asked a senior prosecutor to help. The prosecutor was later unable to help, so the criminal chief came to the rescue and assigned another junior prosecutor, like me, to assist as my second chair. That prosecutor later became a United States Attorney and then a United States District Court Judge.

The trial lasted two or three weeks. We, the government, called scores of witnesses and so, too, did Dr. Feelgood and his three attorneys. It was a hard-fought battle with spirited cross examination and various petty disputes where Dr. Feelgood's attorneys repeatedly accused us of wrongdoing. The attorneys for the defense were good, experienced attorneys. One, in particular, didn't typically practice criminal defense. Rather, he routinely defended doctors against medical malpractice cases. He was an expert in the medical profession and medical litigation, but also an incredibly good trial attorney. At one point during a break in the trial I had occasion to talk to a law clerk for one of the other judges in the courthouse. I must have asked at some point why the clerk had been sitting in the back of the courtroom watching the trial for days at a time.

"The judge told me I should come in and watch this trial because there's a great attorney here," the law clerk explained.

Before my head could swell, he quickly clarified that the judge said the law clerk should come in to watch the malpractice attorney in action.

After we rested the government's case, the defense began with their witnesses. The defense theory was twofold. First, Dr. Feelgood's prescriptions were proper in quantity and for proper medical reasons. Second, if any of the prescriptions were improper, it was because the drug-seeking patients had lied to him or feigned conditions that would have justified the prescriptions. Dr. Feelgood had several prominent physicians and experts testify on his behalf but his main expert, the star of the defense, was a doctor who was associated with the Harvard Medical School. This expert testified at length about Dr. Feelgood's prescribing practices and stated that Dr. Feelgood's conduct was within the scope of a reasonable medical practice and was fully appropriate and justified. The expert was very smooth and persuasive, though an arrogant ass.

I had been researching him for months. He was nationally renowned, had written many medical articles and had testified for hire in scores of cases involving medical malpractice (though never in a criminal case). I had a copy of his report and so I knew in advance what his opinion would be and the basis for his opinion.

As a prosecutor, I generally placed experts into one of three categories. The first were hired guns who would say whatever the person hiring them wanted them to say and have no regard for the facts or the truth, trading on their pedigree to fill their pockets. The second category were incompetent experts who might be quite honest, but who were either unqualified to render an opinion on the topic or who had adopted defective methods or relied on inadequate information to arrive at their opinions. The final category were the competent and honest experts. The last category was the hardest to cross-examine. It was my observation that lawyers can successfully cross-examine these competent and honest experts only if the lawyer can show that the experts' opinions are truly flawed not because of anything they did but because the attorneys who hired them provided them with incomplete or incorrect data. I conclude that the defense star expert in my case fell into the first category: a hired gun.

In reading all the transcripts of other trials I could get my hands on in which this star defense expert testified and by digging through all his published articles I could find, I found ten or twelve statements he had made elsewhere that were completely and diametrically contrary to what he had said in his report in this case or were completely in support of the government expert's position. The trick was how to impeach him with all these prior inconsistent statements effectively. I figured that the first time I exposed a prior inconsistent statement of his, he would turn slippery on me and evade answering any other question directly so as to prevent me from impeaching him. The solution, I concluded, was to get him committed to each of the statements first and then expose them all at once. I puzzled long and hard for a way to do this and finally found one.

On the day this star defense expert testified, my criminal chief came to the courtroom to watch part of this expert's direct examination and my cross examination. I hadn't shared my cross-examination strategy with my criminal chief in advance so he had no idea what I was doing. He nearly had a nervous breakdown when he started watching my cross examination.

My first strategy was to lure this expert into overconfidence. He was already highly arrogant, mentioning his connection with Harvard at every opportunity. If I came on strong, I feared he'd become wary and careful. So, I began my cross examination as if I was the unintelligent hick from Iowa that he presumed me to be. My first five to ten minutes of cross examination was bumbling, halting, and unorganized. I intentionally mispronounced some medical terms so that he could correct my pronunciation. The jury, judge and opposing counsel must have been perplexed by my performance because they had seen me in action for days. They saw that I was generally very well organized and my examination of witnesses went smoothly. They knew that I could pronounce the medical jargon properly. But the key was that the defense expert didn't know me and hadn't seen me in action before. After I was satisfied that he was properly cocky, I set my trap.

"Well, uh, doctor, um, ... well, I have some statements here I have written down on a piece of paper, and I want you to go through them with me and see if you don't agree with me that each of these statements is true."

Here, I put the paper on a projector so that he and everyone else in the courtroom could see it. On the paper were the ten to twelve key statements I had found, and then to the right were two columns labeled "true" and "false." The statements were direct quotes from him, either from an article he wrote or from the transcript of a trial or deposition where he testified. The statements were things like: "It is outside the reasonable practice of medicine to prescribe more than 20 hydrocodone pills to a patient per week," or "Prescribing an opiate pain reliever to a pregnant woman constitutes gross medical malpractice."

Once I had his list of statements displayed on the screen, I started down the row of statements. I haltingly read a statement and then turned to him and asked,

"Now, um, doctor, wouldn't you agree that that statement is correct?"

Each time I asked him such a question, his response was consistent: "False and misleading, Mr. Williams!" he'd routinely reply in a snide tone and with a look of smug superiority on his face. Then he'd pontificate about why it was an absurdly incorrect statement and why it was so clearly wrong.

As I worked down the list and he gave the same answer, I acted as if I was reluctantly checking the "false" box for each one and put on a façade as if I was going down in flames but didn't know how to pull out of the dive. Inside, I was growing increasingly elated as I saw that my trap was working flawlessly. The criminal chief, sitting in the back of the courtroom, meanwhile was becoming unglued and, I'm certain, ruing the day that he hired me.

When I got to the end of the list, I slammed the trap shut with a few more questions.

"So, doctor, you don't agree that every one of those statements is true?"

"No, Mr. Williams, I certainly don't! No honest, competent doctor would make statements like those!"

At this point I paused, turned and smiled at the jury, and walked back to my table. From beneath counsel table I retrieved two boxes containing copies of all the articles and transcripts from which I had recovered the expert's prior statements. I proceeded to hand copies of them to the defense counsel and then one by one laid them out. It went something like this.

"Doctor, I want to talk about that first statement, you know the one about how it is outside the reasonable practice of medicine to prescribe more than 20 hydrocodone pills to a patient per week, which you claimed was false and misleading; I'm handing you a copy of a transcript of your testimony in the case of *Smith v. Jones*, dated July 21, 1997. You'd agree that this is a transcript of your testimony, would you not?"

"Uh, yes it is."

"And you were under oath to tell the truth in that case, weren't you?"

"Yes, I was."

"I want you to turn to page 342, and beginning at line 10, you were asked this question and you gave this answer."

Here, I would read the question and then the quoted answer from him that he had just told me, and the jury, on cross examination was false and misleading, and that no honest doctor would say. When I finished I would then ask him each time, "Did I read that question and answer correctly, doctor?"

Of course, he had to answer "yes" because all I was doing at this point was reading straight from the document.

As soon as the defense realized that their expert was about to be eviscerated, they attempted to object but the judge shut them down, with an ever-so-slight smile, stating that it was completely proper cross examination.

By the time I finished with each of the statements, the star defense expert had been destroyed. He was exposed for the charlatan that he was and no effort by the defense to rehabilitate him on redirect examination would be effective.

Although for me that was the highlight of the trial, my co-counsel and I had several other instances of very effective lawyering. So much so that many months later, over drinks with two of the defense attorneys, they told me that somewhere about the middle of the trial they turned to each other and asked how the hell we had become so good. My co-counsel was in her late twenties at that time and I was only in my early 30s, while the defense attorneys were all in their 50s and 60s.

The jury deliberated for more than half a day, but returned verdicts of guilty on 25 counts. That included findings from the jury that Dr. Feelgood's distribution of the drugs contributed to the death of three of his patients. When, at the conclusion of the trial, I called for Dr. Feelgood's immediate incarceration pending a sentencing hearing, the judge was annoyed. He felt that I was being heavy handed and unreasonable, but a statute mandated that a defendant found guilty of distributing controlled substances under these circumstances "shall" be detained pending sentencing. That the defendant happened to be a prominent and wealthy doctor didn't matter. When I explained the legal basis for my detention request, the judge, who was a fair and intelligent man, reluctantly ordered Dr. Feelgood's detention pending sentencing over the vehement objections of defense counsel.

One might think that the most interesting part of this story is over. But that would be wrong. This story has only just begun to become interesting.

Dr. Feelgood was housed in a nearby county jail pending sentencing. While there, he came to know a man I'll call Bugsy. Remember that name because it will arise again in a later story.

Bugsy was originally from Cedar Rapids and had been convicted some time ago for some federal offense. While in federal prison for that offense, he operated a drug conspiracy from inside the federal prison. He was again convicted and this time the court sentenced him to life in prison without the possibility of parole. In prison he befriended a member of a New York mafia family and before long became a "made" member of the mafia. Bugsy's little brother was then a 20-something, low-level drug dealer in the Cedar Rapids area. He wanted to become a high-level drug dealer and asked for his older brother's help. Bugsy pulled his mafia strings and got a member of the mafia family to go to Cedar Rapids to help his little brother expand his drug operation. Once the mafioso arrived in Cedar Rapids and concluded the market was ripe for exploitation, however, he decided to go into business himself and cut Bugsy's little brother out of the operation.

Before long, the mafioso himself came under investigation by the feds in this area. Another prosecutor in my office ultimately charged the mafioso and he was detained pending trial. While those charges were pending, the mafioso hired a private detective to break into a local defense attorney's office to get information about a client who was snitching on the mafioso. That attorney happened to be one of the attorneys representing Dr. Feelgood in my case. The break-in was discovered and that led to more charges against more people. The prosecutor running that prosecution also subpoenaed Bugsy back to Cedar Rapids in an effort to get him to cooperate after the investigation had uncovered the link between Bugsy, his brother, and the mafioso.

The feds housed Bugsy in the same county jail as Dr. Feelgood. Bugsy was a slimy, manipulative operator who worked every angle he could to get whatever he wanted. And in Dr. Feelgood, Bugsy saw an angle. He knew that Dr. Feelgood was a high-profile defendant in a case that was prominent in the local news. Bugsy figured that if he could get more evidence of some crime involving the famous doctor, that the feds might reward him in some way that would get him out of his current troubles and perhaps even result in a reduction of his life sentence. When Dr. Feelgood made some passing comments denouncing some of his former patients for cooperating against him in the trial and expressed a fear of what more they might say at his sentencing hearing, Bugsy saw the opening he was looking for.

I had concerns that Bugsy took the tiny little seed and watered it with manipulation until he had convinced Dr. Feelgood that the way out of all his troubles was to have the two witnesses whacked. Bugsy easily convinced Dr. Feelgood that he was a mafioso and knew other members who would and could easily kill the witnesses for a few grand. When Bugsy decided that he had fully hooked his catch, he told his attorney about it and asked him to call in the feds to negotiate a deal. Bugsy would land the fish for them, and if necessary testify in his little brother's case, in exchange for a reduction in his life sentence.

The prosecutor running the mafia case worked with Bugsy through his attorney and launched an undercover operation. I was kept in the dark about it at the time to ensure that, if during the operation Dr. Feelgood revealed any attorney-client communication about the case, I wouldn't be forced to recuse myself from the prosecution. What I learned later, though, is that Bugsy told Dr. Feelgood that he would arrange for another mafioso to visit Dr. Feelgood in the jail and the doctor could hire the mafioso to kill the witnesses. They discussed the plan while walking in the very small outside yard at the jail; Bugsy was wired. I later listened to the wire and it was clear to me that Dr. Feelgood was reluctant and that Bugsy was using every tool of manipulation to push the doctor to go along with the plan that Bugsy himself had hatched.

Dr. Feelgood eventually agreed and there followed a meeting in the jail visiting room between the doctor and the mafioso hitman. But the hitman was really an undercover special agent who was also wired. During that conversation, the agent was extremely careful not to pressure Dr. Feelgood into anything. The agent said he was here at Bugsy's request, that yes he could easily kill the witnesses and get away with it, and stated his price, but left it up to Dr. Feelgood to decide what to do. After much hemming and hawing Dr. Feelgood finally agreed to have it done and said he'd make arrangements for his wife to get the money to the hitman. When Dr. Feelgood's wife withdrew money as her husband requested and paid the hitman, even though she had no clue of what was going on, that was sufficient to bring the case to a close and charge Dr. Feelgood. At this point the evidence was all turned over to me. I presented the evidence to the grand jury who returned an indictment charging Dr. Feelgood with attempted witness tampering and obstruction of justice.

Even though the evidence was more than sufficient to convict Dr. Feelgood of attempting to have witnesses killed, and even though the facts didn't establish entrapment under the law, I was extremely uncomfortable with Bugsy's role and the degree to which I believe he manipulated a vulnerable man who had no history of violence. Thus, with the criminal chief's approval, I negotiated a global resolution to the case that would wrap up both the original charges and the new charges against the doctor. Dr. Feelgood agreed to a lengthy prison sentence on the charges for which the jury convicted him and agreed not to appeal his conviction or his sentence. In exchange, I agreed to dismiss the witness tampering-related charges.

And thus, it ended. Dr. Feelgood went to prison for more than a decade, Bugsy got a reduction in his sentence from life to something like 40 years, and the case was closed.

A couple weeks after it was all over I hosted a small gathering in the back room of a local bar so that I could properly thank my co-counsel, the agents who worked so hard on the case, and the support staff, especially the paralegal who worked on the case. I presented each with a small token of my appreciation, but to the paralegal I also gave another gift. A rock. But it wasn't just any rock. It was a geode, the state rock of Iowa, the type of rock that from the outside looks like nothing special, but if you break it open there are gems inside. As I handed it to her I told her that she was right all along.

Chapter 4

A Happy Ending

Soon after I started in the United States Attorney's Office, the criminal chief assigned me to take over a drug trafficking investigation in Mason City, Iowa, that he had started but still needed much more work. The agents came to Cedar Rapids to meet with the criminal chief and me so that we could plan the next steps in the investigation. It was then that I met two special agents with the Iowa Division of Narcotics Enforcement (the state equivalent of the DEA) based in Mason City, a special agent with the Iowa Division of Criminal Investigation (the state equivalent of the FBI) also based in the same office, and a special agent with the Internal Revenue Service Criminal Investigation Division (think Elliot Ness) working out of a Cedar Rapids office. This was the beginning of an amazingly productive and rewarding partnership. Over the next decade and a half, I prosecuted hundreds of defendants working with these agents, often working together as a group, and sometimes working with just one or two of them. These agents were outstanding and each became my friend. All have since taken well-deserved retirements.

This first investigation the criminal chief assigned me to work on with these agents involved a complex and extensive methamphetamine trafficking operation based in Mason City. Two large dealers, we'll call them Capone and Moran, had each developed a drug trafficking organization and although they sometimes competed with each other, there was also some overlap and occasional cooperation between them. They imported the methamphetamine from Mexico and the Southwestern United States and distributed it primarily in northern Iowa, but also to some extent in southern Minnesota. They used violence and threats of violence to keep their dealers current on their payments and to deter them from cooperating with law enforcement officers. Over the course of several years, Capone and Moran had earned hundreds of thousands of dollars in drug proceeds. After laundering the drug proceeds, they amassed many expensive toys, including motorcycles, boats, jet skis, cars, and houses. They flaunted their wealth and seeming immunity from prosecution. Capone and Moran also each had in their orbits a bevy of young, attractive women who were happy enough to enjoy the ill-gotten gains and didn't trouble themselves with the source of the cash or the damage the drug trafficking was wreaking on the community.

It took several years, but we dismantled both drug organizations and sent more than a score of drug dealers to federal prison, including Capone and Moran. It took diligent work, long hours, persistence and patience. The IRS agent focused on following the money and developing money laundering charges against the drug dealers, while the DNE agents focused on making controlled buys, executing search warrants, and arresting the bad guys. The DCI agent had his hands in and helped organize and coordinate everything, but his specialty and focus was the drug dealers' violence and firearms. We didn't have a single large trial, but a series of guilty pleas and trials, ripping apart the organizations bit by bit, month by month, year after year.

We slowly chipped away at each operation, but Capone's was the first to collapse when we had flipped enough of his dealers and seized enough evidence. We ultimately seized so many assets from him that the United States marshals had to rent a warehouse in Mason City to store it all and eventually had an auction of all his toys. I attended the sale, along with the agents, for the joy of seeing Capone stripped of the proceeds of his drug empire.

Moran went down about a year later. He became more careful as he saw what was happening to both his and Capone's operations, so it became harder to get to him. We got a break finally when we caught his young girlfriend with a significant amount of methamphetamine. I will call her Sue. She was facing more than a decade in prison. Before we filed charges against her publicly we got the court to appoint Sue an attorney and through the attorney approached her about cooperating.

I remember that meeting vividly. Sue was a young woman of 22, who in high school had been an honor student, a cheerleader and a member of the student government. Somehow she got mixed up with Moran and came to enjoy the money, drugs, trips and toys. He had also introduced her to the use of methamphetamine and her world had spiraled out of control. Sue was estranged from her parents and former friends and caught up in the drug world where she never imagined she'd be. And now she faced a federal prosecutor in her lawyer's office telling her that she had two choices: go to prison for a long time, or cooperate with us and help us take down Moran and possibly go to prison for a shorter time.

She tearfully agreed to cooperate and we developed a plan to have a video camera secreted in her apartment. When Moran came to visit her, she was to steer the conversation to a drug shipment we had recently intercepted that we knew belonged to Moran but couldn't prove it. The undercover operation worked as planned and Moran made incriminating statements on video that became the smoking gun we needed to take him and the rest of his organization down.

Sue eventually pled guilty to participating in a drug conspiracy, but because she cooperated she was sentenced to only a couple of years in prison. By the time she came up for sentencing, she had reunited with her family and they were there in full support of her at the sentencing hearing. It was hard to witness the impact it had on the parents to see their daughter go to federal prison. The collateral impact on a criminal defendant's loved ones was always hard to see.

Many years later one of the DNE special agents was out to dinner with his wife in a city near Mason City. After a while the agent noticed that a woman at another table across the room was looking at him repeatedly. She was seated with a man and two children and the agent didn't at first recognize her. As she and her family were leaving the restaurant, though, she stopped by the agent's table as her family continued on. The agent later recounted the encounter to me and it went something like this.

"Hi," she said to the agent, "you don't recognize me, do you?"

"No, I'm very sorry, I don't," the agent admitted.

"I'm Sue. You arrested me a decade ago and sent me to prison."

The agent then recognized her and became nervous about where the conversation was going to go from there. "I recognize you now, and remember your case," he said, "and I'm sorry for having to arrest you, but that was my job."

"I'm not sorry at all," Sue said. "You arresting me was the best thing that could have happened to me. I had gone down a dark hole and it was only going to end in tragedy. I was hooked on meth and had no values then. I hate to think of what would have happened if I hadn't been arrested. But it turned out to save me. After prison I graduated from college and got married and I have two beautiful children now."

"Oh, that's wonderful," the agent sincerely exclaimed. "I'm so very happy for you."

"Well, I don't want to disturb your dinner any more than I have, but I just wanted to thank you for what you did for me."

Sometime later the agent told me about the meeting. That kind of thing, the justice system intervening in a person's life at a time and in a way that changed it for the better, didn't happen often. But it did happen from time to time. It happened often enough that it gave us hope that sometimes we did make a difference.

Chapter 5

Ocean Pollution in Iowa

One of the dog assignments I received upon joining the United States Attorney's Office was to become the prosecutor specializing in environmental crimes. This was considered a dog assignment for a few reasons. First, there wasn't anything exciting or sexy about environmental crimes. Hollywood doesn't produce shows about the war on environmental crime. Second, this area of law was heavy on science, regulations, and obscure statutes. Last, these cases take a significant amount of work. It was difficult to comprehend the science and law to determine if a crime was even committed and, if so, how to prove it, and it was even more difficult to explain it all to a jury. It was also difficult because it required the development of traditional evidence, such as witnesses and documents, but it also required scientific evidence, such as samples and testing. Given all that, it wasn't surprising that other prosecutors in the office avoided responsibility for the specialty. But each United States Attorney's office had to have a prosecutor trained and dedicated to handle such cases when they arose. It fell to me to be that prosecutor.

I was probably the poorest choice for an environmental prosecutor they could have selected. I graduated from high school with an uninspiring C average, but barely passed my science classes. I had no aptitude for sciences, and no interest in them. Thus, when the Department of Justice sent me to training on environmental crimes, I felt like I was back in high school and wondered what I had gotten myself into. It was a week-long course with several mandatory classes and several breakout sessions on specialized areas from which prosecutors could select the topics they felt fit their needs. I was just happy that there were no examinations and prayed I'd have very few environmental crime cases come to me during my career.

Over the course of my career, I ended up prosecuting about a dozen environmental criminal cases. I actually enjoyed them, for the most part. Several involved Clean Water Act violations by people involved in the agricultural industry. Quite frankly, these cases literally stank as they invariably involved the illegal discharge of animal waste into Iowa waterways. Pig and cattle operations generate prodigious amounts of manure. Manure can be a valuable by-product of the agriculture industry because it is a natural fertilizer. But modern agricultural operations are sometimes so large they generate more manure than operators can sell or properly use as fertilizer. This led some operators to intentionally breach manure lagoons to let the manure flow into a nearby creek, or to have truckers back their trucks of manure up to streams and dump the contents. When large quantities of manure enter waterways, it pollutes them and kills off fish and other wildlife.

Several notable environmental cases, however, arose outside the agricultural industry. The first environmental case I handled involved a violation of the Resource Conservation and Recovery Act, known by the acronym RICRA. A "cradle to grave" statute, this environmental act was designed to govern the generation, storage, and disposal of hazardous wastes. "Hazardous waste" is the subject of statutory and regulatory provisions and interpretation in scores of cases. Generally speaking, though, a hazardous waste is the type of industrial byproduct that will harm you. It is the worst of the worst industrial waste that must be carefully handled. If someone involved producing, transporting, or storing such wastes either intentionally or recklessly fails to handle the waste as required, it can constitute a criminal offense.

The one case I had involved a company that ironically manufactured storage tanks used to treat waste-water to prevent water pollution. The Environmental Protection Agency (EPA) had even conferred an award on the company for its work. The problem was that the company was also dumping hazardous waste in a ravine behind its plant, burying some of it, and burning off more. The waste-water tanks were made of fiberglass. Fiberglass is made of matts of interwoven glass fibers which create a lightweight but solid surface ideal for holding liquid. A byproduct of fiberglass manufacturing is waste from chemicals used to bond fiberglass matts together. That waste qualifies as hazardous under RICRA because it is highly flammable, among other reasons.

The company generated huge quantities of this waste byproduct. At first, the company contracted with another company to properly dispose of the waste. But that was expensive and became increasingly expensive as its operations grew. The owner decided to dump the waste behind the plant. But as the ravine behind the plant soon began to fill with these waste buckets of semi-solid sludge, he turned to burying the waste in the small lot behind the plant. That, though, took time and equipment like backhoes and the space was limited. Eventually he turned to having the employees burn the waste in 50-gallon metal drums behind the plant. The employees were instructed to dump the sludge into the drum and when it got full, light a match and throw it into the barrel. The owner instructed the employees to burn the waste at night, when possible, so that the smoke wouldn't be seen.

We wouldn't have learned of the crime had one of the employees not been slightly injured when a flash fire erupted and singed his face to the point of burning off his eyebrows and requiring medical treatment. That led a supervisor to make an anonymous call to the EPA to report what was happening.

The owner was represented by a powerful law firm whose lawyer felt that I was being too aggressive enforcing the law. The investigation and prosecution ultimately ended in guilty pleas by the company and the owner. In connection with the sentencing hearing I filed a motion that allowed me to see the company's financial documents to determine the amount of fine the company should pay. When reviewing the documents in their attorney's office I came across billing records from the law firm. In them I discovered that the law firm had billed the company to research the ability to sue me personally on a theory that I had exceeded my powers as a federal prosecutor. The guilty pleas showed I hadn't. Nevertheless, I thought it advisable after that to pay for malpractice insurance.

Another significant environmental case came at the very end of my career and was really an offshoot of a massive fraud investigation that I was conducting. Again, it involved a company that purportedly was endeavoring to reduce pollution, but actually was generating it. The company was involved in producing ethanol, an alcohol-based biofuel designed to move us away from more environmentally-damaging fossil fuels. The production of ethanol, it turns out, generates an incredible amount of wastewater that contains contaminants. A well-run and well-equipped plant can recover most of the wastewater in a way that reduces it to a manageable and cost-effective quantity that can be properly and legally disposed of.

The plant I was investigating was anything but a well-run and well-equipped operation. My focus in the investigation was actually the financial crimes committed by the executives who lied and stole from investors to fund this disaster of a company. It was one of my largest fraud cases, but I became a judge before it was ready for indictment and so I handed the case off to another prosecutor who saw it to a successful conclusion.

In any event, while investigating the financial fraud, I stumbled across the environmental crime. It seems that when the plant generated too much wastewater, the plant manager/co-owner decided that the best solution was to dump it in the storm sewer. His unsophisticated fix was rather simple; he had his employees run a large diameter hose from the holding tank out through a bathroom window in the plant, across the property lot, and down into a storm sewer grate in the street that ran in front of the plant. Chemical tests of the river where the storm sewer eventually discharged showed incredibly high levels of contaminants. Upstream fish swam; downstream they floated. That was one case where it wasn't so difficult to prove the source of pollution or criminal intent.

But the most interesting and important environmental case I handled involved ocean pollution. Yes, I'm quite aware that there are no oceans within a thousand miles of Iowa. Indeed, I recall that one of the breakout courses offered at my basic training on prosecuting environmental crimes focused on ocean pollution. I remember crossing that class off my list, certain that topic had nothing to do with me and instead attending a riveting breakout session on manure.

As it turns out, though, a company in our district, Company X, happened to own a fleet of American-flagged, ocean-going vessels and two of the ships became involved in polluting the ocean. Thus, despite my distance to any shore, I found myself enmeshed in the investigation of two ocean pollution cases.

There is a section within the Department of Justice in Washington, D.C., that specializes in prosecuting environmental cases. These prosecutors, though few, are highly trained in this area and many have backgrounds in environmental studies or working in private practice on environmental cases. When an environmental crime case is sufficiently large or significant, or spans multiple districts, or, as here, involves crimes on the high seas, a prosecutor from this section is assigned to head up the case, often working with the local environmental crimes prosecutor from the United States Attorney's Office in the district where the case arose.

Thus it was that one day I got a call from such a prosecutor introducing himself and telling me that we'd be working together on a couple very significant cases arising in my district. Company X was involved in the purchase and resale of grain, wheat and other agricultural products in massive quantities, the D.C. prosecutor explained. Company X sold the products to third-world countries, typically to fulfill contracts the United States government had made with the countries through international aid programs. A couple years before this case arose, Company X had purchased another company that owned a small fleet of ocean-going vessels. Company X intended to integrate vertically. The idea was to own companies involved in the distribution chain of Company X's product so as to achieve greater profits. Instead of paying another company to ship the agricultural products, Company X would pay its own subsidiary. Toward that end, it purchased a company that owned a fleet of ships.

The D.C. prosecutor explained that the Coast Guard had brought two cases to the attention of the Department of Justice involving ships from Company X. Over the course of the next three years, we conducted an extensive grand jury investigation into the two cases, and in the process discovered a third case involving the death of a sailor. The investigation took me to San Francisco to interview the captain of one of the ships, to Fargo, North Dakota, to work with an expert to show how wheat can become contaminated by oil, to Tampa and Fort Myers, Florida, to indict and try the cases, and many trips to D.C, the last to receive an award for my work on the cases.

Here, I will summarize the three cases and how they each turned out.

Contaminated Wheat

The first case involved a vessel that was hauling thousands of tons of wheat to Bangladesh. When the vessel made port in Chittagong, stevedores began unloading the wheat from the holds of the ship using giant vacuums to suck the wheat out of the holds and transfer it into lighter vessels. As they got toward the bottom of one hold of the ship, the stevedore supervisor noticed that the wheat was discolored and smelled of petroleum. He immediately stopped the unloading and the ship's crew investigated.

They discovered that a pipe that supplied diesel fuel to the engines and ran through the bottom of the hold had sprung a leak. About 440 metric tons of wheat had become contaminated with diesel fuel and was inedible. After the rest of the ship was unloaded, Company X arranged with a company from Singapore to off-load the contaminated wheat and lawfully dispose of it in compliance with international environmental laws.

When the ship docked in Singapore, an employee from a disposal company came on board and inspected the wheat and wrote up an estimate. The ship's captain faxed the estimate to Company X's corporate headquarters in my district. Proper disposal of the contaminated wheat, it turned out, would cost approximately $125,000. That would eat up all the profits Company X made from this shipment, and then some. Company X's owner was livid and concluded that he'd find another way.

A week or so later, the ship left port in the dark of night and without authorization. A few days before, a dozen laborers from Bulgaria had come on board. Once the ship was in international waters, the ship's captain put the Bulgarians to work. Over the course of the next two weeks, as the ship sailed from Singapore to Seattle, the laborers emptied the hold bucket by bucket, hefting the contaminated wheat out of the hold and dumping it overboard into the ocean. It was described as dirty, god-awful work because the wheat had by now begun to rot in addition to smell overwhelmingly of diesel fuel. The laborers reported often being overcome by fumes. When a female cook onboard ship complained to the captain, she was threatened with being fired and told to mind her own business. She didn't and sent a message to a family member to alert the Coast Guard. When the ship arrived in Seattle, Coast Guard investigators were waiting for it.

We were able to find internal company documents which showed that the owner of Company X and several other high executives, including corporate counsel and the captain of the ship, made a conscious and intentional decision to dump the polluted wheat at sea, even though they knew it violated international law and, by extension, American law. The motive was pure greed. The cost of proper disposal was simply more than the owner wanted to pay. The company tried to claim the crew had "washed" the wheat by pumping sea water into the hold, siphoning off the contaminated sea water, and pumping it back into the bilge tank for later disposal on shore. Hence my visit to Fargo. I worked with an expert in wheat at the university there who conducted experiments for us with wheat and diesel fuel. We were able to prove that swishing the wheat in sea water didn't remove diesel fuel from the wheat.

Ultimately, Company X, the captain, the owner, and several executives and crew members were prosecuted. All except the owner pled guilty. Company X paid a fine in excess of $2 million for this and the crime involved in the next case I will discuss. Some of the individual defendants received short prison sentences or probation, depending on the extent of their involvement. The owner was tried on this and the next case in Miami.* He was convicted and sentenced to a short term in prison and fined. Unfortunately, I couldn't try that case with the D.C. prosecutor because I was then occupied trying a long death penalty case. That is another story for later.

*Although the case was properly venued in Iowa where the company and all the defendants who pled guilty were prosecuted, we prosecuted the owner in Miami because we believed a jury from a city next to the ocean would understand the evidence better than an Iowa jury. The law in this area is complicated, but venue in these cases can be either where the ship makes port or where the corporation is located. In the second case, the ship made port in Miami. Thus, we had a choice of venues and chose to prosecute the owner in Miami.

Oil in the Bilge

The second case involved a supertanker hauling oil. (Although Company X purchased the subsidiary company primarily to use its dry cargo ships for grain, the fleet also included a couple of supertankers involved in the petroleum trade.) After the ship had offloaded petroleum in New York and was heading back to Houston, the crew discovered that a crack had formed in the wall between the cargo tank and the bilge tank. A large volume of petroleum had leaked into the bilge tank. Again, it would cost a significant amount of money to properly dispose of this on shore.

Thus, only about two months after the discharge of the contaminated wheat into the Pacific Ocean, Company X's owner instructed the crew to pump the bilge water into the Atlantic Ocean. Now, as a practical matter, ships invariably have minor leaks and the law recognizes the costs/benefit ratio of prohibiting any pollution whatsoever by a ship. Thus, the law permits a ship to discharge contaminated bilge water into the sea, but it must pass through a pipe that contains a device measuring the extent of pollution. If the amount of petroleum in the bilge water exceeds so many parts per million, it cannot be discharged into the sea. This bilge water would clearly exceed that limit, so the first mate had crew members bypass the proper discharge pipe and pump the bilge water through a hose hanging over the railing of the ship.

One of the crew members observed the discharge and filmed it with his cellphone camera. When the first mate spied the crew member filming the discharge, he threated the crew member, telling him that if he reported it to the Coast Guard the first mate would break his legs and throw him overboard. The crew member was so frightened that he spent most of the rest of the trip locked in his cabin. When the ship docked in Miami the following morning, the crew member immediately reported the incident to the Coast Guard.

Here, again, Company X, several crew members and the company's owner were prosecuted. On this and the prior case, part of the company's financial penalty went to pay whistle blower awards to the two crew members who risked their jobs and possibly their lives to report the incidents.

Our last case, alas, ended in failure.

Death in the Hold

While we were investigating the second case, several crew members told us that the first mate was a mean and bad man and mentioned how the year before he had forced a crew member to enter the hold of the ship when it was full of chemical vapors, resulting in the crew member's death. These crew members explained that the ship had just offloaded a cargo of methyl tert-butyl ether, MTBE, a highly volatile, flammable, and colorless chemical used as an octane booster for gasoline. The ship was headed back to Houston for another shipment, but of oil this time. Thus, the hold had to be cleaned out of any residual MTBE so that it wouldn't contaminate the next shipment.

The first mate was in charge of getting the hold cleaned out. I don't recall now exactly what they did to clean the hold, but it required a crew member to descend into the hold of the ship, some three or four stories down, to remove any remaining MTBE. The hold is supposed to be vented for days and allowed to air out before the cleaning is attempted, but on this particular trip there was no time for proper venting given the schedule for the next load. Already the effort to clean out the hold has resulted in one crew member collapsing halfway down the ladder. He had to be rescued and resuscitated, but didn't suffer lasting injuries.

The following day, the first mate approached another crew member and ordered him into the hold to clean it. The crew member resisted, but the first mate insisted. It was hard for me at first to understand, but on board a ship, even a civilian ship, it is like a military operation in the sense that a superior officer's instructions are orders, not suggestions, and must be followed. It isn't like in civilian jobs on land where an employee can just say no. Failure to follow a superior officer's command on board ship wouldn't only result in losing that job, but likely being unable to work on board any ship ever again.

The ship's own procedures barred the cleaning of the hold under these circumstances. It required either the proper airing out of the hold or that the crew member be equipped with a self-contained breathing apparatus. Here, the first mate prohibited the SCUBA equipment, asserting it would interfere with the crew member's work. He argued that the hold had aired out another full day since the previous crew member had been overcome by the fumes. Brooking no more defiance, the first mate again ordered the crew member down into the hold.

The crew member made it down about two stories on the stairway when he was overcome by fumes. By the time a rescue team wearing SCUBA equipment pulled him out, he was dead.

As it happens, there is a federal statute making it a crime for a superior officer to place another crew member in danger. The statute dates to the mid–1800s and has been seldom prosecuted since then. The statute contains no wording on the exact *mens rea* requirement. That is, it didn't expressly indicate what state of mind the defendant must possess to be found guilty of the offense. In other words, it was left unclear whether the officer violated the statute if he knew of the risk, or whether the officer had to act recklessly, or whether the officer had to intend to place the crew member in danger.

Our interpretation of the statute was that it was sufficient if the officer simply knew of the risk and ordered the crew member to engage in the conduct anyway. The judge agreed with us. On the morning we were picking the jury in Fort Myers,* the first mate decided to plead guilty, conditioned on the right to appeal the judge's order finding that a "knowing" *mens rea* showing was sufficient. We agreed and he pled guilty and was later sentenced to prison for a few years. Before he went to prison, though, he appealed and the court of appeals reversed the judge, finding that the government would have to show that the officer acted in reckless disregard for the safety of the crew member. This was a much higher burden of proof, so instead of going to trial and losing, we dropped the charges against the first mate.

One of the most interesting parts of these series of cases was the model that craftspeople at the FBI built for us. There is a section in the FBI, called the Special Projects Unit if I recall correctly, specializing in creating demonstrative models, videos, photographs and the like for use in trials. At our request, they built a model of the front quarter section of the second ship (the one with the oil in the bilge water and the death). When complete, it was about three feet long, and two feet high, with a cut-away section so that on one side one could see into the hold of the ship. Made primarily of balsa wood, the model was to exact scale

*That is the port where the ship first stopped after the crew member's death.

and had all the pertinent details, including the stairs going down into the hold of the ship, a crack in the wall between the bilge and cargo tank, and deck hatches that opened and closed. It was painted the correct color and had the name of the ship on its side. It was quite impressive. I wanted to keep it after the case was over, but the Special Projects Unit wanted to keep it to display as an example of the type of work it can do. They won that battle.

There are times when I think about what a great job the Special Projects Unit workers have. I liked building models as a child. I think perhaps I missed my calling.

Chapter 6

"Shoot the Bastard, Rico, Shoot Him!"

During my career, I prosecuted only one juvenile. He was a drug dealer who sold heroin that killed users. But the teenaged criminal that stands out most in my memory was a guy I'll call Rico. Rico began selling marijuana at 15 and by the time he celebrated his 16th birthday he was selling ounce quantities of methamphetamine. At 17, he dropped out of school, moved into pound methamphetamine deals, and expanded into selling cocaine, LSD, and other drugs. Rico had an organization of a dozen or more people working for him or at his direction. By the time he was charged, he had just turned 18.

Rico came by his criminal behavior honestly, as the saying goes. His father was in prison for drug dealing. His uncle was a drug dealer, as were two cousins. His older sister was dating a drug dealer and felon, who also worked for Rico.

Rico himself was rather thin and short, but nevertheless he was a very cocky guy. And remarkably violent. He achieved his prominence in the drug world so quickly in part because he had no qualms about using violence to attain his goals and no empathy for his victims. Too physically small himself to strike terror in others, he used firearms and henchmen working for him to be his enforcers. The slightest delay in repaying a drug debt resulted in threats and often destruction or theft of property. Any hint that someone was assisting law enforcement resulted in death threats and severe beatings.

Rico and his organization quickly became the bane of law enforcement officers in the area. Because he was a juvenile at the time, the courts did little to punish him. His mother protected him and swore the police were just harassing him. Because of his violence, people caught with drugs they bought from Rico would rather go to prison than turn snitch and cooperate with the cops. Given the prior murders of so-called snitches by other drug dealers in the recent past, people tended to believe Rico's threats. If they had any doubts, they were dismissed when Rico shot his sister's boyfriend.

Rico had a driver because Rico lost his license shortly after getting it due to multiple driving offenses. Rico was being driven around one summer afternoon in between drug deals when they drove by an alley in the downtown area. Rico suddenly called for his driver to stop and back up to the alley. Rico had spied his sister and her boyfriend standing outside her car, halfway down the alley. He could see they were fighting and saw the boyfriend slap his sister across her face.

When the driver backed up and into the alley, Rico jumped out of the passenger side of the car in time to see the boyfriend strike his sister across the face again. Rico's sister saw Rico at the same time and screamed out "Shoot the bastard, Rico! Shoot him!"

So, Rico reached in the small of his back, pulled out a .45 caliber pistol, and shot the boyfriend five times from about ten feet away, striking him in the chest, stomach and one leg. The boyfriend crumpled onto the pavement as a pool of blood spread beneath his body. Rico hopped back into his car and had his driver take him away, leaving his sister to fend for herself.

Emergency personnel responded to multiple reports of shots fired. They rushed the boyfriend to the hospital where he underwent emergency surgery. They dug four slugs from his body (one was a through-and-through wound and officers never found that slug). Amazingly, the medical personnel saved the boyfriend's life. Officers tried to question him when he came out of anesthesia the next day. As he lay in the hospital bed, tubes coming out of his arms and nose, the boyfriend looked the cops in the eye and claimed he didn't have any idea who shot him. Remarkable, given that all the entry wounds were in the front of his body, he was shot from ten feet away, and it was broad daylight.

Bystanders reported Rico's car in the area at the time of the shooting. Officers found the car a short time later, but when they searched it they found no gun. Rico and his driver admitted being at the scene but claim they fled when some unknown person started shooting.

Shortly after the shooting, the drug task force began concentrating on making a case against Rico and his organization. It was hard going, given his strongarm tactics. Eventually, though, the task force was able to chip away at his organization, slowly making a case. Finally, they developed enough evidence to approach me asking for help in getting a search warrant and bringing charges against a couple of his dealers to provide them with motivation to cooperate. Rico had turned 18 a few months before.

Soon, agents searched Rico's house, along with other locations associated with him and his dealers. They were early morning raids, with the use of full tactical teams. At one house, officers rushed in announcing "Police! Police!" and ordered everyone to the ground as, firearms raised, they tactically moved room to room throughout the house. As the agents reported it to me later, they burst through the door of one bedroom where they encountered a man having sex with his girlfriend, who was tied to the bed, surrounded, the agents later told me, by sex toys of every description.

The agents screamed, "Get on the floor! On the floor!"

The man turned and looked at them without pausing in his task at hand and said, "just a minute." I don't think the officers did.

In Rico's house, agents found a large supply of drugs, including methamphetamine and thousands of units of LSD, along with several firearms.

Rico ultimately pled guilty to a drug charge. The crime carried a mandatory minimum sentence of ten years and a maximum sentence of life in prison without parole. The guidelines called for a sentence of about 11 to 12 years. The matter came up for sentencing. I thought Rico a real danger and that the sentence was too light, but the judge presiding over the case was known to be lenient and pro-defendant generally, so although I could have asked the judge to sentence Rico above what the guidelines recommended, I decided it'd be a lost cause. On the other side, Rico's attorney was asking the judge to sentence Rico to the mandatory minimum sentence, emphasizing his tender age.

On the day of sentencing, the back of the courtroom was packed with Rico's family members and those members of his organization we hadn't yet prosecuted. As I sat at the prosecutor's table with my agent before the hearing started, it was frustrating to observe how Rico and his family and associates were treating the matter. Rico was holding court in a manner of speaking. He had turned his chair toward the back of the courtroom and was laughing and talking loudly with his followers. He cockily proclaimed the whole proceeding a joke and assured them all that he'd be out in no time. He spoke of the system being rigged and that Five-0 (street slang meaning law enforcement, taken from the old television show *Hawaii Five-0*) was corrupt and would get theirs soon. His followers egged him on, parroting his lines.

Then the clerk struck the gavel, commanded everyone to rise, and announced the opening of court. Rico slowly got to his feet, making it clear that he was doing so only because he felt like it, not because he was told to, and then slumped down in his chair pointedly ignoring the proceedings as court got underway.

The judge opened court, stated the name of the case, and indicated that the matter came on for sentencing. Then he surprised us all by announcing a continuance. Then he said something like the following, as I recall: "Under the United States Sentencing Guidelines," the judge began, "if a judge on his own motion is considering departing upward from the guidelines range, then he must provide advance notice to the parties and give the parties an opportunity to brief the issue."

"Having reviewed the presentence investigation report in this case," the judge continued, "I have concluded that an upward departure in this case is appropriate, given the size of the criminal organization, the amount of drugs involved, and the extreme violence the defendant has used in his criminal conduct. Indeed, I believe a substantial upward departure is appropriate."

Here, the judge paused for effect as he glared at Rico, who by now was actually paying attention, his mouth open in disbelief. "In fact, I'm thinking that I may depart upward to life in prison without parole!" the judge dramatically announced.

"Belahhh!" was the inarticulate gasp that escaped Rico's mouth when he heard the judge's pronouncement, sounding something between the bleat of a sheep and the sound someone makes when the air is knocked out of them.

With that, the judge recessed court. The sentencing hearing was rescheduled and a couple of months later we were back in court. All of Rico's cockiness was gone this time around. He and his family were somber, and his drug associates were conspicuously absent. The judge did depart upward, as he said he would, but to 15 years, not anywhere near the life sentence he had threatened. By the time of this writing, I'm sure Rico has served his sentence and is out of prison and back on the street. It would be pleasant to think that he learned his lesson and was rehabilitated. I have my doubts.

Chapter 7

A Tattoo Artist, a Chef, and a Civil War Buff

On occasion, state law enforcement agents approached the United States Attorney's Office requesting help to break a state case. Often, this involved determining if the target of the state investigation violated some federal law even if it wasn't the crime under investigation. The goal in these cases is to ensure that a dangerous suspect was incarcerated for some crime, any crime, even if it wasn't the suspect's most serious crime. The prosecution of the real Al Capone, the Chicago gangster, is a prime example. Capone's operation was responsible for many murders, including of innocent bystanders. Capone was never convicted of any violent crime, however; he was convicted of federal tax evasion. Another goal in these cases, when there was more than one suspect, was to hopefully build a federal case against the least culpable target with the hope that that person would cooperate against the more culpable target who was the subject of the state investigation. Many of my most interesting cases came to me in this way.

One such case involved a divorced man who collected Civil War memorabilia. He had a vast collection, worth several hundred thousand dollars. He lived in a small town near the Mississippi River. One day he went missing. His adult children, a son and a daughter, lived in other states. When they hadn't heard from their father for several weeks, they asked the police to conduct a welfare check on him. When the police got no response at the door to the man's house, they peered through the windows and saw that the interior looked as if it had been ransacked. The officers forced entry and found the house empty. The man lived in a remote and heavily wooded hilly area and the neighbors, none of whom lived close to the house, had no information of value.

The children filed a missing person's report and traveled to their father's house to investigate. They discovered that their father's vast Civil War collection was missing. The children were aware that their father had recently let another man live in one of his spare bedrooms for a period. Their father had explained that he met the man through a mutual friend and the man was down on his luck. The man was a tattoo artist and their father liked and had several tattoos. That's all the children knew of Tattoo Man.

The agent had obtained from the children a list and description of all the items in the Civil War collection. The collection was insured, and so the list was thorough and complete. The agent then contacted all the auction houses and other places in the United States that he could identify that traded in Civil War memorabilia to be on the lookout for items on the list. A few weeks later the agent was contacted by an auction house in northwest Missouri. The week before, the salesman reported, a couple had come to his business offering many Civil War artifacts for sale. The salesman purchased several of them for several thousand dollars in cash. It was only after the transaction that the salesman saw the communication from law enforcement about the stolen collection and realized the pieces he purchased were on the list.

A follow up investigation led to a description of the couple and the vehicle they were driving. The vehicle was a used moving truck. Surveillance photos from a security camera at the auction house captured the license plate. Tracing the records led to the discovery that the truck had been converted to include a small sleeping room in the back and that it had been sold in Illinois about a month before the victim and his collection went missing. The records showed the buyer was a woman who worked as a chef in a town near the victim's residence. The car salesman stated that a man accompanied the woman, though, when she purchased the truck.

In the next few days more calls came into law enforcement officers from other museums and auction houses about the couple selling or attempting to sell pieces that were on the list of stolen property. Charting the locations and dates of the contacts revealed that the two were heading southwest through Oklahoma, Texas, into New Mexico and on to Arizona. The Iowa agent sent out word to law enforcement officers in Arizona to be on the lookout for the truck. About a day later a deputy sheriff in Arizona spotted the truck parked in a truck stop parking lot south of Tucson, Arizona. Based on the information the Iowa agent had gathered, he worked with police in Arizona to get a search warrant for the truck.

When officers executed the warrant they found the rest of the Civil War collection in the back of the truck, minus pieces the couple had sold. Officers also found several loaded modern handguns. The man had a criminal record for theft and assaults, and there was an active warrant for his arrest for parole violations.

Through more investigation, officers learned that the man was the tattoo artist who had been living with the victim. Both Tattoo Man and the woman insisted that the victim had given them the collection to sell with an agreement that they'd all share in the proceeds. They claimed they hadn't seen or heard from the victim since they left Iowa a month ago. Tattoo Man was held on the outstanding warrant, but the woman was released because she had no criminal record or pending warrants.

A thorough investigation convinced the agent that the missing man was dead. His car was found abandoned in a city in northeast Iowa, about 20 miles from his home. A records check with his bank and credit card companies showed absolutely no activity since he went missing. There was no use of his ATM cards, his health insurance company reported no doctors' visits, and no friend or relative had heard from him for more than a month. It was as if he simply disappeared into thin air. The agent had no body, but he remained convinced that the couple murdered the victim. Law enforcement officers had scoured the house, but couldn't discover any blood or other evidence that the victim had been murdered in his house. The house was in disarray, but more as if it had been searched for valuables, not as if there were a struggle. Drawers were left hanging open and such, but nothing was knocked over or broken. Leads dried up. It became a cold case.

And that's why the agents needed our help. The case was assigned to me and the agent asked me to see if there was anything I could do to bring pressure to bear on the female companion, the girlfriend of Tattoo Man. The agent was sure that she knew a lot more than she had said and was somehow complicit in the murder.

I quickly determined that I could charge the girlfriend with aiding and abetting the interstate transportation of stolen property. Although both she and Tattoo Man claimed the victim gave them permission to take and sell the collection, that explanation didn't hold water. The victim's family told us that the collection was his pride and joy, he intended to pass it on to his heirs, and that he'd never willingly part with it. There was also nothing in writing, emails, or any other form of documentation to support the couple's claim. Finally, in selling some of the collection on their trip, Tattoo Man and the woman gave various explanations for the source of the artifacts; if they truly had permission to take and sell the belongings they'd have simply said so.

Thus, I presented the case to a grand jury who returned an indictment against the woman for aiding and abetting the interstate transportation of stolen property. This charge was similar to the interstate transportation of a stolen vehicle except with this statute the value of the goods had to exceed $5,000 in value to be a federal offense. There is no similar value limitation on the interstate transportation of stolen vehicles; hence my prosecution of the man for transporting a stolen $85 motorcycle across state lines. Here, it was easy to meet the additional value requirement because the victim's Civil War collection was worth well over a quarter of a million dollars.

After the woman was arrested and appointed an attorney, I contacted her attorney and proposed the woman cooperate with us in exchange for the possibility of a lower sentence. After some back and forth, she eventually agreed to cooperate. We sat down together for a debrief. At first she claimed to know nothing about the victim and maintained the same story she had given before. The agent and I told her that we knew she was lying and presented her with examples of major inconsistencies with her story and problems with her explanation. After a long time, she finally confessed that Tattoo Man had killed the victim and they then decided to steal the Civil War collection.

She told us that Tattoo Man, her boyfriend, was abusive to her and that she was afraid of him. She said Tattoo Man and the victim didn't get along well and fought over rent money Tattoo Man owed the victim. She stated the two of them got into a physical fight and that Tattoo Man eventually got the upper hand and strangled the victim. She claimed Tattoo Man then dragged the body out of the house and to the victim's car and drove away. She swore she had no idea what he did with the body. She said she met up with Tattoo Man in Dubuque where they left the victim's car and then drove back to the house. They left early the following day on their trip to the southwest. She claimed the murder wasn't planned.

We were skeptical about this story, finding it hard to believe that she knew nothing about what happened to the victim's body. There were discrepancies that made her story seem unlikely. For example, she and her boyfriend had purchased the converted moving van weeks before the murder, suggesting that they had anticipated the need for a large vehicle to hold the Civil War collection, which was inconsistent with her claim that stealing the collection was an afterthought. Nevertheless, we had nothing to prove that she was lying. We had no body, no witnesses, no evidence of what happened to the victim.

Ultimately, the girlfriend pled guilty to the interstate transportation of stolen property charge and a few months later the case came on for sentencing. At the sentencing hearing I filed a motion with the court asking the court to reduce her sentence for her cooperation. At the same time, I moved for an upward departure because of the extreme nature of how the girlfriend and Tattoo Man came into possession of the stolen property. In other words, the crime punished only the interstate transportation of stolen property; it didn't take into account that the property was stolen from a murder victim. Nor did it take into account the historic and priceless value of the Civil War collection.

In an effort to obtain a lighter sentence, the girlfriend testified at the sentencing hearing. She portrayed herself as an unwilling victim of Tattoo Man's violence, argued that she was coerced to participate, emphasized that she had a minimal role, and in particular focused on her lack of knowledge or role in having anything to do with the disposal of the body. The judge arrived at a sentence somewhere in the middle of where each side was seeking.

About a year later, the State of Iowa charged Tattoo Man with murder. When, many months later, the case came on for trial, the prosecutor approached the girlfriend through her attorney and offered complete immunity from prosecution for her role in the murder if she'd testify against her former boyfriend. She accepted. I knew nothing of the immunity deal and wasn't consulted. Under a little-known Supreme Court decision called *Murphy v. Waterfront Commission*, though, the federal government was bound by the immunity deal even though it wasn't a party. That would come into play later.

Then, remarkably, the week before the case came to trial we learned of new evidence. Several months before, a man in a truck stop in Missouri made a grisly discovery. He had found a five-gallon bucket full of cement filling a very deep pothole in the parking lot of a truck stop. He was repairing the potholes in the lot, so he removed the bucket and properly filled the hole. Once he had the bucket back in his shop, he decided to salvage the bucket by chipping the cement out of the inside. After chiseling away at the cement for a short time he discovered the top of a human head.

When officers finally cleared away the cement they discovered a man's decomposed, severed head. Using a new computer modeling program, state criminalists created a three-dimensional reconstructed image of what they believed the man looked like based on his bone structure. They then distributed the image on a state website for missing persons.

Before this case I didn't know there were people who search the internet for images matching missing people. Many of these private individuals do it as a hobby, but also out of a sense of mission. Often they have a family history involving missing persons and they are willing to devote countless hours comparing images of missing persons against similar images found in the public domain on the internet. In our case, a woman in Utah (as I recall) found what she believed was a match. Our victim.

Missouri state police eventually forwarded the information to the agent I had been working with. A DNA test confirmed it was our victim's head. This was critical evidence in a murder case where the state didn't have a body. From my standpoint, it also told us that the girlfriend had lied to us. Given the timing of the murder and her and Tattoo Man's departure on their trip, and the location of the head in a parking lot in Missouri, it meant that they must have dismembered the body before they left on the trip and placed the head in the bucket of wet cement at that time. The discovery of the head was completely inconsistent with her story that Tattoo Man drove off with the body the night of the murder and they left the next morning without her knowing anything about it.

Although I wasn't involved in the state murder prosecution, apparently the state officials confronted the girlfriend with this evidence and she broke down and gave a full confession. Unfortunately, it was after the state had already granted her full immunity and the language of the agreement didn't contain a provision that would have rendered it void if she lied, which she had.

Here's what she said actually happened: She admitted that they had plotted to murder the victim to steal his collection. She claimed that on the night of the murder Tattoo Man told her to lie down on a weight bench and bare her back so the victim could admire the latest tattoo that Tattoo Man had added to her skin canvas. As the victim leaned over to look at the tattoo, Tattoo Man wrapped a wire around the victim's neck and choked him to death. They then dragged the body to the basement where they had already lined the walls, floor, and ceiling in plastic. They placed his body over the washing machine, pulled back his head, and slit his throat so that the blood would drain into the washer. Once the victim's body was drained of blood, they dismembered his body. She, a chef by trade, used her high-quality knives to cut up his body as if it were a side of beef. Tattoo Man also used a chainsaw to cut off the victim's limbs. They placed parts of his body into garbage bags, making sure to separate the hands and fingers so as not to be in the same bags. The torso was placed alone in its own bag. The severed head went in the bucket of wet cement.

After that, they cleaned up the basement, taking down all the plastic and placing it all in garbage bags as well, along with the chain saw. She cleaned and kept her chef's knives. They spent the next several hours driving around back roads in northeast Iowa throwing bags of body parts into deep ravines in remote areas. The torso they threw off a bridge over the Mississippi River in the early morning hours. She drove the victim's car to Dubuque and Tattoo Man picked her up. After loading up the truck with the Civil War collection and grabbing a couple hours' sleep, they took off the next morning on the trip to the southwest. Their plan was to go to Mexico. The officers had found and searched the truck the day before they had planned to cross the border.

After a lengthy trial, in which the girlfriend testified, a jury convicted Tattoo Man of first-degree murder. She was done serving her federal sentence already by the time of his trial. The judge sentenced Tattoo Man to life in prison. His defense was that his girlfriend had actually stabbed the victim to death and he only helped protect her by disposing of the body. The jury didn't buy it.

A thorough search was made of northeast Iowa in an effort to find the victim's remains, but it was largely unproductive. Only a few of the bags were found. The girlfriend had no idea where they had driven or where they threw the bags, it was at night, and they were driving back roads. Thus, in the end we were only able to provide the grieving family with limited remains for burial.

I was incensed at the girlfriend's lies and obstruction. Had she come clean earlier, we might have been able to recover more of the victim's remains. Her memory would have been fresher and perhaps the remains would have been more easily found before grass and brush grew up to conceal them. Further, the delay prolonged the suffering of the victim's family who for more than two years had no idea what happened to their father's body. The woman had also lied at her sentencing hearing in my case.

The immunity agreement she reached with the state prevented me (and the state) from prosecuting her for her role in the murder and disposal of the body. But nothing in the agreement barred me from prosecuting her for perjury. So, I did.

She pled guilty to the charge. At the sentencing hearing I argued for a sentence above the advisory guidelines range and to the statutory maximum of five years in prison. The judge granted my motion. The Eighth Circuit Court of Appeals later affirmed the sentence, finding it justified both because of the seriousness of the conduct about which she lied (which led to a shorter sentence) and also because her lies prolonged the suffering of the victim's family members.

CHAPTER 8

Trouble in River City

Meredith Wilson, the famous writer and composer, is best known for the Broadway musical hit and later movie *The Music Man*. Wilson set the play in River City, a town modeled on his own hometown of Mason City. There is a refrain in one of the songs that refers to "Trouble with a capital 'T'" that "rhymes with 'P' and that stands for pool."

Written in 1957, the play was set in 1912, when the parents feared young boys were being corrupted by playing billiards. By 1993, the trouble in River City was more serious: methamphetamine; starts with "M," as does murder.

The Nerdy Drug Dealer

In the early 1990s a nerdy young man from Iowa in his early twenties studied chemistry at a community college. He came from a normal family in a normal small town.

His parents had divorced when he was very young, but his mother remarried to a good man who, though perhaps distant, provided well for her and her three children. The Nerd participated in normal school activities, and his mother was the den mother of his Cub Scout troop. The Nerd's biological father had a drinking problem and some criminal history, but was largely absent from the Nerd's life. The Nerd did well in high school. He scored very high on IQ tests. And he looked the part; he looked like a nerd. He had short, wispy blond hair and thick glasses that were too large for his face.

The Nerd's story took a dramatic turn from normalcy, however, sometime between high school and college. After graduating high school, the Nerd took courses at a community college. Though unlike most students who take classes to learn a profession or to prepare for a career, the Nerd took chemistry classes with the goal of learning how to make controlled substances, in particular methamphetamine. He got straight A's.

At the time, criminal, clandestine manufacturing of methamphetamine was imprecise; purity levels of methamphetamine manufactured in the very best criminal labs turned out perhaps 80 percent to 85 percent pure. The typical street-level purity was around 10 percent to 25 percent. The Nerd was eventually able to manufacture 99 percent pure methamphetamine, reputedly purer than the DEA lab could make it at the time. The Nerd had one goal in mind; to become a very wealthy drug dealer.

The Nerd was also very clever in ways other than chemistry. He rented a remote house in rural Arizona where he and his childhood friend built a clandestine meth lab. He created a fictitious company that allowed him to order complex laboratory glassware and base chemicals from companies who believed they were dealing with a legitimate chemical company. The lab produced pounds and pounds of highly pure methamphetamine.

The Nerd also carefully structured his criminal organization. He had been a small-time marijuana and cocaine dealer in high school before he learned how to make methamphetamine, and so he had learned from prior mistakes. He determined to keep the number of his associates small, and to limit the information anyone knew. The Nerd trusted only his best friend from high school to work closely with him. Only he and the Nerd would be involved in the manufacture and distribution of the methamphetamine to the Nerd's dealers. And the Nerd limited his number of dealers to two people living in Mason City, then I'll call George and Tom. He wouldn't sell to anyone else. But to these two dealers he sold pounds of methamphetamine for hundreds of thousands of dollars. Only he and his childhood friend would deliver the drugs and collect the drug proceeds. He trusted no one else. And George and Tom didn't even know of each other. Only the Nerd and his childhood friend knew the identify of both dealers.

Even the most carefully structured criminal organizations will eventually fail, however, and his did too. In 1992, agents in Minnesota made controlled buys of methamphetamine from a drug dealer. When they arrested him, he cooperated to get a break on his sentence and turned on his supplier. Agents made a controlled buy from that dealer, who in turn cooperated. Eventually agents worked up the chain until a dealer turned on his supplier: George. Working with the Minnesota agents, a Mason City Police Department narcotics agent and a DEA agent made a controlled buy from George. Then they executed a search warrant at George's house, finding large quantities of methamphetamine and tens of thousands of dollars in drug proceeds.

George, too, decided to cooperate. He told the agents everything he knew, including the identity of his source. Moreover, he told them that his source was traveling to Iowa in the next couple days to collect drug proceeds from George.

The agents set up a controlled delivery of drug proceeds. They put a wire on George and recorded the meeting between him and the Nerd. George lived in a home with his wife and two young daughters. When the Nerd arrived, George's wife sent him to the basement where George, a musician, hung out and practiced. George delivered thousands of dollars to the Nerd and in their recorded conversation they talked about past and future drug deliveries and the amount of money they were making. When the Nerd left the house and got in the car with his childhood friend, agents descended and arrested them. Ultimately, the agents let the friend go for lack of evidence, but the feds charged the Nerd with felony drug charges.

Agents searched a hotel room where the Nerd had been staying, but found nothing of any real evidentiary value. On the bathroom mirror, however, was a message written in red lipstick inside the outline of a heart. It thanked the Nerd for a good time and was signed "Angel."*

The Nerd was brought to federal court for his initial appearance and arraignment. He had no criminal history, so the court released him pending trial. The court appointed the Nerd a defense attorney who

*This wasn't her real name and she was no angel.

then reviewed the government's evidence and shared it with his client. The Nerd thus learned that George had snitched on him and wore a wire. The case was scheduled for trial and eventually the Nerd's attorney filed a notice that the Nerd was going to plead guilty. A plea hearing was scheduled. The Nerd was looking at probably ten years in federal prison.

On the day in late July 1993 when the plea was to take place, though, the Nerd and his attorney showed up and announced that the Nerd wouldn't be pleading guilty after all. The federal prosecutor* met with the Nerd and his attorney and asked why the Nerd had a change of heart. The lawyer mentioned having a videotape of George exonerating the Nerd. The Nerd said something like "You're case isn't as strong as you think it is."

A Witness Disappears

A few days later, the DEA agent working the case learned that George was missing. When they looked into his disappearance, they learned that George's wife, previously unaware he was selling drugs, had kicked him out shortly after police searched their house. George then met a woman through a mutual friend and endeared himself to her in such a way that she let him move in with her and her two little girls, ages 6 and 10. She was a divorced, single mother who moved back to her hometown after a stint in the Navy. She worked in a local factory. Her parents lived a few doors away, across the street. The woman, and her little girls, were also missing.

Law enforcement officers conducted a thorough investigation into the disappearance of George, his girlfriend, and her daughters, but there was no sign of them anywhere. It was as if they vanished into thin air. The prosecutor managed to get the judge to continue the trial for a few months while he desperately tried to salvage the case in some way.

When they had arrested the Nerd after his meeting with George, they recovered a drug note from the Nerd's pocket that listed "G-man"

*This was not me. This occurred four years before I joined the office. As will be seen, I became involved in this case much later.

and "T-man" with dollar figures under their names representing their drug debts to the Nerd. Although George didn't know who T-Man was, further investigation led the agents to believe it was Tom. They also knew that Tom had a girlfriend, Angel, who was also reputedly involved in the methamphetamine trade. Angel was a former stripper and now worked as a waitress at a country club. She was subpoenaed to appear before the grand jury, along with a number of Tom's other associates.

In the grand jury, Angel denied knowing anything about drug dealing, the Nerd, or any connection between Tom and the Nerd. The prosecutor didn't know that she was then pregnant with the Nerd's child.

Another Witness Disappears

A few days later, Angel called up Tom and asked to meet with him. She told him that they needed to talk. Tom, still in love with Angel, even though she had recently dumped him, readily agreed to meet with her. It was Tom's weekend to spend time with his ten-year-old daughter. He picked up his daughter from his ex-wife's home and then dropped her off at his mother's house that Friday evening, telling them both that he'd be back in a few hours. He never returned. A thorough search ensued for him in the following weeks, but again without a single lead. Tom, too, seemed to have disappeared into thin air.

Several more months passed with the government constantly seeking continuances of the trial date, but eventually the court granted the Nerd's motion demanding a speedy trial. Lacking evidence, the government had no choice at that point but to drop the charges against him for lack of evidence. It appeared that the Nerd was untouchable.

A New Investigation and Prosecution

The agents wouldn't give up. In particular, one of the state narcotics agents and a DCI agent from Mason City, part of the team that I worked with in the Capone and Moran cases, kept investigating the Nerd. The narcotics agent focused on the Nerd's past and continued drug dealing; the DCI agent spearheaded the investigation into the missing people.

Eventually, the agents got a break. A felon who was out on parole approached the county attorney one day to complain about the police trying to set him up. He said he wasn't doing anything wrong and was trying to lead a lawful life, but that the police had an informant at his job who kept pushing the parolee to get involved in making methamphetamine. The county attorney contacted the police who said they weren't involved, but they offered to talk to the parolee.

When the parolee sat down with his attorney and the police, he explained that a man approached him at the factory where they both worked and kept trying to recruit the parolee into helping the man manufacture methamphetamine. The parolee stated that it was clear to him that the man was an undercover agent because he was too clean-cut. The officers asked the parolee for the man's name. It was the Nerd. The officers assured the parolee that the Nerd wasn't working for them and that they weren't trying to set him up. The officers called in the narcotics agent, though, to speak further with the parolee about the Nerd. The narcotics agent also assured the parolee that the Nerd wasn't an undercover informant and wasn't working for the police. The agent eventually persuaded the parolee to work with them to investigate the Nerd.

Over the course of several months, the parolee reported back to the agents everything the Nerd was doing. The parolee told the police that one of the first things that happened was that the Nerd took the parolee to see the Nerd's girlfriend, Angel. The Nerd told the parolee that she had to approve the parolee's involvement. The parolee told the police afterwards that meeting was tense, but that he apparently passed Angel's approval because the Nerd soon got the parolee started with him and the Nerd's childhood friend in setting up a meth lab. The parolee went along with the Nerd's requests, pretending to help him in his meth lab. This time the Nerd set up a new laboratory in a rental house in Mason City.

In late 1996, after gathering evidence over several months—sufficient evidence that the case could withstand the disappearance of witnesses—the agents executed a search warrant at the house and arrested the Nerd and his best friend on federal drug charges. When the Nerd and his best friend appeared in court, the judge appointed attorneys for them. Over the government's objection, the court released both of defendants on bond pending trial. The judge did, however, confine the Nerd to his mother's home, monitored by an electronic ankle monitor. The case was set for trial. The defense attorneys got access to the government's evidence, which they appropriately shared with their clients. As a result, however, the Nerd again learned what evidence the government had and about the parolee being a snitch against him.

Over the course of the next couple months, the Nerd plotted his way out. He had his best friend come to his house and they met and talked in the garage. They also met and talked with Angel, the Nerd's girlfriend and the mother of his child. Although generally confined to his mother's home, the Nerd could go to doctor's appointments and the like, so he had some ability to move. The Nerd told his friend and Angel that they needed to kill the informant. The Nerd also wanted to kill the narcotics agent. The Nerd had done some research and learned where the agent lived, and knew the agent had a wife and children. He planned on killing the agent's family in front of the agent—to make him watch—before he killed the agent. The Nerd also developed a plan for blowing up the law enforcement building where he believed the evidence against him was stored. One night the Nerd even had Angel drive him and his friend by the building and drop them off where the two of them, dressed all in black, conducted reconnaissance around the fenced-in building to determine how to blow it up. He asked his friend to start purchasing fertilizer of the type Timothy McVeigh used to blow up the federal building in Oklahoma.

The Nerd also spoke of the murders in 1993, though in vague and imprecise ways, such as talking about "the problem back then" or "the issues." He was callous in his tone and treatment of the topic. He noted that he originally feared he'd have nightmares after what he did, but was very relieved that he didn't. He said that, frankly, he gave it no thought at all. He called the "incident" a little bump in the road.

What the Nerd didn't know was that his friend had turned on him. When the Nerd started talking about killing people, it was more than his friend could handle. The friend was a real follower and generally did anything the Nerd told him to do. But even he had his limits. And then he remembered some of the things that the Nerd said and did back in

1993; he concluded that the Nerd must have killed those people, including the children. So he wore a wire. The conversations in the Nerd's garage were all recorded.

Eventually, the government disclosed all of this and asked the court to detain the Nerd pending trial. This time the judge agreed and the Nerd was placed in a jail in Sioux City. The Nerd now came up with new plans. He plotted the murder of his best friend (in addition to the parolee and the agent) and his escape from the jail. He had his girlfriend, Angel, pay a bondsman to bond an inmate out of the jail whom the Nerd had hired to kill the Nerd's childhood friend. The Nerd gave the inmate a map with directions to the friend's house. Angel bonded the guy out as directed, and the guy later testified that he'd have carried out the plot except the moment he got out he went on a meth binge and was re-arrested before he could kill the Nerd's friend.

Stymied at one attempt, the Nerd tried to hire another inmate to kill his friend. The inmate agreed. The Nerd had Angel take money to the bondsman to bond out this inmate as well, but this time the bondsman smelled something wrong about the whole thing; this woman had no known connection to the inmate she was trying to bond out and didn't even have his name correct. The bondsman refused. The inmate later testified that at that point in his life, had he been bonded out, he'd have killed the Nerd's friend.

In the meantime, the Nerd had broken off a piece of metal on a stair step in the jail and used the piece of metal to chip away at the grout between the cinderblocks in his cell. He got to the point where he was going to be able to get to the outside at least the size of one block, but it would be too small for him to fit through, plus he was on the second floor of the jail. So he arranged for Angel to drive down the alley of the jail one night. The plan was for him to push through to the outside and lower a makeshift rope through the opening. Angel was to tie it around a package containing a gun, a hacksaw, and a climbing rope. The Nerd planned to then quickly saw through the bars on his cell window, break out the window, and lower himself down on the rope. The gun was for use if any guard tried to stop him.

A routine cell inspection, though, uncovered the damage the Nerd had done to the cell wall before the night of his escape arrived, even though he had cleverly hidden it with a mixture of toothpaste and toilet paper to resemble mortar. He was immediately moved from the cell and placed in a more secure cell. When the government investigated, they uncovered his plots to bond out the intended hitmen.

The Nerd finally realized he had run out of options. He pled guilty to the drug charges. At a sentencing in 1997, the prosecutors tried to persuade the judge that the Nerd had killed the witnesses in 1993 and sought a stiffer sentence, but the judge found the evidence insufficient. Still, the judge sentenced the Nerd to more than twenty years in federal prison.

The Murders

A couple of years later, the government caught a break on the investigation into the disappearance and probable murders of the witnesses in 1993. The DCI special agent had repeatedly approached Angel's best friend, a good woman who, in her youth, had been a little wild and hung out with Angel. The agent repeatedly interviewed Angel's friend, and the woman repeatedly claimed to know nothing. But this agent was very good at reading people; he knew that she knew more than she was telling him. So the agent patiently kept at it, slowly developing trust with her. Finally, one day, she came clean and told all she knew. She broke down crying at the end, relieved to get off her chest a weight that had been pressing down on her for years.

Rather than repeat what she told the agent, I will shift now and tell the reader what we ultimately learned not just from her, but from every other source about what happened in 1993. As I tell the rest of the story, the source of some of the other evidence will become apparent.

When, in 1993, the Nerd learned that George had snitched on him, the Nerd started to hunt him down. The Nerd quickly learned that George had been kicked out of his house, but for a while he couldn't find out where he went. George, it turns out, had seen in the Nerd's eyes the cold bloodedness that lurked in his soul and was justifiably afraid for his life. So, George intentionally wooed the woman he met through a mutual friend because he knew he needed a place to hide out with someone that the Nerd wouldn't connect with him. When George moved into the woman's house, he made sure the blinds were all closed and told her not to tell anyone about him. He lay low there for a couple months. But not so low that the Nerd didn't eventually find out where he lived.

Together with Angel, the Nerd developed a plan. Late in the evening on a hot day in July 1993, Angel approached the woman's home holding an Avon bag. When the woman answered the door Angel claimed she was selling Avon, but was lost and wondered if she could use the phone to call her customer (this was before cellphones). When the woman opened the door, Angel produced a machine gun from her bag. At gunpoint, she held George, the woman, and her two daughters for a few minutes until the Nerd arrived.

Once the Nerd was inside the house, he got the video camera out of the Avon bag and took George into an adjoining room, telling George that he'd kill the woman and children if George didn't do as he was ordered. He then filmed George making a statement claiming that he made up everything about the Nerd's involvement in drug trafficking, saying that none of it was true, and that the Nerd was innocent.* Once the statement was filmed, the Nerd announced that they would all be going for a ride. He told them that he was going to take them out of state and hold them there until the charges were dropped. Then he'd let them go.

The Nerd then used duct tape to bind the hands of George and the woman behind their backs. He removed one shoe from each of their feet. With a rope, he tied one of George's ankles to one of the woman's ankles. With another rope, he tied one of George's arms to one of the woman's arms. He then stuffed a child's sock into each of their mouths and wrapped a piece of duct tape around their heads and across their mouths to hold the sock gags in place. He forced them out of the house and into the back of George's pickup truck, which had a topper. The children he put in the front seat. While Angel drove the truck, the Nerd sat in the back with the machine gun trained on George and the woman.

Angel drove out into the country and down several gravel roads,

*The Nerd apparently thought the video would be admissible in court. It would not have been under the Federal Rules of Evidence, but he had no way of knowing this at the time.

coming to a stop near a copse along a small stream. There, the Nerd forced George and the woman out of the truck and marched them into the woods. They walked awkwardly in the dark, tied as they were to each other and each missing one shoe. About fifty yards into the woods, the Nerd put the gun up against the back of George's head and pulled the trigger. A medical examiner later determined that the first bullet probably killed George immediately. As George fell, the woman desperately tried to get away, but it was hopeless tied together as they were. As both George and she were falling to the ground, the Nerd let loose with a spray of bullets.

Each of them was hit multiple times in the torso and arms with bullets from the cheap semi-automatic gun the Nerd had converted to a machine gun. As they both lay on the ground, George probably already dead, the woman severely wounded, the Nerd walked up to her and placed the barrel of the gun on her temple. The Nerd pulled the trigger and ended her suffering.

Back in the truck, Angel sat with the two little girls. When the girls heard the gunshots, muffled though they were by the Nerd's home-made silencer he had attached to the weapon, she told them it was the sound of fireworks. The Nerd came back to the truck, got the girls out, and marched them into the woods. The oldest girl was dressed in a t-shirt and shorts; the youngest in a swimsuit—she had been swimming at a friend's house earlier in the evening—over which she was wearing a t-shirt from her mother's workplace. Neither had shoes. When they reached the bodies, the Nerd put the gun up against the back of the head of the ten-year-old girl and pulled the trigger one time; then he moved the gun to the back of the six-year-old girl's head and pulled the trigger again. Her facial bones were so small and brittle that the blast from the gun literally blew out the front of her face. The bullet holes in the back of each child's head were in the same exact spots, dead center and about three inches up from the base. What I eventually told the jury this meant was that the younger child was so frightened and vulnerable that she didn't even run when the Nerd shot her older sister. She stood there, still enough for the Nerd to bring the gun barrel to the back of her head and calmly place it in the same spot.

Over the course of the next hour or so, the Nerd and Angel dug a shallow grave near the bodies.* The Nerd threw the littlest girl's body into the bottom, followed by her older sister's body. He dragged their mother's body and threw her in on top of her girls. Then he dragged George's body over and laid him face up on top of the other three bodies. The Nerd and Angel covered the grave with about a foot of soil, covered it with other debris, and then left.

They later disposed of George's truck at an abandoned gas station and drove back to Angel's apartment. Angel's best friend was staying at Angel's apartment to babysit Angel's 10-year-old daughter while the Nerd and Angel were out. She had done this babysitting several times before while, she was told, the Nerd and Angel were looking for a guy named George. They usually returned after a couple of hours. This time they were gone all night, arriving home about 4:30 a.m. Angel's friend was asleep on the couch in the living room. She woke when they came home, but pretended to still be asleep. Angel's friend heard the Nerd and Angel come in the house quietly, whispering, and then heard them shower. After that night, Angel never again asked her friend to babysit so they could look for a guy named George.

A few months later, Angel was called to the grand jury and questioned about the drug connection between her former boyfriend, Tom, and the Nerd. She claimed to know nothing to the grand jury, but then ran back to the Nerd and reported to him that the feds knew about his connection to Tom. So, the Nerd plotted Tom's murder. They used Tom's love for Angel to lure him into a meeting with Angel. Tom picked Angel up at the country club where she was working as a waitress and they drove out into the countryside. Angel directed him to drive to an abandoned farm out in the country, down a gravel road. What she said to get him there we don't know. What we do know is that once they arrived, the Nerd was there waiting, holding the machine gun.

Tom thought that the Nerd was angry about the drug debt he owed the Nerd and began promising to pay all he owed him. The Nerd shot him. Tom was a very tough and strong man. He didn't go down with one shot. He begged the Nerd not to shoot him again, promising again

*Either that, or they had already been to the site before the murders and dug the hole. We never learned which.

to pay the Nerd all he owed him. The Nerd responded by shooting Tom again and again until he emptied the magazine. Tom went down, but was still alive, still struggling. The Nerd went back to Angel's car where she had remained sitting. She handed the Nerd a baseball bat. The Nerd returned and beat in Tom's skull. When, finally, Tom was dead, they buried him face down in a shallow grave on the edge of a cornfield behind a collapsing barn.

Seven Years Later

Seven years passed without anyone finding the murder victims' remains. As noted, the Nerd was prosecuted on drug charges thanks to the help of the parolee and the Nerd's best friend, and was sent off to federal prison. But, then Angel's best friend told what she knew about the night of the first murders, and about later finding the machine gun in the apartment they shared, and about Angel confessing to her about participating in the murders. The agents tracked down Angel's purchase of the gun at a pawn shop. The pawn shop owner remembered the Nerd picking it out. The Nerd's best friend told about how he helped the Nerd cut the weapon apart with a welding torch and disburse the parts by throwing them in ditches out in the country. Using this and other evidence, in 2000 the government charged Angel with murdering witnesses.

Agents arrested Angel and put her in a local jail. The prosecutor asked the marshals to move her to a different county jail where he believed her mail and phone calls could be more easily monitored. This was the same prosecutor in charge of the case against Bugsy and his brother; the same Bugsy who had cooperated against Dr. Feelgood. As it happened, Bugsy was still housed in the same jail. And, by chance, the Court appointed the same attorney who represented Dr. Feelgood to also represent Angel. When that attorney met with his new client at the jail, he warned her about Bugsy. He told her that Bugsy was a government snitch and that she shouldn't to talk to him.

Bugsy, however, already had his hooks into Angel. Her arrest was all over the news and in her case Bugsy recognized another opportunity to earn points for getting out of prison by cooperating against her. Despite the separation of male and female inmates in the small county jail, Bugsy still managed to make contact with her. At first, they yelled back and forth to each other down the hallway of the same cell block. The guards then moved her to another cellblock. Her opaque cell window, though, looked out on the small exercise yard. Bugsy discovered this and began talking with her through the window, though they couldn't see each other. They also resorted to sending notes to each other by hiding them in books borrowed from the jail library. He would check out a book, write a note, hide it in the pages of the book, and when he turned the book back in, she would check it out, and vice versa.

Through this convoluted and tedious means of communication, Bugsy told Angel that he was a member of a mafia, which was true. He told her that he knew of another mafia member doing a life term in prison; also true. He persuaded her that she should work with him to have his mafia buddy claim responsibility for the murders. His buddy was already doing life, Bugsy explained to Angel, so the government couldn't do anything more to him even if he was convicted of killing five people. Though the government had announced it might seek the death penalty against Angel, Bugsy convinced her there was no legal basis for the death penalty and that it'd be thrown out. Further, Iowa, didn't have the death penalty, so the worst thing that could happen to Bugsy's friend is more life sentences. Once his mafia buddy was found guilty of the murders, Bugsy explained to Angel, the government would have to drop charges against her and release her; then she could sue the government for millions of dollars on the grounds of false imprisonment. Bugsy promised to help her, so long as he got half of whatever she won in the lawsuit.

In the exchange of notes up to this point, Angel had made some incriminating statements. It was also at about this time that Bugsy was being pressured by the prosecutor to either plead guilty to the drug conspiracy charges he was facing or go to trial. So Bugsy played a card and told the prosecutor that he had information from Angel and would help the government if the government reduced his sentence.

The law gets complicated here, but suffice it to say that when the government attempts to get information from a person, like Angel, who is represented by an attorney, the government must be very careful not to violate that person's Sixth Amendment right to counsel. A cooperator can listen to what such a person has to say, but cannot actively question the suspect about the crime for which the person is currently represented by an attorney. The government instructs informants about these conditions with what are called "listening post instructions," meaning they can listen like a post, but cannot solicit any information from the person. In case something goes wrong, a taint team is established with another prosecutor and another agent to work with the informant. Any information from the informant is then filtered to remove any information obtained that would violate the defendant's Sixth Amendment rights.

The whole process of working an informant under these circumstances is extremely delicate. Here, it didn't work as it should have, in part, perhaps, because the prosecutor put in charge of the taint team was new and inexperienced. For example, the prosecutor did not create a separate taint team but continued to use the DCI case agent as the primary agent working with Bugsy. Further, Bugsy didn't follow directions. He was told he could only listen to Angel, but not ask her questions about the crime. He ignored those directions. What followed was a near disaster narrowly averted.

Bugsy actively worked Angel, despite orders to the contrary, pumping her for information about the murders and ultimately persuaded her that the only way their scheme could work was for his mafia buddy to take the authorities to the bodies. That, he insisted, was the only way the authorities would believe the mafia buddy was the real murderer. To do this, Bugsy told Angel, he needed maps to the locations of the bodies. Stupidly, despite her attorney telling her that Bugsy was an informant, Angel fell for it and drew maps to the locations of the bodies, then sent them to Bugsy in a library book.

With his hands on the maps showing the location of the bodies, Bugsy thought he was now in the driver's seat. Bugsy told a jailor he had maps to the bodies and wanted to negotiate with the government. When the young prosecutor working the case learned of the maps, she sent word to the jailor to tell Bugsy to hand over the maps. Bugsy refused and demanded a meeting with her, his attorney, and the DCI agent so that he could negotiate a deal before he turned over the maps.

At some point, the criminal chief learned what was going on. He immediately sensed that things were out of control and that an informant was trying to call the shots, running roughshod over the young prosecutor. So, he called me in. The meeting with Bugsy was to take place the next morning. I remember reading over the file that night, everything I could about Bugsy's cooperation in the investigation, and realized we had a major problem.

The next morning we met in a conference room at the jail. I had called in an FBI special agent telling him that we had an emergency and that I needed him to run a taint team for me. He showed up at the jail, as did the DCI agent. Before Bugsy and his attorney were brought in, I told the DCI agent the bad news. I told him he was being cut off from working with Bugsy. I told him I believed that the maps had already likely been obtained in violation of Angel's Sixth Amendment rights and to protect him and allow him to remain the lead investigator in the murder case, he'd be barred from access to anything coming from Bugsy, including the maps and, if they were accurate, the victims' bodies, until we could litigate the matter and determine if the evidence could be used against Angel. I reminded him that the goal was still to go after the Nerd, and even if we couldn't use the evidence against Angel, we could still use it against the Nerd.

The DCI agent was understandably upset. I was telling him that he'd be barred from participating in the recovery of the murder victims' bodies after he had worked for seven years on the murder investigation. Instead, the FBI agent would take over as the lead on the recovery of any bodies, if the maps proved accurate. The DCI agent left upset and likely remains upset about it to this day. He understood the reasoning, but he didn't like it. In the end, through a legal technicality I will explain shortly, I was able to save the evidence so that it could be used against Angel. Thus, we didn't need the taint team because of that legal maneuver, but I didn't know it at the time.

After the DCI agent left, Bugsy and his attorney were brought into the conference room. I told them I was taking over the taint team and the FBI agent would be working the case with me. Bugsy said he didn't want to work with me. I said it wasn't up to him. Then the conversation went something like this: "I understand you got maps from Angel to the location of the bodies," I said. "You need to provide them to me now."

"Fuck you. I don't know what you're talking about," came the reply.

"You told the jailor you have maps. You need to turn them over now."

"I want immunity on the drug charges and a reduction in my current sentence, then maybe I'll think about it."

Bugsy's attorney tried to reason with him, but Bugsy shrugged him off and told him to shut up.

"Look, that's not how it works," I interjected. "You give us the evidence and then the government and the judge will determine what benefit you receive for your cooperation," I tried to explain.

"Fuck you," Bugsy replied.

"Well, Bugsy, I thought you might say that," I responded. "So, what I have here is a search warrant to search your cell and, if necessary, your body, including your body cavities. You can either turn over the maps peacefully now, or we'll take them from you."

At this Bugsy exploded with a string of expletives that I won't repeat here. I had the jailors, whom I had prepared ahead of time for this, remove him from the conference room. He was taken to a cell and, though he resisted, was stripped and searched, including his body cavities. At the same time, agents searched his cell. The maps were found hidden in his cell.

The Victims Are Found

The maps were written on small slips of paper. In addition to crudely drawn maps Angel had included a description of the condition of the bodies when buried so that Bugsy's mafia buddy could tell the authorities and when they found the bodies in that condition it would appear that he was credible. She described, for example, how George and the mother were gagged and bound; she described how Tom was buried facedown.

The following week is a blur. I presided over several meetings with the FBI and a number of other agencies to organize a search. There was some minor bickering and turf battles that I quickly squelched. Time was of the essence. It was late October. Soon snow would fall and the ground would freeze. Search teams from the FBI's elite unit in D.C.

were sent to Iowa. We secured the airspace around the sites to keep press and others away. Then the search began.

The maps proved to be remarkably accurate. Although Angel had the burial site of George, the mother and girls on the wrong side of a railroad track, all else was accurate. When a core sample came up with bones, a grid was formed and the dig began. The dig was overseen by a forensic archeologist, an FBI agent, who conducted the dig in a manner very similar to an archeological excavation of an ancient historic site. Using hand tools, he dug down inch by inch, taking notes and making detailed drawings along the way. For 19 hours he worked straight through the night, taking only very short breaks to drink coffee and go to the bathroom. Lying on his stomach for hours at a time, he dug down until he recovered every last bone of the 6-year-old girl buried at the bottom of the grave. It was an amazing and unbelievable feat of skill and endurance.

One of the first things the forensic archeologist noted was the presence of bones from a small animal on top of the first body. He wrote in his field notes something along the lines of: "Dog? Possible satanic sacrifice? Placed to throw off cadaver dogs?" Oddly, it later turned out they were the bones of an opossum who had dug a burrow and nest on top of the bodies. Why the opossum chose that particular location is somewhat of a mystery, but the bones were sent to a national lab and confirmed, and the agent found and documented changes in the soil composition showing the direction of the opossum's burrow. All of this was documented in the agent's final reports and in lab reports.

The elite search team was needed on another case on an emergency basis the following week, so it wasn't available to conduct the search for Tom's body. We were told the team would be available to come back out in two weeks, but the weather forecast for northern Iowa was dire. So, the DCI took over the search for Tom's body. The contrast in methods was somewhat humorous. Instead of employing a forensic archeologist who worked with fine hand tools and brushes, the DCI team hired a local backhoe operator. At the site marked on the map, the backhoe operator started scrapping back the soil a half-foot at a time until the bucket pulled part of a leg and boot out of the ground. Then the agent resorted to shovels and hand trowels to recover Tom's body. Although there were no meticulous notes and detailed drawings, the agents took many photographs as they progressed. This, too, was a testament to the dedication of the agents. The day of the search was bitterly cold with snow flurries. They erected a tent over the grave site which at least blocked the winds to some degree, but not the cold.

The remains were taken to the state medical examiner's laboratory where, luckily, an amazing woman was completing post-doctorate work. She was a trained forensic anthropologist. She very carefully documented, cleaned and sorted all the many bones. In the first grave the bones were largely comingled in the grave, and there are many small bones in the human body. The forensic anthropologist identified every bone and sorted them to go with the correct victim, and then studied them for signs of trauma to determine, if possible, cause of death. Each of the bodies from the first site had evidence of head gunshots, which established readily enough the cause of death. The forensic anthropologist also discovered signs of other gunshot wounds to the adults in their torsos and on arm bones. She also noted that the mother's right ring finger had a spiral fracture that, because of the lack of any sign of healing, the expert determined occurred at the time of the murder. This was noteworthy because several months after her disappearance some children playing in a creek many miles away from Mason City found the mother's purse and ring. Her family testified that she never removed her old wedding ring from her right hand. It was clear that the Nerd had ripped the ring off her finger after killing her with the plan to throw off the authorities as to her location by discarding it and her purse at another location far away.

As for Tom, the forensic anthropologist put his bones back together as best she could. His skull was so shattered, she never could quite make all the tiny pieces fit together. Her findings confirmed that he was shot many times in the torso.

The Nerd Is Charged, Tried and Convicted

Because of the Sixth Amendment issue surrounding recovery of the maps, Angel's case was sidetracked as we charged her with different crimes, dropped the old ones, and defended it all on appeal, all of which I will explain shortly. In the meantime, with discovery of the bodies the time had come to charge the Nerd with the murders. A grand jury indicted him, charging him with many counts, including murders in furtherance of a Continuing Criminal Enterprise. The charges were death penalty eligible and the Attorney General ordered us to seek it. I was brought onto the prosecution team now, and not just the taint team. The lead prosecutor was the same one who originally charged the Nerd in 1993.

As part of the ongoing investigation, the agents identified inmates with whom the Nerd had been housed in federal prison and approached as many of them as they could to seek their cooperation, to find out if the Nerd had made any admissions while incarcerated. Many of the inmates told the agents to go pound sand, but enough of them cooperated that we learned some startling and very incriminating information.

When the government charged Angel with the murder a year before, the Nerd knew it was only a matter of time before he was charged. The Nerd had joined a white supremacist organization in prison. The organization had members in and out of prison. He began to develop a new plan. He recruited a number of convicted murderers to be part of his plan. Among them was a former state court judge who had his wife executed in front of his children, a drug dealer from Kansas City who had two drug couriers killed by duct taping their mouths and noses shut and letting them slowly suffocate, and a Vietnam war vet who, among other things, had stolen a helicopter and landed it in the yard of a female federal prison to rescue his girlfriend.* There were many others, some of whom cooperated, many of whom didn't.

The plan the Nerd developed was this. He would list all his gang members as character witnesses. That would require them to be flown to Iowa and held in the county jail with the Nerd during the trial. Together, they'd overpower the guards in the local county jail and escape, killing whomever they needed on the way. He planned to flee to Canada from whence he planned to head back to Iowa on trips to wreak vengeance against the authorities and those who snitched on him. Among others, he planned on killing the lead prosecutor, the

*I have to note that this guy later told us that when he landed in the prison yard, his girlfriend ran to the helicopter as planned, opened the door, looked in, and said, "Is that you, Bill?" He replied, "Just who the hell do you think it would be?"

narcotics agent, his best friend from childhood, the parolee who cooperated against him in the last drug case, and the judge who sentenced him. He and his gang would rob banks as needed to finance operations and to live large.

This wasn't just pie-in-the-sky planning. Indeed, the Nerd and his group bribed a prison guard to loan them handcuffs, leg irons, a belly chain used to hold the cuffs next to the body, and a black box. A black box is a device made of hard plastic that locks with a special pin around the chain and handcuffs so that an inmate cannot gain access to the handcuffs to pick the locks.

In light of this information, several things happened. First, because the lead prosecutor was now an intended victim and also a witness to the Nerd's comment back in 1993 that "your case isn't as good as you think it is," combined with the prosecutor's likely call-up for active duty in the military (the Iraqi war had begun), it was determined that he should withdraw from the case and I'd take over as lead prosecutor. Assisting me would be a prosecutor from the State of Iowa who was an experienced murder prosecutor. The former lead prosecutor had brought him in a couple years before to help prosecute the case.

Second, the marshals determined that security had to be substantially increased for the trial. A security detail was assigned to the presiding judge (the same one who sentenced the Nerd in 1997) and to the judge's wife and daughter. Special Operations Teams armed with machine guns and sniper's rifles would provide security for the courthouse, while a separate team would be assigned to transport and secure the Nerd. We also placed several of the cooperating witnesses into the Witness Protection Program. Each was assigned his own security team.

We charged the Nerd in 2001. His case didn't come up for trial for three years. During that time the defense filed scores of motions seeking dismissal of the charges, suppression of evidence, and countless other challenges to the prosecution, the death penalty and everything else. The judge had appointed two of the very best defense attorneys in the state to represent the Nerd. He also appointed a defense attorney from Kansas City who had tried death penalty cases. These attorneys put up a hell of a fight, and appropriately so. We fought long and hard over many legal issues, and the judge issued scores of written opinions on every aspect of the case.

In the leadup to trial, we had to prepare witnesses. Witnesses in the Witness Protection Program can only be reached through handlers and for those incarcerated in the program, we had to travel to the prisons where they were held to prepare them, because for trial they'd be flown in and out on the same day and wouldn't be around to prepare during the trial. This required my co-counsel and the agents and me to travel around the country on two road trips to visit the many prisons where the inmates were held to prep them. It took a couple weeks to do this.

The case finally came up for trial in the late summer of 2004 and it lasted two and a half months. I won't recount here all the details of the trial. Rather, I'll share just few things that stand out in my memory.

First, my trial team was outstanding. The DCI agent was the lead case agent, while the narcotics agents focused on the drug trafficking side of the case. Sali was our paralegal, and I had the assistance of a victim/witness coordinator and an IT and trial presentation software expert. The team worked very long and hard hours, day after day, week after week, and far from home (the case was tried in Sioux City). I will always remember Sali's amazing organization and memory and mind-reading skills. During trial I'd often turn to her and utter a few disjointed words, like "Sali, a photograph, it showed a sock, lower lefthand corner." Invariably, she'd reply with the exhibit number off the top of her head and hand me the exhibit.

Second, jury selection sucked. In death penalty cases a juror has to have an open mind to consider both the possibility of imposing the death penalty or life in prison, the only two options. Jurors who insist they could never consider a life sentence for someone who killed two little girls cannot serve. Likewise, if jurors insist they cannot consider imposing the death penalty, no matter what crime occurred, because of religious, moral or other beliefs they cannot sit as jurors in a capital case. In addition, this case was highly publicized, so we also had to ensure that jurors hadn't already made up their minds based on what they heard in the news and could remain fair and impartial. Thus, the jury selection process was difficult and required calling a lot more potential jurors (about 500) than in a regular case. It also required that each juror be questioned separately and individually about the juror's beliefs about the death penalty and about the publicity. Jury selection took three and a half weeks. Each morning we'd start out with a panel of about 15 prospective jurors, question them about general matters, and then send them all out of the courtroom and bring them back, one by one, to question them about the death penalty and publicity. That would take all day. The next morning we'd start with a new panel. If you have seen the movie *Groundhog Day* starring Bill Murray, you have some appreciation for what it was like to go into court each day and ask the same questions over and over again.

By about the third week we were all getting a little punch drunk and tired, and our words didn't always come out exactly as planned. During one session I was addressing the panel. One of the general topics I covered every day was the gruesome nature of some of the evidence the jury would have to see. I wanted to ensure that jurors were prepared for the evidence, but also that they could still give the defendant a fair trial and not vote to convict just based on the nature of the evidence. What I meant to say that morning was something like: "In every murder case there will be disturbing and gruesome evidence of some nature. It is important that jurors be able to consider such evidence and still be fair and impartial and not vote to convict just because they are upset about the nature of the evidence."

What came out of my mouth for the first sentence was instead: "In every murder case there is evidence that a murder occurred."

I went on to elaborate, but my trial team thought my profound insight was so noteworthy that at the end of the day in a mock ceremony they presented me with a framed certificate with my quote prominently displayed, covered with additional post-it notes by trial team members with their comments, like "nothing gets by this guy." I still have that framed certificate. It hangs next to the door in my chambers to remind me to be humble.

Another thing about the trial that stands out in my memory is the testimony of one witness in particular. He was a member of the white supremacist organization that the Nerd had recruited in federal prison. He was one of the inmates who told the agents to go pound sand. But a couple of the others who had cooperated told us that this particular inmate was closest to the Nerd and he'd know a lot. Even though he had told the agents to bugger off, I named him as a witness and had him brought back to Iowa with the idea that we'd make one more run at him to try to persuade him to cooperate.

We spoke with him one evening during the trial. The marshals brought him to a conference room in the courthouse. He was bound by leg irons, belly chain, handcuffs and a black box. He had tattoos everywhere. He was a nasty looking man. If looks could kill, I'd have been dead before he sat down at the table. The DCI agent sat next to me on one side of the table, the inmate was on the other side, the Deputy U.S. marshals just inside the door.

I started in on my best pitch, talking about the murder of children, mentioned the possibility that if he cooperated perhaps he could get a reduction in his sentence, and so on. He listened to me without much patience. Finally, he said, "Are you done?"

"Yes," I replied.

"Good," he said, and then stated something along the lines of the following: "I will testify tomorrow, but not because of anything you have said. I'm serving three life terms for murder. I will never get out of prison and I know that. The reason I will testify is because I had a dream last night."

He told us that dream and repeated it in court the next day. Part of what he also told us that night, though, was about how they trained to get out of the handcuffs and chains and turn them into weapons. "All this shit here," he said, gesturing toward his handcuffs and chains, "I could get out of this in less than two minutes. Want me to show you?"

"No," I quickly replied, "No, thank you, please don't, not here, not now. But please do me a favor. When you get back to the jail, show the marshals."

He did. More than once. And they filmed it for training purposes for marshals and prison officials all over the United States. It started with him removing a portion of a paperclip from his mouth. He had been strip searched at least twice before they brought him to see me that evening, including a search of his body cavities. The authorities had missed the paperclip because he had created a cavity between his molars and his gum by repeatedly cutting away at his gum on the inside his mouth so that the half-inch long piece of paperclip would slide in the groove he gouged. Once he removed the paperclip, he banged the black box against the wall at a particular angle, causing the pins in the hinges to come loose. Once the black box popped open and fell off, he used the paperclip to pick the lock on his handcuffs and then leg irons. True to his promise, in less than two minutes he had escaped his bonds and was holding the steel chain between his hands as a weapon.

He testified the next day. He testified at length about the escape and vengeance plan, and in detail about admissions the Nerd had made about the murders. The Nerd thought he had found in prison this one person he could really trust; another man who had killed snitches against him. But the Nerd hadn't counted on a dream.

At the end of his testimony, I asked the man why was willing to testify; that surely he recognized that it was very unlikely the authorities would reduce his sentence. He told the jury why he was testifying. As I recall, he said something like this: "I look at you and I look across the room at the jury, and the judge, and I see you all looking at me and I can see in your eyes that you all think I'm a very bad man. That I'm evil. You know the awful crimes I committed and you think I'm scum. But a few nights ago I had a dream. The two little girls came to me in the dream. They asked me to help them. They told me, 'you are a good man. A good man.' So, I know right now you all think I'm a bad man, but those two little girls (here, he looked at the ceiling), those two little girls are looking down on me now, now that I have helped them, and they believe I'm a good man." He paused.

"So you ask me why I'm testifying here today? It's for those two little girls, the only people who have ever thought I was a good man."

You could have heard a pin drop in the courtroom.

I could go on and on and on about the guilt-phase of the trial, but will spare the reader too much detail. The jury returned a guilty verdict after only a few hours' deliberation and we began the penalty phase of the trial the following day.

I remember the importance of the evidence we presented in the penalty phase of the trial. In death penalty cases, there are two phases; the guilt phase and, if the jury finds guilt on a death eligible count, a penalty phase. The penalty phase is like a whole new trial. There are opening statements, evidence, and closing arguments all over again. Here, the focus isn't on whether the defendant is guilty but on whether he deserves death for the murders. On the eve of trial, the state governor prohibited my co-counsel from participating in the death penalty phase of trial, so I had to handle that portion on my own. It lasted a couple weeks. During this phase we presented some startling new evidence for the jury.

The most startling new evidence involved a bank robbery. When the Nerd was a senior in high school, his father was convicted of robbing the bank where the Nerd's mother worked as a teller. The robbery took place early in the morning, when a cleaning lady came to clean the bank at 6:00 a.m. She was overpowered the moment she got in and turned off the alarm. The Nerd's father was found a day later, sitting drunk in a parked car, with half the loot. In the back seat were several coats, dark glasses, and shoes that were two sizes too large for him. He went to prison for a few years, got out, and never committed another crime. What no one knew at the time, and we only learned later, was that the Nerd had planned the robbery.

Initially, the Nerd planned to commit the bank robbery with three high school classmates: two brothers and a third not-too-bright kid. During the penalty phase, these former classmates testified about it. The Nerd had approached them all with the plan to rob the bank. He had stolen and made a copy of the key to his mother's cash drawer. He told about the cleaning lady and the activation alarm. He planned to have the not-too-bright kid actually commit the robbery while the rest of them looked out for the police. He'd have the not-too-bright kid wear oversized shoes to throw off the cops following any shoe prints, and have him wear many coats so the cleaning lady, if she caught any glimpse of him, would estimate him to be much heavier and taller than he really was.

What the Nerd then suggested separately to the two brothers was that as soon as the not-too-bright kid committed the robbery, they'd kill him. The Nerd said they'd dump his body in the water treatment lagoon where, he assured the brothers, the chemicals would eat away all the flesh and bone. The brothers, both of whom would later join the military, at first thought it was all a joke and big talk, but when the Nerd spoke of murder, they told him that they wanted no part of it and quit talking to him.

The closing argument in the penalty phase was hard to make. It's hard to ask others to sentence a man to die. I argued, though, that so long as we have a death penalty, then this case of cold-blooded murder of children warranted that penalty or no case did. The jury returned three life sentences for murdering the adults, and two death penalties for murdering the little girls.

Angel's Trial

Angel's case came on for trial about eight months after the Nerd's trial, and took just as long. The jury selection was just as painful. The trial testimony just as compelling and disturbing. Although we had no evidence and never claimed that Angel pulled the trigger to kill any of the victims, we emphasized that but for her assistance and urging the murders would likely never have occurred. The Nerd's best friend testified that he was more afraid of Angel than of the Nerd because she was just plainly vicious and out of control. He and other witnesses testified about how very strong-willed she was, how she manipulated people, and how she constantly berated the Nerd and told him that she'd be damned if their baby would be without a father because he was in prison.

The jury returned a guilty verdict against her after only a couple of hours' deliberation, just as the Nerd's jury had done. I wasn't there to hear the verdict. I flew to Florida as soon as the arguments were over. The judge had graciously continued the penalty phase of the trial for a few days. My mother, who had been suffering from cancer, had died the day before closing arguments on the guilt phase. I flew to be with my father and brothers for a few days before we started the penalty phase. I got a phone call from my trial team members as they celebrated the guilty verdict that night in the hotel bar. I also received calls from the defense attorneys from the Nerd's case expressing their condolences. Though we fought hard against each other in that and in other cases, we became friends. It was very thoughtful of them.

The closing arguments on the guilt phase occurred on a Tuesday. We started the penalty phase on the following Monday. I was again the only attorney to handle this portion of the trial because my co-counsel's boss had again barred him from participating. A couple things stand out in my memory from this phase of the trial.

First, I remember during the penalty phase that, as we did in the Nerd's penalty phase, we presented some evidence we had held back on during the guilt phase. We presented evidence that, after the Nerd was sent off to a federal prison, Angel continued to distribute methamphetamine. Further, when one of her dealers ran up a debt she tried to hire two thugs to beat up and kidnap the dealer and bring him to her. The thugs happened to be a cooperator and an undercover DEA agent. The conversation she had with the thugs was recorded and the jury heard it. They also heard that when the DEA agent went out to Angel's car with her afterwards to get directions, he saw duct tape in her trunk. A couple days after the undercover operation though, she spoke with the Nerd in prison and he warned her that the thugs were probably cops; after that, she no longer spoke with them. But the evidence showed who she really was, and that she was capable of violence on her own regardless of whether the Nerd was around.

I also remember the defense called a psychiatrist to testify as a mitigation expert during the defense presentation. The same expert had also testified in the Nerd's case for the same reason. He didn't really do any testing of either defendant or know much about them. But that didn't stop him from relying on second-hand knowledge to proclaim that neither defendant was a danger and that their conduct was driven by societal and psychological stressors beyond their control. It was frankly a lot of psycho-babble with no substance and based on no evidence. In the Nerd's trial I had cross-examined him at length and I think effectively ripped him apart. In Angel's trial, as I listened to this insufferable witness go on and on for four and half hours of direct testimony my mind was going numb. I watched the jury and sensed that they felt the same way about his testimony.

When, finally, the defense attorney ended the direct examination, the judge called on me for cross examination. "Mr. Williams," the judge announced, "you may now cross-examine the witness."

I sat in my chair for a few moments, just looking at my notepad.

"Mr. Williams?" the judge said.

"Your honor," I began, then paused. "Your honor, there's nothing I want to ask this man."

Several of the jurors guffawed and snickered, while all smiled at me. As did the judge, just a little, before he quickly regained his neutral composure.

Last, I remember sadly that the defense called the daughter of Angel and the Nerd. By the time of trial, she was about 10 years old. She testified about her love for her mother and what her mother had done for her, even though her mother had been in prison for the last several years. I recall that the defense attorney, who was very good, handled her testimony expertly. I declined to ask the girl any questions.

We presented closing arguments on the penalty phase and the jury left to deliberate. Late the following afternoon they came back with a verdict of death. It was the first time a woman was sentenced to death in the federal system since Ethel Rosenberg in 1951.

Until the second trial was over we had refrained from speaking with the press about the cases. Now, the United States Attorney asked me to read a statement to the press who were waiting outside the courthouse. As I walked down the courthouse stairs, I glanced to my right as I reached the first floor and before I turned to head outside to confront the press. There, down the wide and cavernous central hallway of the Sioux City courthouse, was the daughter of two people I had tried and had been sentenced to death. She was by herself, quietly twirling in the sunlight streaming in from the windows at the far end of the hallway. In that moment, she was blissfully unmindful of the setting and situation, just being a little girl, not thinking that both of her parents had been sentenced to die. It is an image, like the image of the little children her parents killed, that will never leave my memory.

The Ultimate Punishment

Both cases resulted in years of appeals and post-conviction relief litigation. The Court of Appeals affirmed both defendants' guilty verdicts and death penalties, and the United States Supreme Court denied certiorari on both cases. Both defendants also filed civil habeas petitions challenging their convictions. These post-conviction cases typically involve allegations that trial counsel was ineffective. Both defendants made those claims, and others, in their post-conviction petitions.

As for the Nerd, the trial judge asked another judge to handle the post-conviction litigation to provide a new and different set of eyes on the case to ensure that justice was done. The hearing took the better part of two weeks. Because the Nerd was challenging the competency of his defense counsel, in part, it allowed me an inside view of what his attorneys did for him and what they knew. Interestingly, the mitigation expert the attorneys hired, a person whose job is to dig up as many facts as possible to show the defendant wasn't all bad and to mitigate the seriousness of the crime he committed, came very close to telling the attorneys that she could find nothing mitigating. Indeed, when she researched the Nerd's background she found evidence that he had raped a girl when he was in high school. We hadn't discovered this, but she had.

The Nerd's post-conviction challenge was rejected and the Eighth Circuit Court of Appeals affirmed the denial. The Supreme Court declined to hear the case. In 2020, the government executed the Nerd by lethal injection. In his final words he uttered not one apology. He is one of the few men in whose eyes I saw no soul.

Angel's death penalty verdict was overturned by the trial judge in the post-conviction litigation. That litigation took several months—indeed, it generated more pages of transcript than the trial itself. The key development was discovering what a very poor job her defense attorneys did in researching, developing, and presenting evidence about her mental health. This evidence, the judge found, would have been highly mitigating had it been presented to the jury. The judge ultimately concluded that the jurors might not have sentenced her to death had they known about her mental health problems. Thus, while he didn't reverse the finding of guilt for the murders, he ordered a new penalty phase trial so that new attorneys could present evidence of her mental illnesses.

The United States Attorney General later concluded that the government shouldn't seek the death penalty in light of the new evidence. Thus, Angel's death penalty verdict was overturned and she was sentenced to life in prison without the possibility of parole, where she remains to this day.

Chapter 9

White Knight Bleed-Out Scheme

A white knight is someone who comes to the rescue of another; a savior. A bleed-out scheme is a very sophisticated type of bankruptcy fraud. It involves the depletion and diversion of corporate assets through complex and deceptive means, and then the liquidation of the corporation and cancelling of debts through bankruptcy forgiveness. A white knight bleed-out scheme, then, is when someone purports to come to the rescue of a corporation, but instead bleeds it dry of its assets and then declares bankruptcy, walking away from the corporate debts. Among the many bankruptcy fraud cases I prosecuted in my career, I had one white knight bleed-out scheme. It was fascinating, and depressing.

In the 1920s, a family-owned trucking company began in northeast Iowa, starting with a single truck. By the 1980s, it had grown tremendously to a regional powerhouse with hundreds of trucks and trailers, depots scattered throughout the Midwest, and repair shops with inventories of spare parts, skilled mechanics, and expensive tools. Then came the deregulation of the trucking industry. Whether deregulation was a good or bad thing for the country or the trucking industry as a whole is unimportant. What matters for this story is that the Iowa trucking company, like many others, struggled in a deregulated market. By the end of the 1990s, the family-owned business was upside down financially. It had treated its employees well, including matching employee contributions to fund a generous pension program. When the company fell on hard times though, the company borrowed money from the pension fund to keep the company afloat. It also borrowed extensively from the bank.

By the mid–2000s, the company had massive debts amounting to tens of millions of dollars in unfunded pension liabilities, loans, and accounts payable. The family trucking company was now run by the third generation of family members who were aging and lacked the passion and power of earlier generations. They wanted out and began looking for someone to purchase the failing trucking concern. They considered, but rejected, bankruptcy because the family was still loyal to its employees. If the company went bankrupt, the pension would likely still be largely funded through the sale of the corporate assets, but scores of employees would be out of jobs, some of whom had known no other employment and had worked at the company their entire careers. The family members wanted someone to take over the business and turn it around, someone knowledgeable about the industry and with sufficient capital to infuse and revive the company so that it'd once again be competitive.

In walked our White Knight. He was in his 50s, and a large, stout man with a booming voice and a swagger to accompany it. He had been in the trucking industry for decades and claimed to own a holding company that in turn owned several other trucking companies. Having learned that the family had put out feelers in the industry looking for possible buyers, he arranged a meeting with the officers and board of directors of the Iowa company. White Knight showed up with an assistant, a slick-looking position paper, and documents purporting to show his substantial assets and income. After meeting with the company personnel for several days and pouring over their financial disclosures, he made a proposition to them.

If they turned over all the company stock to him, he'd assume all the company's debts. He pointed out that as a privately owned corporation, where the family members had personally guaranteed the company's debt on bank loans and the underfunded pension plan, the family members personally were on the line if the company failed. He showed that the company's assets at present was many million dollars less than its total debt. He explained that if the company even declared bankruptcy at this point, not only would the family lose the entire company, they'd have their personal assets seized to pay the company debts. In short, he explained, this was an opportunity for the family to walk away debt free from the debacle that had become the trucking company. Their personal fortunes would be preserved and they could move on.

He, on the other hand, would assume their debts and infuse tens of millions of his own funds into the company. He convinced the family members that their failing company would actually fit perfectly into the group of trucking companies he owned. Together, the synergistic effect of combining the assets and distribution routes of the companies under his control would make them a regional powerhouse in the trucking industry once again. To assuage the family's concern about ensuring the vitality of the pension fund upon which all their workers depended for comfortable retirements, the White Knight said that he'd guarantee the fund by pledging his own personal assets as collateral. The paperwork he provided the family showed that he had a net worth of many millions of dollars.

The family members were vastly relieved and quickly agreed to the deal. True, they'd get no money in selling the company to the White Knight, but overnight their liabilities would decrease by millions and their net worth increase a corresponding amount. Soon the paperwork was prepared and signed and the deal closed. White Knight took over as the owner, chief executive officer, and chairman of the board of directors for the trucking company. Although he and his wife lived in an adjoining state, he took up residence in a suite of rooms in a local hotel.

Within weeks, the White Knight began executing his scheme. First, he brought in two co-conspirators. The first would later claim to us that he once worked for the CIA, which might have been true. We'll call him CIA man. The White Knight hired him as a consultant for $100,000, paid for by the trucking company. We were unable to find any paperwork afterwards showing that he did a day of work for the company. What it appears he did do for his money is help the White Knight orchestrate the rest of the transactions I'll discuss shortly. The other co-conspirator was set up as the purported owner of a trucking company (we'll call it Company X) that was part of what the White Knight claimed was his group of trucking companies. Company X never existed as an actual going concern with assets; the corporate address turned out the be the private residence of one of the low-level company employees. We also later discovered that the White Knight didn't own any trucking companies. He and his wife did own a corporation that appeared to have no assets of its own, but through its bank accounts much money flowed.

Soon, the White Knight began letting people go from the corporate headquarters, claiming it was part of a cost-savings effort and need to trim an overweight management team. The one person he did keep on, though, was an elderly secretary who had served as secretary to the CEO and chairman of the board of directors when the family owned the business. She kept the same position after the White Knight took over and became complicit and integral in helping him execute the scheme.

Over the course of the next 18 months, the White Knight bled the company dry through many complicated and complex transactions. I will give you only a taste of them here because a full explanation would be a book unto itself. First, he and his co-conspirators fabricated invoices and other documents purporting to show that Company X hauled freight for the Iowa trucking company. The accounting department dutifully paid the invoices, funneling hundreds of thousands of dollars to Company X for fictitious services that were never provided.

The White Knight also secretly diverted funds from the company, in the form of bogus consulting fees, to purchase another small trucking company (we'll call it Company Y) in an adjoining state. The White Knight, along with CIA man, were the owners of Company Y, although all the paperwork showed that CIA man was the owner. For a while the two companies began doing business together, sharing routes and loads such that sometimes the Iowa company hauled freight for Company Y and vice versa. Again, though, the White Knight and his co-conspirators dummied up documents and falsified the books so that it looked like about an equal amount of money was flowing into the Iowa company's coffers from Company Y as was flowing out of it to Company Y. The reality was that almost no money was coming into the Iowa company. The White Knight was essentially shifting all the business and customers from the Iowa company to Company Y. Finally, toward the end, the White Knight again diverted funds from the Iowa company to purchase part of another trucking company in a different adjoining state (Company Z). This time his other erstwhile associate was listed as the purported owner, though records later showed that the White Knight was the owner.

This type of shell game can only last so long before it falls apart. Company accountants start asking too many questions, questioning too many documents, and bank examiners concerned about their collateral started looking too closely. Knowing time was running out, the White Knight decided it was time to declare bankruptcy. He visited with a bankruptcy attorney, bringing along one of the company accountants and another executive. They met for hours with the bankruptcy attorney, going over all the records. At one point, though, the accountant and executive noticed that none of the debts that Company X and Company Y owed the Iowa company were included in its disclosure of assets as accounts receivable to the trucking company. The two insisted that these accounts receivable added up to hundreds of thousands of dollars on the company books and needed to be listed. The White Knight knew, though, that these companies didn't actually owe the Iowa company anything; the alleged accounts receivable were premised on fictitious documents and phantom loads. At this point in the meeting the White Knight sent the two trucking company executives out of the meeting so he could talk alone with the attorney. About a half hour later they were invited back into the meeting and were told that those alleged accounts receivable wouldn't be listed as company assets. The attorney gave no explanation. The White Knight later claimed the lawyer gave him blank bankruptcy forms to sign and that he didn't know what the lawyer ultimately reported.

In the days just before and following the filing of the corporate bankruptcy, the White Knight began the more labor-intensive effort of stealing the physical assets of the company so that they wouldn't be seized by the bankruptcy court. He had some loyal workers back up empty trucks to the loading docks of the main repair shop and fill them with all the company's spare parts and expensive tools, including forklifts. Then he had his workers drive the trucks and offload the contents at Company Y's location. From there, he and others worked to sell the spare parts and tools to third parties, with the funds being funneled back to the White Knight. The Iowa company rented many rigs and trailers as part of its operations, but it also owned quite a few itself. These the White Knight had driven away from the company headquarters and other area terminals in the dark of the night. Some were taken to be quickly sold, some repainted and disguised to be included as part of the fleets belonging to Company Y and Company Z. Others were hidden in various locations to be gathered later when the dust settled.

When the bankruptcy court appointed a trustee to oversee the liquidation of the company and creditors began filing claims, it rapidly became apparent that this bankruptcy estate was a disaster. The company owed tens of millions, but had almost nothing left in assets. Although when he bought the company the White Knight swore he'd infuse his own funds into the company, the records showed that he didn't contribute one dime. Although he assuaged the family's concerns that the pension fund be taken care of by a pledge of his personal assets to guarantee the debt, the records showed it never took place and the pension fund was virtually unfunded at the time of bankruptcy. An assistant United States bankruptcy trustee, whose role it is to protect the integrity of the bankruptcy system, quickly smelled a skunk. She latched on to the case and never let go.

When a company or business declares bankruptcy, the creditors can call for a meeting of creditors in bankruptcy court where they have an opportunity to question the debtor under oath. The case trustee, the lawyer assigned to seize and liquidate the assets, presides over the hearing. An assistant bankruptcy trustee can appear at these meetings and ask questions as well. Our bulldog assistant United States trustee showed up and questioned the White Knight at length at the meeting.

When asked if Company X was a going concern with assets, he swore it was. When asked details though about where it was physically located, who owned it, who ran it, and the like, he was unable to provide answers.

When asked if he had any interest in or connection with Company Y or Company Z, the White Knight swore under oath that he didn't.

When asked what work CIA man and the other cohort had done for hundreds of thousands of dollars in consulting fees, he blew smoke about claimed evaluations and consultations of which no record was ever found.

When asked about the location of missing spare parts, tools, trucks and trailers, the White Knight pled ignorance.

The assistant bankruptcy trustee soon brought the case to me, and I as quickly recruited an IRS special agent to help me unravel the crime. It took many months and reviewing thousands of pages of documents and bank records, but we eventually got to the bottom of the scheme. We followed the money trail, but by the time we came into the case the money had dissipated so far that much of it was beyond seizure. But we did know where most of it went and would be in a position to seek restitution from those responsible.

In every complex fraud case I worked, whether it was bankruptcy fraud, bank fraud, or any other kind, I always searched for evidence of blatant personal enrichment by the target. I knew it would be difficult sometimes for the average juror to fully comprehend complex fraud schemes. But if I could show that the target took money for his own personal gain in some explicit and often egregious and devious way, the jurors would understand that and see the target for who he was. Sometimes this evidence ended up being funds diverted by the fraudster for a luxury car, other times for prostitutes or mistresses. In this case it was a $5,000 stickpin.

Among the suspicious transactions was a $5,000 check from Company Y to Becker's Repair.* When we searched the company records for an invoice for services performed by Becker's Repair, though, we found none. Indeed, we found no record of Becker's Repair ever doing work for the company. We did, though, see a corresponding transfer of $5,000 from the Iowa trucking company to Company Y at about the same time. We eventually got a copy of the check and saw that it was endorsed on the back by Becker's Jewelers. When we spoke with the owner of Becker's Jewelers, he told us that he sold the White Knight a $5,000 diamond stickpin. He provided us with the receipt for the transaction. He recalled getting a check in the mail from a trucking company for the stickpin, but the White Knight had told him he owned a trucking company and so the jeweler didn't give it much thought. He also noticed the check was made payable to Becker's Repair, which he thought odd, but he figured it was just a typographical mistake. In any event, the check cleared so he didn't think anything more of it.

One of the last steps in a fraud investigation often involves having

*I have changed the name here to avoid referencing an innocent business in this book.

agents question targets. One of two things will happen if the targets talk to the agents, both of them good for the government. First, the targets could tell the truth and make incriminating admissions. Second, they could lie. When they lie, we could investigate the lies and show them to be lies. When a target lies about criminal conduct it is as good or better than when he tells the truth because it shows deception and a consciousness of guilt.

In this case, the IRS agent interviewed the White Knight, who lied. Among the things he lied about was knowing anything about the stickpin or the payment from Company Y to pay for it.

The grand jury returned a lengthy indictment against the White Knight charging him with multiple counts of making false statements and fraud in connection with the bankruptcy. He eventually pled guilty and the judge sentenced him to ten years in prison without parole, and ordered him to pay about $2 million in restitution. We charged a couple of his cohorts as well, who received lesser sentences. His loyal secretary lied through her teeth when questioned and was complicit in many of the fraudulent transactions. But for her advanced age (I think she was 75 at the time), I'd have charged her, too.

The case was fascinating and, from an intellectual standpoint, fun to unravel and solve. It was depressing as well, though. The family members who sold the business were heartbroken when they learned they had been fooled by the fraudster. In 18 months the White Knight destroyed a company that had been around for almost a century and wrecked the lives of scores of loyal employees so that he could line his pockets and wear his stickpin. Ten years in prison doesn't seem like enough.

Chapter 10

Cold Dish, Hot Jeep

There is a tiny town in northern Iowa out in the middle of nowhere. Its grain elevator dominates the skyline for miles in any direction. The business district is a block long. It contains a bank, a few store fronts, most of which are empty, a town library, and a small post office. Only two people worked at the post office. The postmaster who ran the building and manned the front desk, and a lone mail carrier. Every day at noon the postmaster locked the inner door, leaving the lobby door open so people could access the post office boxes, and went to lunch with her best friend, the librarian.

One day when she returned from lunch there was a package sitting on the lobby floor in front of the inner door. It already had postage on it, so she unlocked the door and carried the package inside. She set it down on her desk and then got to work on some other matters, finally returning to the package about an hour later.

When she focused on the package, she began to feel uneasy. It was a cardboard box, about two feet long, a foot high and a foot and a half wide. It was wrapped in brown paper. There were excessive postage stamps on the package; far more than was necessary given its weight. Neither the sender nor the addressee were from the small town. In fact, she had never heard of the company name listed as the sender. The return label was printed with an address and a telephone number. When the postmaster looked them up on the computer, though, the address was invalid, the company name didn't come up in an internet search, and the telephone number was invalid. She called the addressee who lived in a town about fifty miles distant and asked her if she had ordered something from this company. The woman was short with her and said she hadn't, didn't know anything about the package, but nevertheless insisted the postmaster send it to her.

The postmaster hesitated, though. Every year the United States Postal Service provided updated training on suspicious packages, and just a few years before she had attended an in-person training in Minneapolis that included a lecture on suspicious packages and bombs. This package, she believed, had all the hallmarks of containing a bomb.

So, she called the Postal Inspection Service in Des Moines. Postal inspectors are the law enforcement arm of the United States Postal Service. She spoke with a person in that office (never subsequently identified) and explained what she had and what she suspected. Whoever it was on the other line told her to put it in the mail to the Postal Inspector's Office in Des Moines and they'd look at it. She reported something like the following conversation took place: "But it might contain a bomb," the postmaster pointed out.

"Just mail it to us and we'll see," came the response.

When the mail carrier returned to the post office at the end of the day, the postmaster filled him in on the package. The mail carrier was equally concerned and rather than leave the postmaster alone to place the package into the mail bag and deliver it to the regional office in Mason City for shipment to Des Moines, the mail carrier volunteered to take over that part of the job and drive it to Mason City himself.

A couple days later the package arrived at the Postal Inspector's Office in Des Moines. It was on July 3, which fell on a Saturday that year. A supervisor called one of the postal inspectors and asked him to look at the package. There was a breakdown in communication somewhere because the postal inspector was told that it was suspected to contain drugs. The postal inspector planned on taking Monday, July 5, off work, so he decided to come in on Sunday, July 4, to check out the package before he went home and took his kids out to watch the fireworks that evening.

The postal inspector arrived at about noon in the empty office located on the top of a four-floor commercial building on the northwest side of Des Moines. He found the package on his desk. He took it into the conference room, flipped it over on its top, and set it down on a conference table. This was a common approach when dealing with packages suspected to contain drugs. If the package contained drugs, officers would typically remove all but a small quantity of the drugs, substitute some other substance like flour, seal it back up, and then make a controlled delivery of the drugs to the intended recipient with a device inside the package to let the officers know when it was opened. At that point, the officers would enter the house with a warrant and arrest the recipient. By opening the package on the bottom, law enforcement hoped the recipient wouldn't notice that the package had been tampered with.

This time when the postal inspector opened the bottom of the package, he didn't find what he typically found in drug packages. Instead, it appeared to be an antique radio of some sort. The inspector poked around a little, but didn't take the radio out of the package. Instead he resealed the bottom of the package and flipped it over. At this point he decided to use a portable X-ray machine to look inside the package, suspecting he'd find the radio box to be empty of electronics and full of drugs.

When he set the X-ray machine before the package, what he saw set his heart racing. Clear as day on the X-ray image was a large pipe bomb. Wires from the bomb appeared to run to the knobs of the radio controls, but it was hard to see because the bomb itself blocked the view. In short, it wasn't clear what the triggering mechanism was. It was possible that it would explode upon opening the top of the package. The inspector snapped a photo of the X-ray image, then quickly removed the X-ray machine and ran to the phone to call the bomb squad. Then he called his wife and told her that he'd be late and wouldn't likely make the fireworks that night. Or, at least he wouldn't be watching the fireworks he had intended to watch.

The bomb squad arrived in short order and, after viewing the X-ray image, concluded that the only safe way to disarm the bomb was to blast it with a water cannon. The bomb squad sent a remote-control robot into the postal inspector's office where the robot retrieved the package and brought it out to the parking lot outside the building. In the meantime, the bomb squad had built a bunker of sandbags with one end open. The robot placed the package into the bunker. More sandbags were placed across the opening and then from a truck parked 30 feet away, the bomb squad hit the package with a blast from a water cannon. The blast was so powerful that it ripped the package, the radio, and the bomb apart. When it was over, the bomb was separated from the trigger device and it was rendered safe.

In the process, though, the package and radio had been shredded. Agents were only barely able to later reconstruct most of the address and return labels, and part of the radio. A bomb expert was unable to reconstruct the bomb completely, but he ultimately opined that the bomb was wired to the electronics of the radio such that when a person plugged it in and turned it on, the bomb would explode. The expert stated that the bomb contained so much gunpowder and shrapnel that it would have killed anyone within fifty feet.

Now the question was who sent the bomb and why. The case was referred to the United States Attorney's Office. A postal inspector was assigned to the case. He turned out to be an amazingly good investigator, a driven and dedicated agent, a tactful and thoughtful man, and a guy with a great sense of humor. A great agent from the Bureau of Alcohol, Tobacco, Firearms and Explosives (ATF) was also assigned to the case. In our office, the case was initially assigned to my good friend. He and the postal inspector began investigating the case, conducting interviews, subpoenaing documents, and questioning some people before the grand jury. At some point, a new United States Attorney was appointed to head our office and she appointed my friend to become the new criminal chief. With his new responsibilities, my friend could no longer handle this case and so it was reassigned to me.

As was often the case, when one prosecutor hands a case off to another, the two meet with the agents and the team briefs the new prosecutor about the case and answers any questions. Here's what they told me they knew about that case at that stage, in a nutshell.

The postmaster didn't see anyone suspicious in the post office the day the bomb was left and hadn't noticed anything suspicious. The agents canvased the town and no one saw anyone leave the package. The post office itself had no security camera. The lone bank in town, located two store fronts away from the post office, had a security camera inside and the camera faced the street. The camera angle was such, though, that through the front glass doors it captured only the first five to ten feet of the street. Reviewing the video revealed the passage of several vehicles between the time the postmaster left for lunch and when she returned. But only the tires and the lower half of the vehicles were visible. In short, there was almost no evidence of any value to be gained from the crime scene itself.

A forensic examination of the bomb revealed no fingerprints or DNA or any other biological evidence. From the adhesive side of the tape holding the package together agents did recover several marks that showed that the bomber was wearing rubber gloves. The gunpowder in the bomb was somewhat unique black powder, the type used in old black powder type firearms. Gun powder manufactures are required to include trace elements of marking material in every batch of gunpowder. This means that if the agents could locate the bomber and find gunpowder in his or her possession, they could test the gunpowder to see if it had the same marking material as the gunpowder in the bomb.

The agents had learned that the intended target was a supervisor at a manufacturing plant. Many years before this supervisor began working on the line as a newbie, but very quickly was promoted to position after position until she became the foreman of the welding department, even though she didn't know how to weld. After interviewing a number of people at the plant, the agents were left with the general impression that the intended victim was extremely disliked and that there were any number of people who'd like to see her dead. Several men who were passed over for the promotions she received spoke poorly of her. No one expressed any sympathy for the fact that she was the intended victim of a bomb and several said they weren't surprised. The agents found the intended victim quite unlikeable and reported that she swore like a sailor. She did collect antique radios, and her collection was well-known by the other employees. The agents had received a list of employees that the intended victim had fired going back ten years when she first became a supervisor. There were several people on the list, any of whom could have a motive to kill her. The agents and my fellow prosecutor had spent a significant amount of time investigating these suspects and generally eliminated all but one because the suspects had alibis or for other reasons.

The one person who couldn't be eliminated as a suspect was a man the intended victim had fired ten years before. He was described by others as a misogynist who was deeply offended when she was promoted over him and became his boss. There were reports that they exchanged words on many occasions, ultimately leading to his firing after working at the factory for 19 years. On the day he left employment, he went to the plant manager's office to complain about the woman and report what he claimed was a number of acts of her misconduct. The manager remembered that the man had each incident written on an index card. Nothing came of the man's claims.

This man lived in rural Iowa, between the city where the plant was located and the tiny town where the package was mailed. He lived out in the country. He had no criminal history, though, and since his firing he had created his own welding business. He even had a contract with the same factory to manufacture storage racks. He had a hunting license and belonged to a group of re-enactors who portrayed frontiersmen. We'll call him Grizzly Adams.

From the package, the agents examined the to/from labels and determined the manufacture of the labels. Through subpoenas, the agents obtained a list of all businesses within a hundred miles of the plant that sold that brand of label. From there, the agents subpoenaed those businesses (about twenty) for records showing the sale of such labels within 60 days of the date the bomb was placed in the mail. This reduced the number of businesses to two or three. The agents then visited those stores to get the underlying receipts and to determine if there was any other evidence. At an office supply store, a receipt showed the purchase of the labels and the stamp kit similar to the one used to address the labels; nothing else. The purchase was made five days before the bomb was placed in the mail. The customer paid cash. The store had no internal or external surveillance cameras and, not surprisingly, no one remembered the sale. Records showed that Grizzly Adams had shopped at that store in the past, though, using a credit card.

The agents canvassed the nearby stores to see if they had security cameras and one did. The store was located across the parking lot from the office supply store. They still had the video of the day in question, but it was of poor quality. Using the time stamp on the receipt for the sale of the labels, the agents isolated the portion of the video and made several still images of a white truck entering the parking lot shortly before the labels were purchased. It didn't capture the truck leaving the parking lot; there was more than one entrance/exit.

My friend and the agents showed me the still images of the truck. The camera was facing the passenger side of the truck and captured it as the truck turned into the parking lot driveway. The photos were so poor that, despite efforts to enhance them, the truck was mostly a blur and there was no way to read the license plate. A records check showed that Grizzly Adams owned a Jeep and a white truck, but this one had a topper on the back. The records the agents had, showed that as sold to the defendant years ago, his truck didn't have a topper. Of course, a person could buy a topper and add it later.

As I flipped through the blurry photos of the truck I noticed something in the passenger window. I laid the photos out on the conference room table and placed several of them side by side, each image capturing the truck as it moved foot by foot from the road and into the entrance. In the passenger-side window was something blurry and white. And if one looked very carefully, the white aberration at one point crossed the front door frame ever-so-slightly. In other words, it appeared that the window was open and whatever it was came out of the window a little bit so as to block the view of the door frame. "I think that's a dog," I said.

Dubious, my friend and the agents looked closely, going back and forth over the photos. The skepticism soon faded as they began to see what I saw. It was a dog in the passenger side of the truck. A white dog. And as dogs like to do, at one point it stuck its head out of the window as the truck was passing into the parking lot.

My colleague, in fact, recognized it as a Springer Spaniel. The agent exclaimed that Grizzly Adams bred Springer Spaniels.

I also went back to the photos from the bank, hoping that we'd see an image of the white truck passing in front of the bank on the day the bomb was left.

"Don't bother," my friend said. "We already thought of that; no match. Of course, he could have approached the post office from the other direction, so the absence of a photo of the white truck doesn't eliminate him."

"Have you attempted to interview Grizzly Adams," I asked.

"Not yet," the postal inspector answered. "We wanted to eliminate all other steps first. If we approach him and told him we're investigating the bomb, he could destroy any evidence there may be."

The meeting ended with a request that the agents conduct some surveillance of Grizzly Adams' house to see if his white pickup truck had an after-market topper like the one in the photo. I spent a significant amount of time over the next week reading the file, including the transcripts of several witnesses taken before the grand jury. After the agents confirmed that Grizzly Adams' truck did have a topper, we concluded that we had sufficient probable cause to execute a search warrant on the white truck for evidence of, among other things, the dog, so that we could definitively tie Grizzly Adams to the truck in the video. Quite frankly, we concluded we didn't have much else to go on.

On the day the agents executed the search warrant, they arrived at Grizzly Adams' house to find him gone. Grizzly Adams' adult son was home, though. The agents left a copy of the search warrant with the son, as required by law. Included with the search warrant was a list of the "items to be seized" by the agents, as approved by the judge. This listed things like "microscopic evidence." By that we meant dog hairs. As the son watched, the agents searched for several hours with a forensic team using a vacuum to suck up any microscopic evidence that might be on the truck seat or in the carpet. They did find a dog bed on the front seat, passenger side of the truck.

The agents called me after the search and reported that they didn't find anything of evidentiary value, at least yet. It looked like we struck out.

Then the next morning, about 11:00 a.m., I got an excited call from the postal inspector. A neighbor reported to dispatch that as he passed Grizzly Adams' house that morning on his way to work he saw Grizzly Adams' Jeep fully engulfed in flames in an open space next to the large workshed Adams used for his welding business. The Jeep was sitting upright. The neighbor reported his observations to the police, who passed it along to the postal inspector.

The next report the postal inspector got, about two hours later, was that a citizen had seen Grizzly Adams driving down the highway towing a trailer on which sat the remains of his Jeep, with the Jeep still smoking. Grizzly Adams was seen taking the Jeep to a salvage yard. The postal inspector called the salvage yard and the woman confirmed that Grizzly Adams had brought in a Jeep that was still smoldering, dropped it off, and paid her. She stated that Grizzly Adams told her that it caught on fire because of faulty wiring. The woman stated it'd be crushed later that day, as soon as it quit smoldering.

My conversation with the agent went something like this: "We got the wrong vehicle," the postal inspector said when he excitedly called me with the latest report. "Don't you see?"

"No," I replied. "What do you mean we got the wrong vehicle?"

"He drove his Jeep to drop off the bomb, not his truck. He took his truck to buy the labels, but that doesn't mean that he took that same vehicle to deliver the bomb. When he found out we searched his truck yesterday looking for microscopic evidence, he must have thought we were looking for bomb evidence. He didn't realize we were just looking for dog hairs. He knew we searched the wrong vehicle because he knew he drove his Jeep to deliver the bomb. That's why he was out at the crack of dawn burning his Jeep; he was afraid we'd be back to search it."

"Damn," I said as it began to sink in. "Let's put together a search warrant first to seize the remains of the Jeep before they crush it and search it."

"Right," the postal inspector said. "I already asked the woman at the salvage yard not to crush it."

"Then I think it's time you paid Grizzly Adams a visit," I said. "I think we interview him and then search his house."

"Roger that."

We did seize the remains of the Jeep. The only thing noteworthy about what we found was that the battery was missing, as were the wheels. When the agents interviewed Grizzly Adams the next day, he refused to let them into his house and spoke to them in his front yard. About midway through the interview, his wife joined him. She also worked at the factory where he used to work, but in another department, and she knew the intended victim as well.

The interview didn't result in a confession or any direct evidence. The postal inspector started off explaining that they were there to talk with him about a bomb that had been sent to his former supervisor. Grizzly Adams denied any knowledge of it. Grizzly Adams gave the agents the same story about how his Jeep caught on fire. When asked about the missing battery and wheels, he claimed that after the Jeep caught on fire he decided he should salvage the battery and wheels so he removed them. When asked about his relationship with the intended victim, he claimed he had quit and she hadn't fired him. He stated he had no hard feelings about it and mentioned that he even had a contract to build racks for the factory. He claimed he always got along with the woman, didn't know where she lived, and had no contact with her since he left the factory. Grizzly Adams admitted shopping at the office supply store, but denied he was there the day the labels were purchased and denied buying such labels. Grizzly Adams also denied visiting the town where the bomb was mailed. Grizzly Adams said on that day he was working all day in his shop, but admitted that he had no one who could verify that.

At the conclusion of the interview, the agents produced a copy of the search warrant and called in additional agents who were waiting nearby. During the search the agents found postage stamps matching the same type used on the package. They recovered electronic devices, radio components, soldering guns, and drill bits. Material found in the grooves of one drill bit, still in the drill press, exhibited similar physical and chemical characteristics to the composite-wood back of the radio that housed the bomb. Agents also seized gunpowder matching that recovered from the bomb. Last, agents found the collection of index cards filled with hand-written complaints Grizzly Adams had about the victim that he had written ten years before.

The following day, agents interviewed Grizzly Adams' son. The son stated that his father was a big fan of CSI shows. The son related that his father said the Jeep fire started after Grizzly Adams drained the vehicle of motor oil and ran the engine to test how long the motor would last. Grizzly Adams said he removed the battery and tires before the fire and then pushed the vehicle on its side before it was engulfed in flames.

A grand jury ultimately charged Grizzly Adams with mailing, possessing, and transporting a pipe bomb, and possessing a bomb in furtherance of a crime of violence. The case went to trial. At the conclusion of the government's case in chief, the judge came close to granting a judgment of acquittal, stating that he was very concerned that the evidence was insufficient to prove the defendant's guilt. I distinctly remember the closing argument I gave. It was the only one I presented during which I observed changes in expressions on the jurors' faces. Yes, the case against Grizzly Adams was built entirely on circumstantial evidence. And as I presented our evidence during the trial, I intentionally didn't point out how each piece of evidence fit together with all the other pieces of evidence; that would have been impermissible and would have provided too much insight to the defense attorney.

During closing arguments, though, I methodically went through the evidence, piece by piece, showing how each piece led to the other, and how they all fit together to point to only one logical conclusion; that Grizzly Adams had sent the bomb. I argued that he was motivated by revenge, that he was a misogynist, and that being fired by a woman supervisor was emasculating to him. As I fit everything together, including the motive, I saw lightbulbs turn on in the jurors' heads. I saw in the judge's expression the same revelation of understanding exhibited by the jurors. When I put it all together, he saw it clearly for the first time too.

The defense presented a closing argument criticizing the government's case, focusing properly on the total lack of direct evidence like fingerprints or DNA. As for motive, the defense attorney said it was a huge stretch to allege that this man would try to kill a woman over the loss of a job ten long years before. He argued, reasonably, that if the defendant was really that upset he'd have taken action against her long before.

I began my rebuttal closing argument with a saying: "Revenge is a dish best served cold." And then I explained what that meant to the jury. I argued that the defendant nursed his grudge for years, thinking and plotting his revenge. I summarized for the jury the plot of the Edgar Allan Poe story, "The Cask of Amontillado," in which a man, Montresor, plots revenge against someone who insulted him and finally obtains his revenge years later, when the man least suspects him. In Poe's story, the murderer chains his nemesis to a wall deep in a cellar where he lured the man by promising him an excellent drink from his cask of Amontillado for which the victim had a fondness. Then I pointed out to the jury that the defendant had kept his notes about the victim for a decade. That was a man, I argued, who held a grudge, just like Montresor in Poe's story. The antique radio was the defendant's cask of Amontillado.

The jury returned guilty verdicts on all counts.

Chapter 11

Snatching Victory from the Jaws of Defeat

During my career as a federal prosecutor, I lost three cases. That isn't really to brag, because federal prosecutors shouldn't lose many cases. Prosecutors have the luxury of being able to decline prosecution of any cases they don't believe have sufficient evidence to convict. Thus, most federal prosecutors win 90 to 95 percent of the cases they charge because they only charge the ones they know have overwhelming evidence of guilt. The questionable ones seldom get charged, absent extenuating circumstances. In some instances, a subject of an investigation poses such a danger to the community that taking the risk charging a relatively weak case is necessary to protect the public.

My first loss occurred in a case wherein both a man and his girlfriend were charged with possession with the intent to deliver drugs. The evidence against the man was overwhelming; that against the girlfriend much weaker. They were tried together and the jury acquitted the girlfriend. I take some comfort that the defense attorney later became a judge on the Eighth Circuit Court of Appeals.

The next case I lost involved a case in which about 25 people were charged in connection with the Capone/Moran drug conspiracies I wrote about in a previous chapter. One particular defendant was by far the least culpable of any of the people involved and my case against him turned almost exclusively on the testimony of one cooperator. When, at trial, that cooperator changed his story and exculpated the defendant, the jury voted acquittal. I again take some comfort that the defense attorney later became a state court judge.

I learned from these experiences early in my career to be more selective about whom we charged and to look more carefully at the evidence to ensure it was overwhelming as to each defendant.

My last loss I don't really count as a loss. I had charged a man with distribution of methamphetamine, possession with the intent to distribute methamphetamine, and with possession of a firearm in furtherance of a drug crime. The evidence of his drug trafficking was overwhelming and he pled guilty to those charges. But he went to trial on the firearm charge which carried a mandatory minimum sentence of five years. The firearm, a loaded handgun, was found in the back of his truck that was parked in the backyard of the house of one of his co-conspirators. The pickup truck had a topper and inside the topper officers found some methamphetamine distribution and manufacturing materials and the handgun. The proximity of a handgun and drug materials is typically very strong evidence that the person possessed a handgun in furtherance of drug trafficking. We were unable to recover fingerprints or DNA from the gun, but I was confident the jury would find the defendant possessed the gun; after all, we found it in the defendant's truck.

The case went to trial and I thought all the government's evidence came in well and as expected. Then the defense presented its case. The defendant testified. During his testimony he emphasized that he had pled guilty to the drug charges because he knew he was guilty and accepted responsibility for those crimes. But he emphasized that he wasn't responsible for the gun. He swore that his truck wasn't operable and had been sitting in the yard for more than two months. He hadn't been in his truck since it was sitting behind his friend's house. He testified that his friend, also a drug dealer, carried firearms. The defendant stated that he was afraid of guns and had never possessed one. In closing argument, the defense attorney argued that the gun belonged to the friend, the friend had hidden the gun in the defendant's truck, the truck hadn't moved for months, and that defendant wasn't responsible for the gun. The defense caught me and the agent by surprise. We just assumed that the truck ran and that the defendant had recently driven it. We didn't even think to check, didn't even think to investigate whether it operated or when he last drove the truck.

The jury acquitted the defendant of the firearm charge.

After the trial I was frustrated. It was true that the defendant's friend did carry firearms, but it made no sense to me why he'd hide a gun in the defendant's truck. The friend had his whole house in which to hide a gun. It also didn't make sense because it was unclear how the defendant got around if his truck wasn't operable; there was no evidence he had any other vehicle. The drug transaction to which the defendant pled guilty had occurred only a few weeks before officers searched the defendant's truck. The deal took place across town from where the truck was found and the defendant had to get there somehow. Unfortunately, we had never focused on that detail.

I had the agents do some follow up for me. They interviewed the friend, who denied it was his gun, but of course he'd deny it because he didn't want to be held responsible for it. He denied seeing the defendant with a gun. The friend did say, however, that the defendant had just parked the truck in his back yard the day before the agents searched it. This was helpful, but we needed something to corroborate this otherwise unreliable and unwilling witness. The agents checked public records to see if the defendant had received any parking or moving violations while driving that truck in the month preceding the search, but they came up with nothing. The officers had seized the truck as part of the investigation, but had never tried to start it; they simply had it towed to an impound lot and the defendant's father later retrieved it. By the time the father picked it up many months later, it didn't run. Thus, no one could say whether the truck was operable at the time officers seized the gun.

I kept going over the file again and again. I was convinced the defendant lied and I was sure I was missing some piece of evidence somewhere that would prove it. I went over the photocopies of all the clutter and paper officers had seized from the truck, looking for a receipt dated less than a couple months before the search, but found nothing. I had reviewed photographs of the truck probably twenty times, but I pulled them out, set them on my desk, and looked at them all again. At first, nothing caught my eye. Then I noticed something that wasn't there: tall grass. The defendant had testified vehemently that his truck had been inoperable for more than a couple months. The agents searched the truck in August. I looked at the photos of the truck as it sat in the back yard. The grass under the truck was cut to the same length as the grass in the rest of the yard. If the truck was inoperable, the grass would have been tall under the truck and short where the mower could reach. That was the key. We also canvased several of the neighbors, as I recall, who stated that they didn't remember seeing the truck there except for a few days before the search.

Based on this old, overlooked evidence and the new evidence from the neighbors and the friend, the grand jury charged the defendant with perjury. The case went to trial and a jury convicted the defendant of committing perjury. At sentencing, the defendant received a sentence that was more than he'd have received had he just pled guilty to the firearm charge in the first place.

In this case, justice delayed was not justice denied. Thus, I don't really consider that case in my loss column.

Chapter 12

Ruthless Drug Dealer

One summer evening a pizza delivery boy in a small northern Iowa town reported that he saw several men with guns force another man into a white van. The pizza delivery boy called the police on his cell phone and followed behind the van giving updated information until law enforcement officers converged on the van and brought it to a stop. A newspaper reporter happened to be nearby and captured in still photos the confrontation. The photos depicted a half-dozen officers with guns drawn, several holding machine guns, directing the occupants out of the van and onto the ground. In the van officers found multiple firearms and knives, and the victim gagged and secured by zip ties.

I can count on one hand the people I prosecuted whom I'd consider to be truly evil. One was a drug dealer from a large city in an adjoining state. What made him evil is hard to say. He grew up middle class, attended and graduated from high school, had no mental illness or defect, and there was no evidence of abuse or neglect. But he decided to become a drug dealer, and a ruthless one at that. I'll refer to him as Michael Corleone.

It turns out that Corleone sent the four men to kidnap the victim from his home at gunpoint and return him to Corleone. The kidnapped victim was himself a drug dealer. He and several of his drug dealing friends, all fairly young men in their early twenties, had been selling drugs for Corleone for several years. Although many drug dealers deal primarily in one drug (one is typically a meth dealer *or* a cocaine dealer, for example), Corleone dealt in almost every controlled substance. And he sold to dealers in several of the surrounding states. His operation included stash houses where large quantities of drugs were stored, money collectors who traveled to the various dealers to collect drug proceeds, delivery boys who delivered drugs to the dealers, and enforcers, like our friends in the van, who ensured that everyone working for Corleone did as he commanded.

Our kidnap victim and his friends had decided to rob Corleone, which ended up being a horrible idea. Corleone took great pains to isolate information so that people working for him didn't know more than was necessary. Thus, those running his stash houses didn't know who the dealers were, and the dealers didn't know where the stash houses were located. Only the delivery boys, who picked up drugs from the stash houses knew where both the stash houses and the dealers were located. Our kidnap victim and his friends decided to tail one of the delivery boys so as to discover the location of one of Corleone's stash houses in Iowa. Once they found the house, they broke in, ransacked the house, and stole a haul of drugs. As I recall, there were pounds of methamphetamine, ounces of cocaine, pounds of marijuana, and hundreds of ecstasy pills and other club drugs.

The robbers split the loot and started selling it on their own. Corleone quickly learned of the robbery and heard that some of his dealers were selling larger quantities of drugs than they were paying him for. He quickly figured out who at least some of the robbers likely were. That's when he sent several of his enforcers to Iowa to kidnap one of the suspected robbers and bring the victim back to him.

The victim in this case can be thankful that a pizza delivery boy called the cops, even though it eventually meant that the victim went to federal prison for several years. After an investigation, I prosecuted the victim and his friends and the enforcers for various drug and firearms charges. Most ultimately decided to cooperate and inform on Corleone and his operation. The enforcers told us that this wasn't the first time Corleone did something like this.

Apparently a few months before, in the winter, someone had robbed another of Corleone's stash houses. This one was located in the state where Corleone lived in a palatial house in the woods overlooking the Mississippi River. Corleone was livid and on this occasion suspected the stash house operator. Corleone had his enforcers bring the man to Corleone's mansion where they took him to a part of the basement that had been taped off in plastic. There they tied the young man in his mid-twenties to a chair. Over the course of the following 48 hours, Corleone oversaw his systematic torture. It included many beatings, but also burning him with a soldering iron and cigarettes, and electrocution (with a cord pulled out of a lamp and the wires exposed and then applied to the victim). In my estimation, the worst was when they removed the victim's shoes and then systematically smashed his toes using a ballpeen hammer. At one point they also tied the victim to a tree in the yard at night in the winter for several hours where he was without a coat or any warm clothing. The victim repeatedly swore that he had nothing to do with the theft, knew nothing about it, and begged for mercy.

Eventually, Corleone learned that he was wrong about suspecting this man, having discovered that one of his rivals had broken into the stash house. He had the victim untied and driven home, and gave the victim $15,000 cash to make amends. Corleone also threatened him to keep his mouth shut or he would suffer worse.

I will always remember the enforcer who told me about the torture. He was the leader of the group that went to Iowa to kidnap the dealer. He was in his late twenties and if you saw him on the street you'd think he looked like a nice guy. He readily told us everything in graphic detail. He wasn't proud of his conduct, but neither was he apologetic. He related the events matter-of-factly. He got emotional only once, when he spoke about finding out he had been hurting an innocent guy. He felt bad, he said, because the guy wasn't responsible for the theft.

After more work and investigation, we charged Corleone and several of his top associates. Corleone himself ultimately cooperated against his suppliers, so the agents working with me and I had an opportunity to sit down with him. Talking to Corleone was disturbing. He was a fit, good-looking man in his early thirties. He was articulate and polite. But when he spoke about his drug business, when he talked about people who disobeyed him or stole from him, or about the torture he and his henchmen inflicted on the stash house guy, he was cold as ice. He was without emotion or regret, empathy or feeling. Talking to us, giving us information on his suppliers in an effort to get a reduced sentence, was simply part of the drug trade. After a cost/benefit analysis, he decided snitching on others was worth it. He was polite with us because we could affect his sentence and he wanted something from us. It was clear to me when looking in his eyes, though, that if the control was in the other direction, he'd have been as ruthless with me as he had with others. We danced with this devil, despite how bad he was, because only through him could we go after those above him in the drug organization. In such cases, it is distasteful to work with people like this, but sometimes there is no other way to take down or infiltrate criminal organizations other than working with and through criminals.

There is a very good chance, I think, that he tortured and perhaps even killed others and we just didn't uncover those crimes. If not, if we indeed intervened before he tortured another person or killed someone, then we were just lucky, as were his would-be victims. In the end he went to prison for more than a decade. He is likely out of prison by now. I wonder what he is doing and I worry.

Chapter 13

Money Laundering Professionals

The drug trade is a cash business. Drug dealing generates prodigious amounts of cash. A drug user doesn't pay for drugs with a check or credit card, and neither do the drug dealers at each level of a drug trafficking organization. For the drug proceeds to be useful to drug dealers, at some point in the chain someone must convert the cash to other forms of property. A drug dealer can't walk into a dealership and plop down $50,000 in cash to buy a luxury car without raising suspicions that would bring him unwanted attention from law enforcement. Nor can a drug dealer buy a house with cash without causing a stir. Thus, to be of practical use drug dealers must convert the cash into another form of property or find ways to have it quietly deposited into bank accounts where it can be drawn upon or transferred. This process of converting cash criminal proceeds, dirty money, into usable assets is called money laundering.

Long ago, law enforcement officers realized that where there is a large amount of cash there is likely illegal activity afoot. Beginning in the 1950s, Congress passed laws designed to track large cash transactions for that reason. These laws imposed reporting requirements on banks and business dealing with large amounts of cash so that law enforcement could track the transactions and investigate them when appropriate. A Suspicious Activity Report (SAR), is one such report filed by bank personnel about any suspicious financial transaction they observe, whether it is cash-based or not. Tellers know their customers and come to recognize their patterns of transactions. When an old lady suddenly comes in and withdraws a large amount of cash for several days in a row, for example, when she has never done so before, it may be a sign that someone is defrauding her. Tellers can report these suspicious activities to law enforcement officers who then must sort through the reports and decide which reports merit further investigation. Sometimes when the transactions are investigated there are innocent reasons for the transactions and nothing comes of it. On other occasions, it leads to criminal prosecution.

Another important reporting tool is Currency Transaction Reports (CTRs). Any bank or business, including professionals like lawyers, real estate agents, and others, must report to the IRS any cash transaction in excess of $10,000. In doing so, the reporting entity must provide basic information: who, what, where, when, etc. Again, these CTRs are reviewed by law enforcement agents who then decide whether there are sufficient signs of criminal activity to warrant further investigation.

It didn't take long for criminals to learn that their cash transactions were being monitored and to devise ways to evade the reporting laws. With CTRs, for example, criminals simply decided to structure their cash transactions to come in below the threshold reporting requirement. If a drug dealer wanted to launder $45,000 in drug proceeds, for example, he might make five deposits on five separate occasions into a bank account, each one for less than the $10,000 that triggers the CTR reporting requirement. Of course, money laundering can get much more sophisticated. Clever criminals may have multiple associates each open separate bank accounts and have each one deposit part of the drug proceeds into each of the separate accounts and then sometime later transfer the funds to the kingpin's bank account. Law enforcement officers quickly caught on to the criminals' evasion methods and lobbied Congress to create a legislative fix. Congress responded to the criminals' response to the CTR reporting requirements by enacting a law making it a crime to structure financial transactions for the purpose of evading the reporting requirements.

Several of my more interesting cases involved money laundering statutes. I prosecuted at least two car dealers for either knowingly failing to file Currency Transaction Reports, or helping their customers structure the purchase of a car so that the car dealer didn't have to file a CTR. In these cases, we had learned from drug dealers we prosecuted or from evidence uncovered during the prosecution of drug dealers that certain car dealers were helping drug dealers launder money so the drug dealers could buy either fancy cars or buy cars to be used to transport drugs. These investigations involved undercover operations in which we sent law enforcement officers to the car dealerships posing as drug dealers. In recorded conversations the undercover officers would have explicit conversations with the salesman about being a drug dealer, wanting to buy a car with cash, and not wanting the car dealer to file a CTR. The car salesmen would be recorded agreeing to not file a CTR, despite getting paid more than $10,000 in cash.

I had two other interesting cases involving structuring, though, that didn't involve car dealers. The first involved a real estate agent and the second a lawyer.

A Laundering Realtor

A local drug dealer had accumulated a lot of cash and wanted to buy a house. This particular drug dealer flaunted his wealth, wearing alligator shoes and showy clothes, was bedecked with expensive jewelry, and had a flashy car. He even had another man, his bodyguard, drive him around wherever he went.

The drug dealer, accompanied by his bodyguard, visited a real estate office and met with a realtor. He told the realtor that he was in the market for a house. The realtor asked him some basic questions about what he was looking for, the price, the location, and some background questions about how he'd finance the house. Typically, she'd fill out some paperwork indicating the prospective buyer's employment and financial condition and run a credit check. Based on his answers, though, she decided not to generate the usual paperwork. In response to her questions, he told her he didn't have a job, didn't have credit cards, didn't have a bank account, didn't have a house or apartment in his own name, and would be paying 20 percent down for the purchase in cash. All this should have, and certainly must have, alerted the real estate agent that this particular client was engaged in criminal activity. She later claimed not to recognize any of these signs, though.

There isn't anything illegal about selling a house to a criminal, however, and so she worked with him over the following few weeks showing him a number of houses that she thought he might want to purchase. He finally settled on a house and they sat down (the real estate agent, the drug dealer, and the dealer's bodyguard standing nearby) to fill out paperwork for the purchase of the house. When it came to the topic of the down payment he said he'd bring her cash. She explained to him that at closing they'd need a cashier's check from a bank for a down payment and so he should take the cash to a bank and get a cashier's check in that amount.

"No," he replied. "If you want your commission, you will take the cash to the bank and get a cashier's check."

The next day he delivered to her a paper bag filled with more than $48,000 cash. The real estate agent knew about the CTR requirement and so she structured the deposits. Over the course of the next five or six days, she made several deposits of cash in various amounts, each deposit under $10,000. She made the deposits at six or seven different bank branches. On several days she made two deposits on the same day, within a half hour or so of each other, but at different branches of the same bank. Eventually, once she got all the cash deposited, she obtained a cashier's check in the amount necessary for the down payment, the closing occurred, and the drug dealer moved into his new house.

Months later agents working with me executed a search warrant at the house after a long investigation into the drug dealer's drug trafficking. At the time, we didn't know about the money laundering involved in buying the house. We did know, however, that the house was in his name and as part of the criminal prosecution we sought criminal forfeiture of his house, his car, and some other assets we tied to him. One of the agents working the case with me was a special agent with the IRS and he began to follow the money to find out how the drug dealer bought the house. The IRS agent determined that the cashier's check was obtained by the real estate agent from funds drawn on her own account. This was unusual, which led him to look into her bank account. That's when he discovered the structured cash deposits.

The grand jury charged the real estate agent with structuring and aiding and abetting money laundering and she pled guilty. At the sentencing hearing she testified in an effort to obtain a lighter sentence. She claimed ignorance and gullibility, and although she admitted enough facts to support a guilty plea, she tried to persuade the judge that some of the deposits she made weren't attempts to structure but that she just happened to go to one bank branch and then decided to deposit more and happened to be near a different bank branch a bit later and so made a second deposit there a half hour after the prior deposit.

I don't remember the details now, unfortunately, but I had the only Perry Mason moment of my career during my cross examination of her. We had identified some other suspicious-looking financial transactions in her bank records, but couldn't figure out what she was doing and whether the transactions had anything to do with the drug dealer or were illegal. During my cross examination, though, I pressed her on these transactions and, much to my surprise, she broke down and confessed that they also involved money from the drug dealer and she was helping him convert his cash into other assets.

The realtor was sentenced to a short term in prison and lost her professional license.

A Laundering Lawyer

We were investigating a large-scale drug dealer who was purchasing many assets, including a tow truck and a gas station. He then used the bank account associated with the gas station to launder drug proceeds while posing as a legitimate business owner. Again, I was fortunate to have the assistance of a special agent with the IRS on the investigation team and he dug deeply into the financial transactions.

Eventually, we charged the drug dealer and served search warrants on his home and business, finding large amounts of drugs and cash, guns and other tools of the drug trade. The dealer hired a lawyer from northern Iowa to be his defense attorney. This attorney was relatively young, in his mid-thirties as I recall, and had a small law firm with one even younger associate who had graduated from law school only a few years before. The attorney was sort of a jack of all trades, often a mistake when practicing law, and dabbled in everything from real estate law, tort law, and some criminal defense work. He had never handled a federal criminal case before.

In this particular case I didn't have grounds to seek the drug dealer's detention pending trial, so he was free to meet with his attorney in his attorney's office as needed. I recall on one occasion the attorney came to review the evidence in our office and asked to see me. I met him in the conference room thinking he had some question about the discovery materials (the evidence he was reviewing). Instead, he wanted to talk about a plea deal. He said that he had developed evidence that would show that the agents planted evidence in his client's house and business and would expose them unless I cut his guy a sweetheart deal. I was taken aback at the approach and the accusation. First, my job as a prosecutor was to seek justice; if an agent planted evidence it was my job to expose that as much as it was to prosecute a drug dealer and the attorney here was suggesting that I be complicit in covering up malfeasance by the agents. Second, I knew the agents and had worked with them for years. I was personally confident that they'd never betray their oath of office and commit such an offense.

I no longer remember exactly what I told the attorney, but I let him know I was offended at his proposal, that I'd never cut a deal to cover up another crime, and that he had better be very careful about making accusations. I warned him that if he was fabricating the allegation, it would come back to bite him. Then I asked him to provide me with the evidence of the agents allegedly planting evidence, assuring him that if it was true, the agents would be prosecuted. As for his client, I said that his client would answer for whatever the evidence proved. If he wasn't responsible for drugs allegedly planted in his house, then he wouldn't be sentenced for the drugs. But I emphasized that there would be no quid pro quo of making a deal with his client in exchange for covering up crimes by agents.

The lawyer refused to tell me what evidence he had, and refused to turn it over. In the end, we discovered there was no such evidence other than his client telling the attorney that the agents must have planted the drugs. What we did discover through more investigation, however, is that the lawyer was structuring financial transactions and laundering money for his client.

In some drug cases when a criminal defendant hires a private attorney, and the evidence suggests that the defendant has no legitimate source of funds, the courts allow the government to obtain financial records from the attorney about any financial transactions involving the defendant. Here, through a thorough review of the drug dealer's financial records, personal and business, the IRS agent showed that the dealer had no legitimate source of income. Thus, the court let us get records from the attorney about the money the dealer paid him. This is a tricky area because it isn't illegal for an attorney to receive money from a drug dealer. Further, the government must be careful not to interfere with a lawyer's representation of a criminal defendant by doing something like seizing the money in the lawyer's account, even if it is dirty money. But the financial transaction may still be relevant for determining guilt or for sentencing and the government may be able to seize any money left over from a retainer, for example, after the close of the case.

The records the attorney provided us about the money he received from his client, though, made little sense. We couldn't decipher what money the attorney received when from the dealer and the records didn't line up with any other financial records from the dealer. For example, as I recall the attorney's record suggested receipt of a check from the dealer as part of the retainer, but there was no corresponding check from the dealer's personal or business bank account. It appeared at first that it was a case of sloppy bookkeeping on the lawyer's part. So, we decided to subpoena the lawyer's law firm bank account to get at the underlying transactions.

What we discovered appeared to be structuring. The total retainer was in the mid–$30,000 range, as I recall. The bank records showed that the attorney made several cash deposits into his bank account, each one under $10,000. This could have been the result of the defendant bringing the attorney money on multiple occasions, each time under $10,000 and, if so, then the drug dealer might have been trying to structure the transactions, but the attorney wasn't.

I decided we needed to dig deeper. We questioned the lawyer's junior associate attorney and she told us that she recalled only one time the dealer came to the office. We subpoenaed the attorney's billing records and they, too, showed only one office visit and no entries that he met with his client elsewhere and billed for it. At this point, though, there was enough evidence of structuring that we informed the attorney he was under investigation and that it created a conflict of interest for him to continue to represent the drug dealer. I recall that he resisted withdrawing as counsel and ultimately the court got involved and found that he needed to withdraw. The drug dealer at this point stated that he was indigent and the court appointed him counsel.

With new counsel, the drug dealer decided to cooperate in the hope of receiving a reduced sentence. When the drug dealer debriefed with us, he informed on other drug dealers and his sources of supply, but he also told us that his former attorney had, indeed, helped him launder the money he paid the lawyer for representation. He told us that he brought his attorney all the cash at one time in a brown paper bag. The dealer said that he wasn't involved in making any of the deposits, which we already knew from the bank records and surveillance photos.

We charged the attorney with structuring and money laundering. I recall that he initially denied it and claimed not to know about Currency Transaction Reports and therefore even if he made the deposits in the manner he did, there was an innocent explanation and that we couldn't prove that he deposited the cash with the intent to evade the reporting requirement. A subpoena to the Continuing Legal Education Commission and digging into records of classes he took to comply with his continuing legal education requirements showed that he attended two seminars where CTRs were discussed. I also got records from one of his law school classes that showed that he took a class in which CTRs were covered as part of the assigned reading. Of course, I couldn't prove that the attorney did the reading or listened to the speakers at seminars when they discussed CTRs, but it was certainly pretty good evidence that the lawyer knew about CTRs.

In the end, the lawyer pled guilty. As part of the sentencing resolution, he agreed to surrender his law license.

Both the real estate agent and the lawyer received relatively light sentences, as I recall, of perhaps a year or two. Structuring offenses don't typically carry harsh penalties. But the point I made at each of their sentencing hearings was that if business owners and professionals like real estate agents and lawyers would comply with the law, it'd make it much harder for criminals to launder money and enjoy the proceeds of their crimes, and much easier for law enforcement agents to catch them.

CHAPTER 14

A Bad Cop

One day an FBI agent came to my office to talk to me about a case involving possible criminal civil rights violations. A state narcotics officer passed on information to the agent that he had arrested a woman with a small amount of drugs. She was cooperative with officers and debriefed with them, ultimately receiving a deferred judgment on the possession charge. During the interview, though, she mentioned that there was a bad cop.

She said she had been pulled over by this cop after she left a bar one night. He claimed she was speeding; she was certain she wasn't. He said she smelled of alcohol and she admitted she had been drinking. He had her perform field sobriety tests and though she thought she passed, he claimed she didn't. He told her he was going to have to arrest her for drunk driving. She begged him not to and swore she wasn't drunk. Then he propositioned her. For oral sex, he'd let her go. She was desperate because given the nature of the job she had at the time, she'd be fired if she was convicted of an OWI (operating while intoxicated). Reluctantly, she agreed. They then left the area of the traffic stop and she met him in a park where she performed oral sex on the cop while he was on duty. She said that she later learned that he had done the same thing to a friend of hers.

The FBI agent interviewed this woman who repeated the story to the agent and also gave him the name of her friend. The agent interviewed the friend, who ran with a wilder crowd than the first woman, and she confirmed a similar story. She had intercourse with the officer on the hood of his squad car to avoid getting arrested for an OWI. Like the first woman, she was pulled over shortly after leaving a bar. She said she also recalled that the cop had been in the bar conducting a bar check about an hour before she was pulled over. She said she knew of another woman that the same thing happened to.

To make a long story short, I took the case and after further investigation we found a half-dozen or so women who claimed to have been victimized by the same officer in similar ways. It seemed like each time we talked to one victim we'd get the name of another possible victim. Understandably, some women didn't want to talk to us and some denied anything happened, but enough told us the same thing that it became believable. The pattern appeared to be the same; the cop would conduct a "bar check" during which he'd scope out attractive women and then would wait nearby in his squad car. When the targeted woman left, if she got in a car alone and drove off, the cop would stop her.

We eventually met with the chief of police and the department's internal affairs investigator, both of whom were completely cooperative. They provided additional information about the cop's performance which included at least one complaint by a woman who claimed the cop propositioned her during a traffic stop. She refused his proposition and filed a report against him. The cop denied it and unfortunately the case went no further. The other interesting information the department provided was records about when the officer was "out of service," meaning he had called into dispatch to report taking a bathroom break or dinner break or some other reason to be listed as unavailable for calls. We also obtained records showing every vehicle stop he made. It's hard to explain here without getting into great detail, but the bottom line is that his radio and dispatch records showed suspicious patterns of out of service periods, and remarkably few reported traffic stops compared to other officers working similar shifts. We were also able to confirm that he was out of service on the dates and at the approximate times reported to us by the women who claimed they were having sex with him in exchange for avoiding criminal charges. We also learned that bar checks weren't part of his duties as a patrol officer. That last bit was very helpful because we were able to visit the bars where the women had been (there were only two bars involved) and confirm with employees that, indeed, this cop routinely came in late at night ostensibly to conduct bar checks.

It is a criminal civil rights violation for a person acting under color of state law to use the position to deprive another of their liberty. The officer coerced the sexual acts by his threat to use his official position to sanction them for real or alleged traffic offenses if they didn't have sex with him.

Eventually, we met with the officer and confronted him. At first he attempted to equivocate and deny, but when we confronted him with the results of our investigation, he eventually said that he might have had sex with one or two women he pulled over, but denied that there was any quid pro quo or coercion. After a while we ended the interview and suggested he hire an attorney. He did so and I ended up having several conversations with the attorney and provided the attorney with our evidence.

In the end, the cop agreed to plead guilty to one of the incidents. In this way, it spared the women from having to testify and be embarrassed or exposed to any publicity. The cop also agreed to resign from the police force effective immediately and would be barred from becoming a sworn police officer in the future. He'd also paid a $2,000 fine. Before reaching this agreement, we of course consulted with the victims, none of whom objected to the agreement.

Chapter 15

Death by Heroin

There is probably no pleasant way to die. But dying from a heroin overdose must be one of the worst. Or perhaps not. Perhaps the deceased goes out oblivious to the fact that they are slowly drowning as their lungs fill up with fluid. The deceased are certainly unpleasant to see afterwards, with blood and mucus foaming from their nostrils and mouths. They are often found slumped over, dying as they struggled to move somewhere, perhaps to seek help.

In the last decade, heroin overdoses have become an epidemic. In part, this has been aggravated by drug dealers who have begun lacing the heroin with fentanyl and other synthetic substances to make the drug more powerful; but it also makes it much, much more deadly. By 2020, the Department of Justice had developed a robust response to the problem and had devoted training and resources to prosecutors in an effort to stop the heroin trade and hold responsible those trading in the poison that is killing thousands. Back in 2006, though, this was new territory. We were just beginning to feel the impact of the epidemic and didn't fully understand its cause, let alone how to deal with the problem from a law enforcement standpoint.

In 2006, over the course of about a year, eastern Iowa had experienced more than 25 heroin overdose deaths.* The United States Attorney's Office was asked to step in and help. A driving force of the federal involvement was the bereaved parents of one of the victims. He died at age 22. He came from a good family, was an Eagle Scout, and at the time of his death a college student. His father found his son dead on the couch one morning. The father was livid with the dealer who sold his

*That seemed like a huge number at the time, but by 2019-2020, that was an average monthly heroin overdose death toll.

son heroin. The parents weren't ignorant of their son's struggles with addiction. It began with pain pills prescribed to him after a minor surgery. The parents had sought help for him and had him in and out of drug treatment several times. They thought he was turning the corner. He wasn't.

It happened that the father knew the United States Attorney from their membership in a community benefits program. He asked to visit with the U.S. Attorney about what happened with his son, and the U.S. Attorney asked me to attend the meeting. I had recently opened a file on another case involving a heroin death. During the meeting, the father shared the sad story of his son's untimely death and begged us to do something not just about the person who sold heroin to his son, but all the heroin dealers; he didn't want any other parent to have to go through what he and his wife suffered.

Sometime after that meeting, and after talking with a new and young DEA agent who was working my open heroin death case, I hit upon an idea for a strategy to address the heroin trade and the many deaths in a coordinated effort and not simply on a case-by-case basis. I asked a group of law enforcement agencies to send someone to attend a meeting I was hosting to talk about setting up an ad-hoc heroin death task force. Every agency I asked cooperated. At the meeting I had agents and officers from the DEA, the Iowa Division of Narcotics Enforcement (DNE), the Iowa Division of Criminal Investigation (DCI), the Cedar Rapids and Marion Police Departments, and the Linn County Sheriff's office.

I proposed that we set up a task force consisting of law enforcement personnel trained in narcotics enforcement (primarily DEA and DNE, but also narcotics officers from the police departments) and those trained in homicide investigations (primarily DCI, but also officers from police departments and the sheriff's office) to work together to investigate both past heroin deaths and stop the on-going heroin trade. Those trained in narcotics enforcement would focus on identifying the sources of the heroin and the people involved in the organizations, make controlled buys where possible, execute search warrants when and where we could, and shut down the heroin trade in Eastern Iowa. Those trained in homicide investigations would treat each heroin death as if it were a homicide investigation and try to solve the crime by identifying the dealer who provided the drugs to the victim. Although this latter approach seems somewhat obvious now, it wasn't at the time. Drug overdose deaths weren't treated as crime scenes back then. They were treated as tragic accidents. Law enforcement officers on the scene didn't gather evidence to identify the source of the drugs, such as downloading the victim's phones to find out who the victim called or texted to get the drugs. I was proposing a novel approach. I asked each agency to devote at least one agent or officer to work on the task force for six months with the task force work being their primary duty during that time period.

The agencies all agreed and over time, as we investigated the cases, we had other law enforcement agencies from surrounding communities contribute personnel to the task force. The key to success was coordination and communication between all the agents. We also recruited the county medical examiner, who also worked as an emergency room doctor, to aid the task force in evaluating the medical evidence for us and, when necessary, testifying about cause and manner of deaths. The task force ended up operating for a little over a year, although toward the end the hours devoted by the officers started to dwindle as their agencies pulled them back to work on other cases. We called our coordinated effort Operation Black Widow.

When we finally stood the task force down, we had successfully prosecuted 27 defendants, ten of whom were held responsible for causing overdose deaths, and two of whom were held responsible for causing overdoses resulting in serious injury, but not death. Although we couldn't ultimately prove who distributed the heroin that caused the deaths of 14 of the 24 victims, we were confident that some of the 27 people we convicted and sent to prison were involved. Out of the 27 defendants convicted, six went to trial, each one tied to a heroin death. Each trial was difficult because it wasn't easy to prove who supplied the drugs that killed the user because the users often had multiple sources for their heroin, and it was difficult to prove that death resulted from the heroin and not for some other reason. Every victim had multiple drugs or alcohol in their systems, along with the heroin. The cause of death was most often the result of the combined effect of all the drugs and alcohol, sometimes exacerbated by underlying health issues. What was remarkable to me was the very small amount of heroin necessary to kill a person; each of the victims died by consuming less than a gram of heroin. It is a very deadly drug.

What we found from our investigation is that most of the heroin was coming from Chicago. The distribution network was also fragmented and not terribly organized. Unlike cocaine and methamphetamine operations, which are often highly structured, the heroin trade seemed much more disjointed. Individuals from eastern Iowa would travel to Chicago, buy heroin, bring it back, and sell it. There were no stash houses and seldom tiers of dealers. The people who bought the heroin in Chicago were also the people who brought it back to Iowa and distributed it. Few worked with more than one or two others in the distribution. As a result, it was much harder to stop the trade. Instead of dismantling one or two large organizations, it was like we were trying to stamp out a score of small groups or single actors. It was like trying to step on cockroaches.

Each story was tragic, but I will share a few here to provide a sense of them. The Eagle Scout got his heroin from a high school student, who in turn got the heroin from his older brother. The dealer had just graduated from high school. He was a defiant and cocky man. We had precious little evidence tying him to the heroin that killed the Eagle Scout; we only had evidence of a call between them the night before the Eagle Scout died and some general testimony that would establish that they knew each other and had a drug relationship. No witness, however, could put them together the night before the Eagle Scout died. We decided to attempt a controlled buy from the dealer and hopefully get him into a conversation about the Eagle Scout. The new, young DEA agent worked with a cooperating informant to get introduced to the dealer. They exchanged some phone calls and set up a time for the agent to buy heroin from the dealer. They met in a fast-food restaurant parking lot. The agent, wearing a wire, got into the dealer's car and they made the deal. During the transaction, the agent asked if the heroin was any good. As I recall, the conversation went something like: "It's the bomb," the dealer said.

"That good?" the agent asked.

"Hell ya, man, it's so bomb that a motherfucker O.D.ed on it, man. I sell only the best, dude!"

Despite the agent's efforts to get the dealer to identify the person who had overdosed on his heroin, the dealer wouldn't say and became nervous about the agent's questions. Recognizing he had gotten as much information as he was going to get out of the dealer, the agent said the code word signaling the other agents nearby to swoop in and arrest the dealer.

The dealer was 17 years old. Juveniles are rarely prosecuted in federal court, and equally rarely does the federal government seek to have them prosecuted as adults. To do so, a prosecutor must get approval at the highest levels of the Department of Justice. Here, we felt it appropriate and necessary to prosecute this dealer as an adult on federal charges. He was only two months from turning 18. We had documented proof of him distributing a large amount of heroin, and evidence from the undercover buy that he knew the heroin he was selling was particularly potent and dangerous, and that he didn't care. The Department approved charging him as a juvenile and then seeking a court order to have him treated as an adult. It is a rare procedure and hadn't been done in our district for a long time.

The process was complicated and the rules Byzantine. Under the code, juveniles can be charged with some but not all drug offenses. Thus, we weren't able to charge him with all the crimes that would have applied had he been 18. Although we could charge him for heroin trafficking, we were unable to charge him with distribution causing the Eagle Scout's death. At sentencing, though, we provided enough circumstantial evidence tying the dealer to the death that it likely influenced the judge's decision to sentence the dealer at the top of the advisory guidelines range.

Another case involved a young drug-using couple who got heroin from a source they knew only as Youngblood. They had purchased heroin from him multiple times in the past. On this occasion, they bought a couple of grams and then traveled to a town in southern Iowa to meet up and party with a friend. They were at the friend's house using heroin and drinking when their friend's stepfather, also a drug user, came home. They agreed to share some of the heroin with him. The man shot up a very small amount of the heroin. Within minutes, he was on the floor turning blue. The others tried CPR to no avail. Afraid of getting in trouble, they all left the house, but the couple called 911 from another location to report the overdose. By the time rescue personnel arrived, the man was dead. An autopsy revealed that he had been drinking a lot earlier that evening and had some artery blockage, but absent the heroin the man wouldn't have died. We prosecuted the couple and their friend because they were all responsible for distributing the heroin to the man, but we also went after Youngblood with their help. Youngblood went to trial and was convicted of distribution causing death. He went to prison for about 15 years; the others received much reduced sentences because of their assistance in prosecuting Youngblood. All the same, I felt sorry for them. They were nice people who got caught up in the drug world with deadly consequences and were truly remorseful. I hope their time in prison went quickly and they are now leading productive lives.

Another dealer held responsible for a death was the closest we came to in this task force effort to a higher-level dealer and the person who died was one of his heroin dealers. The defendant came from Chicago one evening and stopped at the drug dealer's apartment. The defendant provided his dealer with what witnesses later said was a half-pound of heroin. While the defendant was present, the local dealer's girlfriend came over to visit. Together, the three of them used some of the heroin. Just before the defendant left, the dealer's roommate came home. He saw the defendant, his roommate, and the girlfriend sitting on a couch and chair. On the coffee table in front of the dealer was a mound of powder on a plate that was a combination of heroin and a cutting agent the dealer was adding to the heroin. This is a common practice among dealers when the substance comes in a powder form; they combine the drug with other similarly colored powdered substances—everything from laundry detergent to laxatives or creatine—so that an ounce of the drug becomes two ounces. That way the drug dealer can sell the drug and make more money from the sale because the end-user has no idea how pure the drug is that he's using.

Soon the defendant left and returned to Chicago. The roommate joined the dealer and his girlfriend and they used some more of the uncut heroin. Sometime around midnight the girlfriend left. About that same time, one of the dealer's customers, also a dealer, came over and purchased an ounce of the heroin. After everyone left, the roommate decided to go to sleep because he had to work the next day. He encouraged the drug dealer to go to bed too and not to use any more of the heroin. The dealer said he'd go to bed. A short time later the roommate heard the water running in the dealer's bathroom and assumed the dealer was on his way to bed.

When the roommate woke up the next morning he came down the hallway and saw the door to the dealer's bedroom open. He looked in and saw the dealer on his knees, awkwardly bent over into a laundry basket. The dealer was in his underwear. At first, the roommate thought the dealer just passed out, but then noticed the blueness of his skin; when he came around to look at the dealer's face, he saw dried, foamy blood emanating from his nose.

The roommate called 911, but not before he first called his mother. His mother came over and before the police arrived removed an assault rifle and the remaining drugs from the apartment. She threw the assault rifle in a dumpster and the drugs she flushed down her toilet when she got home. We learned of the destruction of the evidence only much later when we questioned the roommate. He told us that the defendant, the dealer from Chicago, was storing the assault rifle in their apartment. He was present when the defendant brought it. He stated that he didn't want the gun in the apartment and had words about it with his roommate. We never did find the assault rifle.

After a trial, a jury found the Chicago dealer guilty of distributing the heroin leading to his dealer's death. It was once again a combination of drugs that killed him. In the victim's blood the pathologist found alcohol, heroin, and cocaine.

As a result of our efforts, we effectively staunched the flow of heroin into the community and people stopped dying of heroin overdoses. The price of heroin on the street increased, meaning we had strangled the supply chain. Unfortunately, though, it lasted for only a couple years, at most. Trying to stop the drug trade always reminded me of the whack-a-mole game. As soon as we took down one dealer, it seemed another person would take the dealer's place. I used to describe the enforcement of the narcotics laws as akin to bailing out a sinking ship. Bailing isn't going to repair the hole, but we dare not stop bailing or the ship will surely sink.

In 2008, I was promoted to senior litigation counsel and my involvement in prosecuting drug cases pretty much ended as my new focus became complex cases, most of which were white collar or violent crimes. From 2008 to 2011, the number of heroin deaths started to mount again, not only in Iowa but nationwide. By 2009, heroin and opioid overdose deaths exceeded the number of people killed in car accidents for the first time in history. In 2011, while I was on detail to the Capital Case Section in D.C., another prosecutor in my office took over where I left off. He formed a new ad hoc task force, modeled after the one I had formed years earlier. That task force has more or less continued to operate ever since. This prosecutor has now tried many heroin overdose death cases, and has prosecuted probably hundreds of heroin and opioid dealers. He has become a national expert in the area, providing training for other prosecutors and law enforcement officers from around the country to show them how to work overdose cases like homicides and how to coordinate the work of drug enforcement officers and homicide investigators to prosecute these cases. In 2020, he received a well-deserved prestigious national award from the Department of Justice for his work.

Despite his efforts, and the efforts of others like him and the agents they work with, heroin and opioid deaths continue. There remains much work to be done.

Chapter 16

If It Sounds Too Good to Be True...

Good law enforcement agents will proactively look to uncover criminal conduct and not wait for crimes to occur or to be brought to their attention. I worked with an IRS special agent who was quite proactive. When he was in a city working on one case, he'd often stop by businesses that wired money (such as grocery stores and convenience stores) and look over their books of wire transactions. Under the law, officers have the right to inspect such records. It's part of the money laundering laws Congress passed over the years. Criminals often have to wire money to other locations, often in the drug trade, to pay suppliers for drugs. Sometimes the wires go to source states for drugs, such as the southwestern states and Florida, and sometimes the wires go to source countries, such as Mexico or Colombia. The agent made notes of suspicious wires, or of senders whose names he knew were associated with criminal conduct, and kept track of them, looking for patterns, sometimes conducting a follow up investigation, occasionally leading to a criminal prosecution.

One time the agent called me and requested my assistance to follow up on one such investigation. Over the course of several months the agent had noticed tens of thousands of dollars being wired to a recipient in an African country known for fraudulent scammers who sent faxes, emails, or text messages to people living in the United States promising vast riches if the recipient would wire them a few thousand dollars. The nature of the fictitious stories would vary, but generally they involved a claim that the person was a government official pursuing a claim to recover funds due to the government from some other African nation, typically allegedly to do with mineral rights or some other natural resource. The faxes and emails would be on official-looking letterhead purporting to originate from a government agency. The purported official would explain that they only needed a few thousand more dollars to perfect a lien or claim on the funds worth hundreds of millions of dollars. If the fax recipient sent the few thousand dollars requested, they'd be rewarded with millions of dollars. Often the scammers provided an exact amount of the alleged cash reward, such as $1,257,873, to make it appear as if someone had actually calculated the exact return. If the victim responded and sent a few thousand, the scammers would then ask for more, coming up with some other explanation. Occasionally, the scammers sent the victim some money as a partial payment so as to lull the victim, only to later ask for more money.

Unfortunately, many Americans fell for these scams. I had a highly-educated, shirt-tail relative call me up one time about a scam just like this. She said that she was about to wire the money but then thought perhaps, just before she did it, she should ask me my opinion on the matter. I assured her it was a complete scam and if she just wanted to throw her money away, to wire it to me instead.

Thus, the agent and I immediately thought that some poor Rube in Iowa was being scammed and that we should investigate and at least stop the hemorrhaging. Before the agent went to speak with the apparent Rube, though, he did some further due diligence to look into the matter. He reviewed SARs (suspicious activity reports) to see if the Rube's name appeared. It did. Indeed, the SARs reported that the apparent Rube had attempted to deposit a check for tens of thousands of dollars, allegedly from Walt Disney Corporation, in his business bank account. The Rube wanted to immediately withdraw cash from his account after he made the deposit, but the bank refused until the check cleared. The check didn't clear. It came back as fraudulent. The Rube insisted that the check was good and claimed that his company, a plastics molding company, was manufacturing plastic action figures for Walt Disney Corporation.

This complicated matters tremendously. Something more was afoot here than a case of a simple Iowans being taken by scammers. Our apparent Rube was a business owner and had tried to pass a fraudulent check. A multi-month-long investigation ensued which revealed what really happened and it ended up our Rube was both a victim and a criminal.

The Rube was co-owner of a plastics molding company in Iowa. It made plastic products like golf tees and the like. It had a score of full-time employees. The Rube was the chief financial officer and had an accounting degree; he ran the books. His partner and brother-in-law, the chief operating officer, ran the production side of things. The company generated a few million dollars gross revenue a year and the partners paid themselves six-figure salaries from the profits. So, all in all, it was a pretty good setup and a profitable business.

At some point, the business started receiving these scam requests over the company fax machine. At first, the Rube ignored them. But, after a while he started to think that maybe there was something to them. He talked to his partner about it and, although the partner was highly skeptical, the Rube talked the partner into sending $2,000 in response to one of the faxes. The scammers quickly sent the company a lulling fax, that is a fax intended to lull the victim into believing that they'd soon be getting their huge payout. Alas, a short time later the scammers sent the Rube another fax breaking the news that a complication had arisen and they needed another $5,000 to overcome the new hurdle. The Rube went to his partner again suggesting that they invest another $5,000 in the venture. The partner had enough, however, and said no more. "It's a scam," he told the Rube. The Rube insisted it wasn't and tried to persuade his partner to invest just a little more, but to no avail.

That didn't stop the Rube. The next $5,000 came out of his personal account. Soon, the scammers were "pleased to inform" the Rube that they were successful and he'd soon get a check. But then, alas, another fax would arrive, another complication would have arisen, and there was now a need for $10,000 more. The Rube's wife had gone ballistic when she found out the Rube had taken $5,000 out of their personal account and wired it to Africa, so the Rube realized digging into his personal money wasn't an option unless he wanted to be divorced.

Thus, the Rube turned into a criminal. He began embezzling money from the company. It was easy for him as the chief financial officer. He was in charge of the books and so simply made false entries to cover up the diversion of money into a new bank account he opened up in his name only. Over the course of the next six months, the Rube wired tens of thousands more to the scammers. Each time they told him that the funds were almost freed up and soon he'd be getting his money. They told him that because of his significant assistance, in fact, he was being made a 10 percent partner and would now receive tens of millions of dollars.

But as the months wore on and the money kept flowing out with no return, the Rube began to get frustrated. He threatened not to send any more money and demanded his money be returned. That's when the scammers came up with a new plan. They told the Rube they would send him a check from Walt Disney Corporation for $87,000. They told the Rube that if he cashed the check he could keep half of the money as a partial repayment. He agreed; they sent him the check made payable to his plastics company, and he unsuccessfully tried to deposit it into the business bank account. Although the Rube was himself the victim of a fraud, this was blatant bank fraud on his part. The Rube knew that Disney hadn't sent his company a check and knew that his claim to the teller that he had a contract with Disney to make action figures was a lie. He tried to pass a bad check, knowing it was bad, in a failed attempt to recoup some of his own losses.

When the check scheme failed, the Rube was very upset with the scammers. He demanded the payout, or his money back, or he'd contact the authorities. The scammers played the Rube some more. They sincerely apologized for the misunderstanding, but told him that they had finally succeeded in freeing up the frozen government funds. The money was in a bank in the Netherlands. They asked him to meet them in the Netherlands and there they'd give him his tremendously large payout. He told them he'd be there.

The Rube convinced a friend to fly with him to the Netherlands. When they arrived in Amsterdam they took a taxi to the address he was given. It was in a building in the business district. They found the address easily enough, but there wasn't anything on the outside of the building suggesting that it was an embassy or connected with the African government. When they entered, though, they were greeted by a man in an impeccable suit who fawned over the Rube and treated him as if the Rube were an important official. He invited the Rube and his friend to have a seat in the reception area while he took his seat behind a desk and placed a call. He spoke a foreign language, but he was very obsequious and the Rube could tell that he was talking to some high official. It was a short conversation and when the man got off the phone he appeared crestfallen. He announced that the President of the Interim Government would see him now, but apparently there was a complication.

The Rube and his friend were ushered into a large inner office where, behind a massive desk, sat a large man resplendent in native African dress. Behind him were several national flags and upon his desk stacks of papers he appeared to be pouring over. He was flanked on one side by a man in a military uniform with many gold braids and medals, and on the other side by a man in a formal cutaway coat that the Rube assumed to be the ambassador. Also, in the room was a man who acted as a servant, pouring the President a cup of coffee, while near the door were two men in suits with earpieces, posing as bodyguards.

The President stood and greeted the Rube and his friend enthusiastically, but the Rube could tell that the President was upset about something. He invited the Rube and his friend to sit on a couch by the fireplace while he and his general sat in armchairs opposite. The receptionist served as translator.

The President stated that once again the foreign bankers had thrown up another roadblock, but he was resolute that he'd see it through somehow, although he wasn't sure how quite yet. In any event, he announced, he said he couldn't and wouldn't ask anything more of his loyal American friend. He was prepared to pay the Rube back every cent he had invested and let him be on his way while the President would find some way to free up the millions without his American friend's help. With this, he called upon his servant to fetch the official checkbook off his desk.

The Rube thanked the President, but inquired what more was needed to free up the millions. The Rube wasn't sure he wanted to pull out when they were this close to freeing up the funds. The President looked discouraged and said the bankers were now demanding a $50,000 transaction fee before they'd free up the money. The President said he wasn't sure where they'd get the money because his poor country was financially strapped due to the international bankers' machinations. With this, the President began to write out a check to the Rube.

Hesitantly, the Rube said that he might be able to get the needed $50,000. The President stopped writing and looked up at the Rube with surprise and hope etched on his features. No, the President proclaimed, he couldn't ask more of his American friend, but, was it possible, did his American friend really think he could get the money? They'd need it by noon the next day or the bankers were threatening that the funds would be tied up even longer based on another claim that was pending in The Hague. The Rube said he thought he could get the money. The Rube and his friend left after effusive thanks and smiles all around (except for the bodyguards) and the Rube went back to the hotel where he got on the phone with his bank. It took some effort but by the next morning he had arranged to have $50,000 wired from the business bank account to a bank in the Netherlands. He knew his business partner/brother-in-law back in Iowa would learn of this transaction—there was no time to create false paperwork to cover it up—but he no longer cared. Once he got the millions that was his due, he could easily repay the $50,000 and then gloat over his partner about how the Rube had been right all along.

The next morning the Rube went to the bank in the Netherlands and got the $50,000 converted to a cashier's check in Euros. He and his friend then returned to what the Rube believed was the consulate where he was again greeted with great fanfare, invited to an audience with the President, and presented the check to his Excellency. All were in great joy and said that this was the final key to freeing up hundreds of millions of dollars for his country and that the American friend would be richly rewarded now with an even larger share. They suggested the Rube and his friend go enjoy a hearty lunch while the President would send his ambassador to the bankers to complete the transfer of funds. The President invited the Rube and his friend to return in about five hours when the President would personally provide his American friend with his payout.

The Rube and his friend left the consulate in great spirits and found a fancy restaurant where the Rube ordered champagne. They ate a luxurious lunch and then relaxed in their hotel room for a few hours while they awaited the time to return to the consulate. When the time came, they once again took a taxi to the consulate. The Rube was beside himself with joy, excited to receive his multi-million dollar return on his investment (made with money he embezzled from the company). When they reached the door, though, it was locked. They knocked and knocked, but no one answered the door. They looked through the one window, but all they could see was the reception area. After banging on the door for some time a man finally appeared at an upper window demanding to know what the Rube wanted.

The Rube stated he was here to see the Interim President of the African country. The man was confused.

"What President?" he asked.

"The President of [the African country]," the Rube replied. "This is his consulate."

"That's an insurance office," the man corrected the Rube. "At least it was until it closed a few months ago."

The Rube insisted that it was the consulate for the President of the Interim Government and he had a meeting with him. The man insisted that it was no consulate, it was an insurance office. He knew the landlord, he said, and would call him to come there and show the Rube. A half-hour later the landlord arrived, confirmed to the Rube that the first-floor office space formerly housed an insurance business, unlocked the door, and let them enter. The reception area was as it was before, but when they entered the inner office where the President had reigned, the office was empty. The desk, chairs, and couch were gone. There were no flags. No President, no ambassador, no general, no anyone. The landlord claimed he knew nothing about any Africans and said the Rube was simply mistaken. He suggested perhaps the Rube was lost, as a foreigner, and got the address wrong.

But the Rube knew better. He knew he was in the right office. And he finally knew that he had been scammed.

It was some months after his failed trip to the Netherlands that the agent had completed his review of the financial records and other investigation steps such that we were ready to have him interview the Rube and his business partner. The Rube quickly confessed to everything. His business partner had, as predicted, quickly learned of the $50,000 transfer before the Rube could cook the books any more to conceal it. The Rube and his business partner were already at odds with each other and the partner was threatening to sue the Rube for the $50,000. He had no idea yet that the Rube had embezzled another $78,000 from the company.

We ultimately charged the Rube with attempted bank fraud. As I recall, he received a probationary sentence and was ordered to repay his company for all the money he embezzled. We insisted he provide information to the Secret Service, which is the federal law enforcement agency in charge of trying to shut down and prosecute international scammers. I sat in on the interview. Despite all that had happened to him, despite the disappearing consulate in the Netherlands, the Rube still insisted that there were hundreds of millions of funds tied up by a cabal of international bankers and that he'd ultimately get paid.

Unfortunately, the Secret Service has had little success holding international scammers accountable. They have been more successful in shutting down their communications, but African governments have had little success in finding and prosecuting the scammers.

CHAPTER 17

The Molting Maltese Falcon

Malta is an archipelago in the Mediterranean Sea between Sicily and the North African coast. Less than a hundred square miles in size, it hosts a population of a half a million people in one of the most densely populated countries in the world. It's a popular tourist destination today, known for historic sites tied to the Romans, Moors, knights of the Crusades, and the French and British empires, with numerous fortresses and temples. It is less well known for the Iowa drug dealer who fled to—and then wanted to flee from—there.

Among the drug dealers I prosecuted was a man from Northern Iowa who had ties to a Mexican cartel and was importing pound quantities of methamphetamine. He was an intelligent man with some college education, and he was careful. For years he flew under the radar. He maintained a fulltime job, as well as selling drugs, and never used his own product. He had amassed significant sums of money and purchased several collector cars, motorcycles, and a fine home with drug proceeds.

The government will eventually catch up with every drug dealer, and so it was with him. The task force built a case against him and I worked with them to obtain search warrants and arrest warrants. We also obtained seizure warrants to take all the property he had acquired through his drug dealing. The operation was successful when the agents executed the warrants, seizing large quantities of drugs, firearms, and other evidence, along with all his toys. The agents arrested him and a couple of the dealers he worked with. He had no criminal history, so the court released him on bond pending trial, but he was subject to home confinement monitored by an electronic ankle bracelet.

He hired a good attorney, who obtained several continuances of the trial date as he went through the evidence and filed an unsuccessful motion to suppress evidence. Despite the overwhelming evidence against him, the defense attorney told me that the defendant wasn't interested in a plea agreement and was insistent on going to trial. About two weeks before trial, as we were preparing witnesses and marshaling our exhibits, I got a call from the probation officer supervising the defendant while he was on release pending trial. The probation officer informed me that the defendant was gone. She stated that the signal to the defendant's ankle bracelet had suddenly ceased. She had given him permission to travel to Des Moines to see his dermatologist as he had a severe problem with eczema. The signal went dead in Des Moines. She told me that probation officers found the ankle bracelet in a trash can in the parking lot of the Des Moines International Airport; he had cut it off.

With the help of the probation officers and the United States marshals, we conducted an investigation into his flight. As a condition of his release he was required to surrender any passport he had; he claimed he never had one. The probation office didn't check to find out if that was true. It was false. He boarded a flight to New York where he had a connecting flight to Barcelona, and from there to Malta. We traced the ticket purchases back to a travel agency. The travel agent told us that he came in with his girlfriend, who was from Malta. They purchased one-way tickets to Malta, saying that they were moving there. The State Department informed us, however, that he had obtained a tourist visa from the Maltese Embassy.

When we found that the girlfriend didn't fly with him, but rather was following a week later so that she could collect her last paycheck and see to the sale of their assets, we obtained a warrant for her arrest on a charge of aiding and abetting her boyfriend's flight. At her initial appearance, the judge granted my request to have her detained pending trial because she was a clear flight risk. She was incensed, as was her attorney. It is a felony offense, however, to help someone released on bond to escape. Since we had frozen all the drug dealer's bank accounts, she had paid for the tickets. Video from the airport parking ramp showed that she drove him to the airport. And she was the one with connections to Malta, not him. She clearly aided the escape.

Her case proceeded forward and ultimately resulted in a guilty plea a few months later. In the meantime we went through the laborious process of tracking the drug dealer down in Malta. The FBI has offices in nearly every foreign country and, in cases like this, work with Interpol and the country's law enforcement authorities to locate a fugitive. Once they have confirmed he is in the foreign country and can be located, then we push paperwork through the bureaucracy to obtain an extradition warrant for the fugitive's arrest.

Fortunately, Malta had an extradition treaty with the United States. But that doesn't necessarily mean that the fugitive will be extradited, or extradited quickly. Once he is arrested on the provisional arrest warrant, he'd appear in a Maltese court. There, the drug dealer could fight extradition on various grounds. The litigation could take months or years before a court might grant the United State government's request to extradite the drug dealer. Once we got word of a favorable decision, then United States marshals would fly to Malta and bring him back. It is a long and tedious and not always successful process.

By the time we navigated the process far enough to get a provisional arrest warrant, the drug dealer's girlfriend was coming up for sentencing on her charge of aiding and abetting his escape. A couple weeks before her sentencing hearing we received word that the Maltese authorities had arrested the drug dealer on the provisional warrant. What was even more interesting is that we learned that the drug dealer had waived all extradition rights and had asked to be extradited back to the United States. In fact, we were told that he was begging to be extradited back. The marshals were soon flying to Malta to pick him up.

He arrived back a couple days before his girlfriend's sentencing hearing. The day of her sentencing arrived and the judge sentenced her to two years in federal prison. After the hearing she was returned to the local jail to be held pending a ConAir flight to take her to her prison. That same afternoon I got a call from the drug dealer's attorney. He informed me that the drug dealer wanted to plead guilty and cooperate with the authorities. He'd tell us everything about his sources of supply in the cartel and anything else we wanted to know. He just requested a chance to see his girlfriend one last time before they'd be separated for years.

I wasn't keen on the idea of negotiating with a drug dealer, and was skeptical that jail authorities would allow them to meet; they certainly weren't going to meet in our office. But the agents were adamant that his information could be very valuable and that we should try to make it happen. We arranged with the jail staff to allow the two of them to meet briefly in a visiting room, but they'd not be allowed to touch and guards would be present at all times. That was acceptable to everyone and the brief meeting apparently occurred without a hiccup.

A few days later the drug dealer sat down with his attorney, my agents, and me to debrief. He told us about his sources of supply and connections, all of which proved helpful to law enforcement agents. But the most interesting part of the interview was the tale of his flight. When he first came in the room I noticed that he looked terrible. He appeared to have lost significant weight, and his skin was in horrible condition with his eczema angrily broken out everywhere. He had bandages on his arms and on one hand. That, it turns out, was part of his story.

The drug dealer said that the flight to Malta was long and tedious, but otherwise uneventful. His girlfriend's uncle met him at the airport. Fortunately, English is the official language in Malta, so communication wasn't an issue. But the uncle wasn't happy about the whole matter. He didn't know the whole story; he knew that his niece's boyfriend was coming to Malta on a tourist visa, but the uncle was to hide him. The uncle was savvy enough to know that something illegal was afoot and he didn't like being part of it.

The uncle took the drug dealer to a hovel of an apartment building the uncle owned and put him in a sparsely-furnished, one-room apartment with a tiny kitchen and a bathroom. There the drug dealer stayed and stayed. The weather was fine, but he had nowhere to go, knew no one, and didn't want to be seen by the authorities. Without a television or even books, he spent days in utter solitary confinement. After a week passed and his girlfriend didn't show up, he began to worry. The uncle inquired and found out she had been arrested in the United States for aiding the drug dealer's escape. Now the uncle was particularly unhappy. The drug dealer had come with little money and that had now run out. The uncle found himself having to financially support his niece's deadbeat fugitive boyfriend.

The drug dealer quickly also began to suffer from more than boredom. He was frequently sick from drinking the local water and eating the local food. Stress can cause an outbreak of eczema, as can a reaction to some foods. Soon, the drug dealer was breaking out with eczema in a way he had never suffered before. He tried to buy some over the counter treatments from a local pharmacy, but nothing they had was effective. He had no doctor and no insurance in Malta, and no money to pay a doctor. He tried to visit a free medical clinic for the poor, and received some treatment there, but it was ineffective. By the end of his fifth month on Malta, the drug dealer was as miserable as he had ever been in his life. The itching made it hard for him to sleep, some of his sores became infected, the eczema spread throughout his body, he could hardly keep any food down, and he was becoming mentally unstable.

Thus it was that when the uncle brought the local police to the apartment to arrest the drug dealer on our provisional warrant, the drug dealer was ecstatic. He said he eagerly put his hands out to be cuffed and begged them to take him away. He said all he wanted to do now was escape from Malta. He spent another couple of weeks sitting in a Maltese jail before the marshals came to fly him back. At least in jail he started receiving decent treatment, he said: topical ointments for his skin, antibiotics for his infections, and medicine for his ravished intestinal tract.

As the drug dealer told us about his tale of woe we couldn't help but laugh a little, and he joined in. He, like most of the people I prosecuted, was a decent guy at the core, and he saw the humor in his story. He said it was the worst six months of his life and no prison could possibly be worse. As humorous as his story was, I did sincerely feel sorry for the man as it was apparent that he was still a long way from getting his eczema under control and that he'd continue to be very uncomfortable for some time to come. My sympathy went only so far, though. When his attorney asked the judge to reduce his sentence because of the hard time of confinement the drug dealer had suffered while on the run, I resisted the motion vociferously. The judge lacked any sympathy for the plight the drug dealer brought on himself by fleeing. I don't recall the sentence the drug dealer received, but I do wonder if he and his Maltese girlfriend reunited.

Chapter 18

Slumlord and Damage Deposits

Every criminal case involves interesting facts and personalities. I generally found that the most fascinating, however, were white collar cases. It was fairly easy to understand what motivated most street crimes, such as drug trafficking, firearms possession, and violent crimes. It was often greed, unchecked emotions, or a disadvantaged background in which the offender grew up knowing only that kind of life, or a combination of all the above. More interesting to me, though, was what led people who grew up with all the advantages of life, who had education and careers, family and friends, to risk it all. I guess greed was always the base motivation. But it was a more egregious form of greed because no matter how wealthy these people were, it was never enough. I found it fascinating to try to understand the mindset; what caused them one day to decide to lie, cheat and steal and risk all they had.

The other factor that made white collar cases so interesting was the challenge of discovering exactly what the criminal did and how the criminal did it. To me, white collar cases were like complex puzzles, but with the twist that you first had to find the pieces before you could start to put it together. And, you didn't have the picture on the box to tell you what the puzzle would look like when you finished.

One of the most fascinating and, in the end satisfying, white collar cases I prosecuted involved the single largest property owner in the city. Other than a few large manufacturers, two colleges, and a hospital, this man owned more real estate than any other person or company in the city. He owned literally hundreds and hundreds of properties, the vast majority of which were single family rental homes. Of these, he owned on average between 600 and 800 rental properties, numbering more than 1000 rental units, although his inventory varied from time to time over the two-decade period under investigation. He also owned 25 or so apartment complexes and a dozen or more commercial properties. Of his rental homes, some were decent; indeed, two of my colleagues rented from him temporarily when they first moved to town to take a job with the United States Attorney's Office. By far, though, the vast majority of his rental homes were in various stages of disrepair. He soon gained a reputation in town as a slumlord.

He was quite wealthy. College-educated, he even attended two years of law school before he quit to run his business. He started out with only a few rental homes, but his empire grew steadily. By the time I prosecuted him, he lived in a multi-million-dollar house in a gated community. Bank documents for loans he obtained to fund his property empire reported his net worth at about $34 million. His company office, however, was small and cluttered and staffed by only two people besides himself; an office manager and a secretary. He had scores of others who worked for him, though, on maintenance, repairs, and cleaning.

The case came to me in an indirect way. At this point in my career I was primarily assigned to complex drug trafficking and violent criminal cases. We had other prosecutors devoted to white collar prosecutions, but one of them was in the Navy reserve and was called up during the Iraqi war. This was his case. The criminal chief assigned me to take over the case. I spoke with the prosecutor about it. Our conversation wasn't encouraging. He told me they were investigating insurance fraud. A hailstorm had torn through the city a few years before and the Slumlord submitted claims for damage to hundreds of his properties. The insurance company thought many of the properties hadn't actually been damaged and they suspected fraud. An agent from the Iowa Insurance Bureau and a United States postal inspector (because the claims were mailed into the insurance company) were assigned to the case. The prosecutor said he was about to decline the case, but decided to leave the decision to me. He said there was little evidence of insurance fraud, in his view, and the case would involve a fact-intensive fight over claim-by-claim disputes on each house. He explained that the insurance company had already sued the Slumlord in federal court and it seemed to him best to just let them pursue civil remedies and decline the criminal case.

A few days later I met in the conference room with the outgoing prosecutor, the paralegal (the same one who was so instrumental in the Dr. Feelgood case) and the agents. The agents summarized the evidence for me and, generally speaking, I had to agree with the outgoing prosecutor that there didn't appear to be overwhelming evidence of fraud. In the civil litigation, the Slumlord had produced many documents, including invoices from multiple roofers giving damage estimates and invoices showing the Slumlord had paid for repairs in the tens of thousands of dollars. In total, the Slumlord was seeking approximately $380,000 in insurance proceeds for damage to his properties. Even if some claims were overstated or even completely fabricated, it appeared that most of his claims had some documentary support. A trial would involve a property-by-property fight. Nevertheless, I saw multiple possibilities for our investigation and different leads to follow. His claims all smelled fishy and I suspected that if we dug a little we'd find a lot more holes in his alleged documentary support for the insurance claims.

As the agents were telling me about the case, though, they also told me about the Slumlord. They showed me a newspaper article about the man from several years before, with a photo of him going into the county courthouse with an armful of files. The article spoke about a failed civil lawsuit brought on behalf of some of his renters by the legal aid society claiming he had cheated them out of their damage deposits. Apparently, the Slumlord, or his office manager, were in court almost every week seeking judgments against renters for damages he claimed the renters caused to his properties in excess of the damage deposits the renters had provided him. The newspaper reporter interviewed a number of renters and sat in on some hearings.

The upshot of the article was that the Slumlord almost never returned damage deposits. If a renter sued in small claims court to get the damage deposit back, the Slumlord would file a counter-claim alleging that the renter caused so much damage to the apartment or house that not only was the renter not entitled to return of the damage deposit but actually owed the Slumlord hundreds or thousands of dollars more. The Slumlord would show up with reports from workers about the damage they found to the apartment, photographs of the damage, and invoices showing he had paid companies to repair the damage. Although the renters would deny causing the damage, they had no legal training and weren't prepared for the fight he brought. Most former renters were happy to walk away with an agreement he could keep the damage deposit so long as they didn't have to pay more. In a few cases, judges found for the renters when they came more prepared; in one case the renter proved that the photos of damage weren't to the renter's property, but to another property.

One particularly intriguing piece of information revealed in the newspaper article was that most of the lease agreements, notices to renters, and so forth were signed with the name of R. Gordon Sargent. The Slumlord claimed that Sargent was his partner. But when renters called to complain about something, Sargent was never there. When people attempted to call him as a witness, he could never be found to serve with a subpoena. Indeed, it seems that no one had ever set eyes on this elusive Sargent character. The Slumlord explained that Sargent traveled often and didn't always keep the Slumlord aware of where and when he was going and when he'd be back. The newspaper reporter speculated that there was no such person.

To the agents' surprise, the damage deposit matter interested me as much or more than the insurance fraud angle. There was a pattern of conduct here that we might be able to uncover. It certainly appeared from the article that the Slumlord was systematically fleecing his renters out of their damage deposits. It would be expected that some renters would cause some damage and some wouldn't be entitled to the return of some or all the damage deposit. But the idea that every single renter damaged the rental properties to the extent that none received their damage deposits in return seemed beyond belief. Damage deposits are typically equal to one-month's rent. For many of the Slumlord's properties, then, the damage deposit would be only a few hundred dollars; at most a little over a thousand. Although no single damage deposit amounted to much, if the Slumlord took damage deposits from hundreds of renters year after year, we could be talking about hundreds of thousands of dollars. We had a federal jurisdictional angle because the Slumlord sent notices to his renters about not getting their damage deposits back through the United States mail. If the scheme was fraudulent, we could charge him with mail fraud in federal court.

I realized that we needed some help. This investigation was going to require significant work following the money. So, I called up one of the IRS special agents I worked with often and asked him to join the team. Thankfully, he agreed to come on board.

About a month after I took over the investigation, the civil case brought by the insurance company came on for trial in federal court. The IRS agent and I sat in the back of the courtroom and watched when the Slumlord testified. Among other things, he swore that R. Gordon Sargent really existed and was his partner. Whenever the insurance company lawyers confronted him about some document at issue that appeared to be fraudulent, it was inevitably signed by Sargent. The insurance company lawyers were no more successful than anyone else in locating Sargent and serving him with a subpoena.

A few days later the jury returned a verdict in favor of the insurance company and found the Slumlord defrauded the insurance company out of approximately $230,000 in proceeds. The verdict didn't make our job any easier. The burden of proof in a civil case is by a preponderance of the evidence, meaning that the insurance company needed to persuade the jury only that it was more likely than not that he committed the fraud. In a criminal case, we have a much higher burden of proof—beyond a reasonable doubt—which was going to be much harder to meet without better evidence than what the insurance company had to work with.

After months of investigation, gathering as much evidence as possible without the Slumlord knowing we were investigating him, we put what we knew together in a lengthy affidavit and applied for a search warrant to seize documents from the Slumlord's office. This included not only documents pertaining to the insurance claims and alleged repairs, but also the complete files for 100 of his rental properties going back ten years. In short, whole filing cabinets of documents. When the agents executed the search warrant, they found that the Slumlord's office was a mess. His files were in disarray and completely unorganized. Nothing was filed in chronological order and no file was complete.

We initially seized files for only 100 rental properties to make our task manageable, and even then it proved a herculean task. I concluded that there was no way that we could examine all of his hundreds of properties over more than a decade; we'd never finish the case. Rather, we'd take a representative sample of his properties. If we could discern a pattern of fraud there, we could extrapolate against the entirety of his property empire.

As the agents, our paralegal, and I spent scores of hours going through the files trying to make sense of them, we also pursued other avenues of investigation. We questioned many of his employees under oath. We followed up on every purported invoice for either roof repairs or rental property repairs related to the damage deposits, seeking documentation to support the alleged repairs. We tried to question every person who allegedly performed repairs to the roofs or to the 100 rental properties on which our damage deposit fraud scheme was focused.

What we learned was astounding. First, no one had ever seen or spoken to R. Gordon Sargent. Indeed, one of the Slumlord's former girlfriends stated that she was with him on vacation in Florida one day when he opened a phonebook and picked the name out at random. We even tracked down every person by that name in the United States (there was a half-dozen) to eliminate them as possibilities.

Second, we discovered that 90 percent of the invoices for alleged repairs to roofs and rental properties were fraudulent. Some were made up out of whole cloth when the Slumlord dummied up letterhead from an imaginary company and created a fictitious invoice. In other instances, the companies actually existed, but they had no records that matched up with the invoices in the Slumlord's files. It appeared that he took real invoices and altered the documents as needed. Last, in still other instances, he altered the dollar figures on legitimate invoices. For example, a roofer may have charged a thousand dollars for a roof repair and the Slumlord altered the document to reflect ten thousand dollars. Or a carpet cleaning company charged $80 to clean the carpet in an apartment, but the invoice that the Slumlord submitted to the court showed $280.

We were also able to place the Slumlord's employees into two categories; those who were complicit and those who weren't. Some helped fabricate documents for him and knowingly presented false documents in state court when renters disputed the return of their damage deposits. Two of his workers who cleaned and repaired his rental properties when renters moved out knowingly falsified the paperwork reflecting damage that didn't exist and repairs that were never made. Most of his workers, though, were honest. They'd fill out paperwork showing the condition of the rental property upon inspection after the renter moved out, and then would document the repairs, if any, that were actually performed. This annoying honesty didn't deter the Slumlord. He'd simply alter the paperwork to show damage that didn't exist and repairs never made. For example, if the worker said one window blind needed replacing, the Slumlord would alter the "1" into a "4."

We also learned something very curious about the man. He was a hoarder and petty thief. We were told that he'd often enter renters' properties when they were absent and take things he liked. Also, when he evicted renters for late rent, he'd throw their property out on the curb, but not before he sorted through and took what he wanted. Many people told us of seeing the Slumlord driving around town in his beat-up pickup truck, with the bed of the truck full of various items of personal property he had taken from renters.

At one point before we charged the Slumlord and his complicit employees, we issued a grand jury subpoena for him to submit a handwriting exemplar. The subpoena was a court order compelling the recipient to sit down with agents and write what the agents told him to write, as many times as was necessary. In this case, the Slumlord met in a conference room with two agents. Over the course of the next four hours, they had him write various things allegedly written by R. Gordon Sargent, and in particular Sargent's signature. In legal academic circles, there is a hot debate about whether handwriting forensic analysis is junk science. Whatever the merits of that argument, handwriting analysis is often helpful especially when, as here, the subject attempts to evade the process. That effort to disguise writing so as to make sure it doesn't match the suspect writing shows consciousness of guilt.

Here, the Slumlord repeatedly tried to disguise his handwriting. He tried to use the wrong hand to write with. He attempted to write in cursive when he was told to print and vice versa. The process took four hours because he was trying so hard not to write anything in a natural style. Eventually, the agents just wore him down. Try as he might, after signing the name R. Gordon Sargent several hundred times even the most determined suspect is going to accidentally write the name with natural effort. A forensic examiner later testified that the Slumlord had signed Sargent's name on fraudulent documents, though the Slumlord's attempts to evade the handwriting exemplar was just as incriminating as the forensic examiner's opinion.

A grand jury ultimately retuned a lengthy indictment against the Slumlord. We charged him with mail fraud in connection to the insurance fraud scheme and mail fraud in connection to the damage deposit scheme. We charged him with perjury for lying in the federal civil case about, among other things, his claim that R. Gordon Sargent actually existed. Finally, we charged him with tax fraud on the theory that the wrongfully-kept insurance proceeds and damage deposits constituted income that he was duty bound to report but didn't. In fact, we discovered he hadn't paid taxes for years, claiming a huge loss from flood damage years ago that he had carried forward on his books such that he'd not owe taxes.

The Slumlord hired an excellent defense attorney who worked hard to defend him. It appeared that we were going to trial on all the charges and we spent many days preparing. The trial would take place in Sioux City, so that was an added inconvenience. The Friday before the Monday trial, the defense attorney called me to say that the Slumlord was willing to plead guilty to everything except the tax fraud charges. I told the defense attorney that I'd not drop the tax fraud charges. We got hold of the judge and he scheduled a change of plea hearing before him in Sioux City for Monday and, over my objection, continued the trial on the tax fraud charges for a week.

On that Monday the Slumlord pled guilty to all but the tax fraud charges, and did so without a plea agreement. In short, I gave up nothing in return for the guilty pleas. Everything would be up for grabs at sentencing, meaning that we'd be fighting then about how many renters he defrauded and for how much, which would be the driving force on his sentence. But, at least the guilt part was established.

The following week we were back in Sioux City and tried the Slumlord on the tax fraud charges. The defense attorney did an excellent job, but the facts weren't on his side. The Slumlord mounted an advice of accountant defense, meaning that he claimed he couldn't be guilty because he had relied upon the advice of his accountant. That defense crumbled when his accountant took the stand, though, because she testified that he never told her about illegally taking insurance proceeds or that he wrongfully kept damage deposits. She agreed that all income, lawful and unlawful, must be reported on tax returns, as counterintuitive as that sounds. The jury returned guilty verdicts on all counts on a Friday afternoon at about 4:00 p.m. It was early January and a winter storm had hit Iowa, with many roads closed. But it was my son's birthday, so I was determined to get back home. The IRS agent bravely agreed to trek across Iowa with me in a blizzard, with him helping me see the road. The typical four-hour trip took us seven and half, but I got home in time to wish my son happy birthday as I put him to bed.

Now that we had the Slumlord convicted, we shifted to preparing for his sentencing hearing. He fired his attorney and hired two other good and well-known defense attorneys to handle the sentencing hearing. Everything was contested, so at sentencing we needed not just to prove to the judge's satisfaction that he defrauded the insurance company—the Slumlord admitted he did when he pled guilty—but to prove every dollar of the fraud because that would drive the sentence and the amount of restitution he owed. Similarly, we had to prove how many renters he defrauded and for how much. Because of my sampling theory, we hadn't inspected every file for every rental property for every year he rented them. Rather, we took a representative sample of 100 properties and examined them over a ten-year period, then extrapolated our findings. I hired a forensic accountant (a former, retired IRS special agent, one with whom I had worked on several of the cases mentioned in this book) to conduct the calculations. He calculated that for the ten-year period before indictment, the Slumlord had defrauded more than 2,000 renters out of their damage deposits. Based on the average amount of the damage deposit and subtracting the very small amount for the damage deposits he actually returned, he determined the Slumlord defrauded his renters out of at least $1.4 million and probably more than $3.6 million.

When the day came for sentencing we appeared in court prepared to put on evidence to prove our case and support the sentence we were seeking. At the beginning of a sentencing hearing judges go through certain housekeeping procedures which include making sure that the defendant has reviewed the pre-sentence report (PSR) with his attorneys. The PSR is a document drafted by the probation office that summarizes the evidence of the offense conduct, calculates the advisory sentencing guidelines, and reports on the offender's history and characteristics, including the offender's upbringing, education, employment, physical and mental condition, and criminal history. It is a requirement and a matter of routine that attorneys review the draft PSR with the offender, determine what objections to make, and then go over the final PSR with the offender in preparation for sentencing.

On this occasion, the judge asked the Slumlord if he "had a full and fair opportunity to review the pre-sentence report with his attorneys."

> SLUMLORD: What's a pre-sentence report?
> JUDGE: It's the document drafted by the probation office.

At this point, the Slumlord's attorney placed a copy before the Slumlord and explained that's what the judge was talking about.

> SLUMLORD: Your honor, I have never seen this before in my life.

The judge went ballistic. He was incensed that these two very experienced and well-known attorneys wouldn't have performed this fundamental part of representing a defendant in a federal sentencing hearing. The lawyers were on their feet swearing that they had gone over it with their client many times. The attorneys asked for a short recess during which they attempted to confer with their client. We couldn't hear what was said, but from facial expressions it was clear that the whispered discussion was heated. After the short recess, the Slumlord continued to insist to the judge that his attorneys had never shown him the pre-sentence report. "I've never seen the thing in my life," he insisted.

The judge was about to become very upset when I stood up. I explained to the judge that I had copies of emails and correspondence between the defense attorneys and me, sent weeks ago. I assured the judge that the emails reflected the attorneys discussing the PSR with their client and relating objections that the Slumlord had to the PSR.

At this, the judge cooled down and told the lawyers to confer with their client again. The lawyers bent over and whispered with their client for a long time. I couldn't hear what they were saying, but I could tell that the lawyers were becoming exasperated. Finally, the lead defense attorney stood up and announced that their client had just fired them.

Suffice it to say, the judge wasn't happy but because the Slumlord had privately retained the lawyers, there was little the judge could do but continue the hearing. The judge ordered he Slumlord taken into custody, though, because we had also shown that the Slumlord was violating conditions of his release, including contacting witnesses. After the hearing, the defense attorneys thanked me for coming to their aid.

The Slumlord hired yet another attorney, one of the best in Iowa. After multiple continuances, the sentencing hearing finally took place. The judge adopted our calculation of loss amount and imposed a sentence of 20 years in prison without the possibility of parole. The Slumlord gave a rambling and self-pitying allocution at the sentencing hearing that lasted more than an hour. He had written it and read it aloud in court. Not once in his statement did he admit he did anything wrong; he didn't apologize. Instead, he railed on his renters, claimed they cheated him and that he was a good man for providing these lowly people with housing even though he made almost nothing from it.

Despite our best efforts to contact former renters who may have been defrauded, and to advertise the possibility of collecting past damage deposits, only a couple of hundred former renters applied for restitution. This is unfortunate, but also understandable. The people who rented the rundown and sometimes barely habitable properties were often poor, vulnerable, and transient. They had written off the loss of the damage deposit as just one more lousy hand life had dealt them and moved on.

Although the Slumlord's criminal problems had come to a head, he was also dealing with many other financial issues. The banks had called his loans and foreclosed on hundreds of his properties. With the judgment from the civil case and the anticipated fine and restitution he'd owe in the criminal case, he declared bankruptcy shortly before the final sentencing hearing. The bankruptcy trustee eventually seized control of his house and later shared photos of it with me to see if I wanted to pursue bankruptcy fraud charges against him. I most certainly could have, as he failed to disclose many assets in his bankruptcy filings. Nevertheless, the Slumlord was in his mid-fifties when he was sentenced to 20 years in prison. I saw nothing to be gained by charging him with still more criminal offenses.

The photographs revealed an odd and disturbed man. The

Slumlord's house was a mansion. His foyer, dining room, and living room were spotless and opulent. Indeed, the large dining room table oddly had plates, silverware and glasses set out as if he was expecting a dinner party of twelve. The rest of the house, however, was the total mess of a true hoarder. The trustee could barely find a path through the many rooms. And here we found all the items he had taken from his renters. He had hundreds of Precious Moments figurines in multiple cabinets, for instance. One room was full of Coca-Cola memorabilia, another full of Elvis merchandise. Room after room was full of similar collections. Even his bedroom was full of such junk, piled on every horizontal surface.

When the bankruptcy estate was finally closed, the Slumlord was left with almost nothing and his creditors with far less than what he owed them. In the matter of three years, the Slumlord went from having a net worth of about $34 million to nothing. One positive result of the financial fallout was that banks repossessed the many rental properties and ultimately sold them or, if they were too far gone, had them torn down. I imagine that new owners purchased many of the homes and rental properties, invested in them, and made the long-neglected repairs and deferred maintenance, improving their values and appearance tremendously. The city is now a far better place with these properties out of the Slumlord's control.

Chapter 19

Immigration Raid Leads to Bank Fraud Trial

In the late 2000s, a new administration in the White House decided to take a hard line on undocumented workers and those who knowingly employed them. A decision was made well above my pay grade to undertake a massive "enforcement action" in our district, meaning that an attempt would be made to raid a large employer of undocumented workers, arrest all the undocumented workers, charge them with immigration-related criminal offenses when the evidence supported the charges, and then seek to prosecute everyone in the company that knowingly hired and employed these undocumented workers, using the workers themselves as witnesses against members of management complicit in illegally employing them and helping them obtain false documents. One of my best friends in the office was put in charge of the investigation and operation, but it was going to be such a massive operation that it would require the involvement of virtually everyone in the office.

The employer, a meat processing plant, employed by our best estimate about 600 undocumented workers; in essence almost every single line worker and even a few low-level supervisors were illegally employed there. The undocumented workers comprised roughly 90 percent of the company's workforce. Most of the undocumented workers were illegally in the United States and from primarily Guatemala and Mexico. The company had been on law enforcement's radar for years as undocumented workers were regularly arrested in the community after committing minor offenses or infractions, such as speeding, and found to have been working there. The titular head of the company, the president, lived in New York, but his son who lived in Iowa, was clearly the one in charge of day-to-day operations.

This enforcement operation would involve us arresting potentially hundreds of workers in a single day. It'd take scores of law enforcement officers. Moreover, timing would be crucial because the workers would have to be identified (which would be difficult because most if not all carried false identification), tied to evidence showing they were knowingly working at the plant illegally, charged, and have an initial appearance within 72 hours of arrest. Further, to go after the supervisors and owners of the company, our ultimate targets, we'd need to execute search warrants for documents and search the company's many computers for evidence showing who was involved in hiring and employing the illegal workers. This operation would be a massive undertaking.

In the end, agents arrested about 389 workers. Then, to our surprise, the case evolved into one of the most massive financial fraud investigations and prosecutions our office worked on. It resulted in a trial against the son who ran the plant for the financial fraud, and the conviction of a score or more of the supervisors and white-collar workers for their knowing involvement in the immigration violations and financial fraud.

The Investigation and Planning

The investigation and preparation for the raid and prosecution of hundreds of people took on the appearance of a military operation in its complexity. The raid had to be a surprise or else the undocumented workers were likely to flee and the complicit supervisors in the plant would likely destroy documents. Yet, we needed to recruit and coordinate scores of agents and involve a dozen different law enforcement agencies to pull off an operation of this magnitude. The Bureau of Immigration and Customs Enforcement (ICE) was the lead law enforcement agency for this operation. The bureau was involved at the highest levels of the agency in Washington.

We also had to develop a system for processing the large number of defendants in a very short time frame. There were about a dozen different criminal statutes that undocumented workers might have committed, including illegal re-entry, using false documents, misappropriation of social security numbers, and aggravated identity theft (that is, the knowing use of another person's identity). To move things quickly, we needed to prepare charging documents for all the possible charges, plea agreements to go with them, and every other document we'd need with the ability to fill in the blanks once we figured out what evidence we had for each potential undocumented worker. The ICE people had a special unit of computer geeks and evidence handlers. They had high-speed scanners and copiers and people who would begin to sort through the employment files for each undocumented worker and, using their fingerprints, determine the workers' true identity, obtain their true documentation, and match everything up with their false employment papers, feeding the key documents to the prosecutors. We'd then have a team of prosecutors who would review the documentation, identify the charges supported by the evidence, if any, fill in the form charging documents, and create the paperwork necessary to bring the person to court. The ICE unit said that it could process the paperwork for something like 50 workers an hour, fast enough, they guaranteed us, that we could easily process all the unlawful workers within the short 72-hour time frame we had.

Because we had such a short window of time to complete this massive project, we decided to work around the clock. Agents would work on eight-hour shifts, as would our teams of prosecutors and support staff. My friend and fellow prosecutor was in charge of the entire case. As senior litigation counsel, I was brought in as well. My primary responsibility was working on the search warrants. Once the arrests were made, I'd be in charge of one of the eight-hour shifts of our prosecutors, while my friend and a third prosecutor, an extremely talented and hardworking guy, would be in charge of the other two shifts. The office clandestinely reserved a bank of hotel rooms with three people sharing one room, each person using it for their eight hours of sleep.

This operation was too big for the small courthouse, and for our small court to handle alone without significant advance planning. Thus, we alerted the court about the operation without improperly disclosing any details about it. The court personnel needed some idea of the size of the operation so that they could prepare.

The ICE bureau identified a fairgrounds in Northeast Iowa that had enough large buildings to handle the operation. We'd need one building with several rooms to serve as courtrooms. There was an auditorium we would use to process the hundreds of workers in a series of processing stations looking something like the checkout lines in a supermarket. We'd also need one large building to hold male defendants and another to hold female defendants. In addition, we'd need buildings for agents and prosecutors and staff. Even the fairground wasn't sufficient for all of this and so we had FEMA trailers brought in primarily to be used by our office and the United States Probation Office. We also needed to alert the defense bar that many attorneys would be needed, but, of course, we couldn't tell them why.

The lead ICE agent was, simply put, amazing. He was in charge of coordinating everything on the law enforcement side. He was incredibly efficient and his work was flawless. Most important, he was calm and careful, and his judgment excellent. He also had an unbelievable work ethic. At the remote site we'd be using one large ballroom to process hundreds of workers through initial appearances and pleas, but the following week we'd be holding sentencing hearings for those workers who agreed to the fast-track plea offers. So, we needed a few additional courtrooms to process the hundreds of workers we predicted would accept our favorable plea offers. We used two FEMA trailers for these courtrooms. But the trailers were just large, open rooms. To make it more secure and to have it appear more like a courtroom, the lead ICE agent personally built railings to separate the public portion of the courtroom from the "well" of the courtroom and raised daises for the judges' benches (here, desks). How and when he found time to do this is beyond me.

As you might imagine, this was a complex and difficult operation. Eventually the word got out and about a week before the raid the press picked up that something was afoot. After all, the fairground had been shut down and secured, FEMA trailers delivered, a perimeter fence erected, and scores of law enforcement officers, particularly ICE agents, began flying in from around the country and staying in area hotels. The rumors were accurate that an ICE raid was in the making, but the target was unknown. Fortunately, I guess, there were many plants in Iowa employing at least some undocumented workers. Each plant likely suspected it was the target of the operation, but no one knew for sure. We kept the ultimate target of the investigation a closely-held secret, not even telling most of the law enforcement officers until the last moment. We also intentionally selected a fairground in a city somewhat between Cedar Rapids and the town where the target plant was located, so that it wouldn't be obvious which plant we were hitting. Thus, many undocumented workers began not showing up for work in the plants around the city where we were setting up our remote operations. Because the target plant was located miles away from the fairgrounds, most of the workers there weren't spooked and continued to come to work as usual.

The Raid and the Prosecution of Undocumented Workers

The raid took place about mid-morning on a Monday. The prosecutors and staff then drove to the fairgrounds to set up shop and await the arrival of the undocumented workers.

During the raid, agents arrested about 400 undocumented workers. Some were released because they were the sole parents of minor children or for other humanitarian reasons. Agents also executed search warrants at the plant and at a few other locations belonging to plant supervisors. The son of the owners, who operated as the chief executive officer (CEO) of the company, and some of the managers, owned many apartment complexes in town where the workers lived.

At first, the operation appeared to be going smoothly. The raid of the plant was a surprise and was executed very smoothly and peacefully, with no one getting hurt and no mishaps. The search of the company files and computers went smoothly and the ICE special evidence unit began processing the paperwork.

By mid-afternoon the first workers were transported by bus from the plant to the fairgrounds. In the large arena, scores of agents sat at desks and processed the workers as they began coming through. First, the workers' fingerprints were scanned. Then the agents asked the workers questions about their immigration status. Many of the ICE agents spoke Spanish fluently, but for those who didn't there were interpreters. Once the administrative immigration questions were asked, the agents advised the workers of their Constitutional rights. Then they began asking them questions about their use of false identification documents and the like, questions which could lead to criminal charges. The agents also asked them about where the documents came from, the knowledge and involvement of management in the employment of undocumented workers, and about allegations of abuse and exploitation. These questions were read from a questionnaire that the prosecutors and agents had developed.

Soon, the first workers were coming through processing and then taken to a detention center. Runners collected the paperwork from the agents and took it to the ICE special evidence processing unit. The special unit was to match up the fingerprints to the true identity of the person along with their false identity at the plant, identify the false employment records, and provide all that to our team of prosecutors who'd then review the file to determine what, if any, federal criminal offense the worker committed. If none, the worker would be processed by ICE on immigration violations with deportation proceedings likely to follow. For those workers for which there appeared to be evidence of criminal offenses, the prosecutors would draft up the charging documents, a fast-track plea offer, and the other necessary paperwork for prosecuting the worker. Court was to convene the following morning at 8:30 and we expected by then to have scores of defendants filing through the courtroom.

I was busy working with the agents executing the search warrants and on follow-up warrants that grew from evidence the agents had already uncovered. But I recall at one point going to the arena and seeing all the workers being processed through the conveyor-belt like apparatus set up on the floor of the area. It looked like all was going smoothly. I was responsible for the evening and early morning shift, as I recall. At the end of the first shift and before the second shift began, at around 7:00 p.m., there was a pause in the processing of workers as the team of agents on the floor of the arena changed. The lead ICE agent debriefed the first shift agents to find out if there were any trends becoming apparent from the evidence, like whether the workers were identifying certain supervisors as complicit in obtaining and furnishing the workers with false identification and the like. The other two lead prosecutors and I were present for the debrief. Then together we and the lead ICE agent briefed the agents coming in on the new shift, making sure they knew the rules, knew of the need to advise the workers of their Constitutional rights, and to alert them to any new information that we obtained from the first batch of workers processed so that the agents on the next shift could refine their questioning for the next batch. Over the next three days, we went through this same routine with each change of shift.

Sometime that first night, around 10:00 or 11:00 p.m., we started getting bad news. The prosecutors trying to work through the files were running into problems. The files they were getting from the special evidence processing team were either incomplete and lacking the documentation necessary to determine who the worker really was or to match them up with the false identity they were working under, or the information in the folder didn't match. For example, a file might contain the photo the worker was using at the plant, but it didn't match the photo of the person that the special evidence unit claimed was the same person. When we began reviewing some of the charging documents the line prosecutors were generating for the workers, we saw more problems even for those for whom there appeared to be sufficient documentation at first. In short, around midnight we realized that we had a massive problem.

Between about 1:00 and 2:00 a.m., the criminal chief and the three of us lead prosecutors went to meet with the special evidence unit located in one of the adjacent buildings on the fairgrounds. We told them about the problems we were seeing and provided them with some examples. They hadn't been able to scan in all the information from the company's computers and physical files as quickly as they anticipated and their programs weren't correctly identifying documents to match up a real identity with the false identity accurately or completely. Further, it appeared that the paperwork for the first batch of workers whom we had already processed were mixed up, such that we couldn't be sure that the file we received for any given worker actually matched the worker that had been processed. In short, we were processing people faster than the paperwork connected to them, resulting in errors.

The head of the special evidence processing unit suggested we just try to sort through all the files that had been generated and figure it all out. We prosecutors consulted with each other and decided that the unit's plan would never work. We'd never be sure that the information was accurate when the paperwork had been mishandled coming off the floor of the arena. So, we came to a radical decision. We shut down the operation and decided to start over. We ordered all the files thus far generated be dumped because we had no confidence in their accuracy. Then, at about 2:30 a.m., we went to the floor of the arena and stopped the processing of the workers the second shift of agents had begun. We had the workers returned to the holding cells and then ordered the entire process to begin again once the special evidence unit assured us that they had finally processed all the computer and physical files from the company, a task they had promised us would be complete within hours of the raid. As it was, we started processing the workers again at about 5:00 a.m.

Then the lead prosecutor and I had the unpleasant duty of advising the court that we were behind schedule, that we wouldn't have a single worker to bring to the court when court opened at 8:30. Fortunately, the court was very understanding. We gave the court our best estimate for when we thought the first workers might make initial appearances and promised to keep the court informed about the timing.

The first workers were charged and made initial appearances mid-afternoon on Tuesday. We were now about six or more hours behind schedule. Although I wasn't to have much of a role in the processing of the workers on criminal charges (I was focusing on developing the evidence for charges against management), it became clear that we needed to have more oversight of the criminal files before charges were approved and workers charged and brought to court. Thus, we three lead prosecutors took on the role of oversight of every criminal file once the line prosecutor completed the paperwork for charging a worker. This wasn't part of the original plan, but it was clearly necessary.

The idea that we three lead prosecutors would work separate shifts quickly fell apart. All three of us were essentially needed at all times if we had any hope of processing about 400 workers within 72 hours. I recall sometime Tuesday night I went to the hotel not to sleep but just to take a shower. I hadn't showered for almost 48 hours. I went to the room assigned to me. One of our line prosecutors was sleeping in the room, but I had a key to the room as well and I was just going to use the shower. But, alas, he had secured the door with the chain latch. I tried to call out to him, but didn't want to wake up everyone down the hallway. Fortunately, two staff members of our office came out of their room down the hall on their way to what would be their lunch. They let me use their bathroom to shower. A couple times the three of us lead prosecutors tried to sleep for a couple hours on some army cots set up in the back room of one of the FEMA trailers. Army cots aren't comfortable. I remember at one point the lead prosecutor and I were both trying to sleep at the same time. Every time one of us shifted in an effort to find some comfort on the cot it woke up the other.

Finally, on Thursday morning, 72 hours after the workers were arrested, the last of them were brought to the courtroom for initial appearances. The 72-hour mark passed literally as the final workers were being ushered into the makeshift courtroom and the judge was announcing the opening of court. Everyone from the United States Attorney's Office working the case was sleep deprived to some degree, but we three lead prosecutors had been awake by then for about 85 hours with, perhaps, three or four hours sleep caught in short snatches here and there. I know when I caught a ride home Thursday afternoon I could barely keep my eyes open.

The Financial Fraud

The following week, about 305 of the workers pled guilty and were sentenced as part of the fast-track deals we offered them. A dozen or so chose to fight the charges and their cases proceeded as they would in a regular case. We spent the next several months interviewing scores of these workers about the knowledge and complicity of management in the procurement of false identification for the workers, and other criminal conduct involved with their employment. This part of the investigation was hampered, as was everything else, when about a month after the raid Cedar Rapids was hit by a flood that inundated most of the downtown, including our office and the courthouse. Thus, we ended up holding grand jury in a courtroom adjacent to a jail in Mason City.

The evidence we developed on the criminal case related to the undocumented workers was significant. We uncovered evidence that several of the employees in the human resources department were complicit. They processed paperwork they turned into the federal government claiming the workers were lawfully in the United States and authorized to work, knowing they weren't. They helped direct them to people in the community, including one of the supervisors, to help them obtain false documents, like false drivers' licenses and social security cards. We uncovered evidence that at least one supervisor personally transported illegal aliens to Minneapolis to obtain false documents. We also uncovered evidence that all of this was done with the knowledge and at the direction of management. In short, the company was corrupt through and through. The investigation resulted in the criminal prosecution of about a dozen members of management and the HR department for their involvement in the knowing employment of illegal aliens and the fabrication and falsification of documents to conceal their employment.

One of the chief culprits, the supervisor who was heavily involved in obtaining false paperwork for the immigrants, got away. He fled the country about a week after the raid and traveled to another country where he had dual citizenship. We later uncovered evidence that shortly before the supervisor fled, the CEO transferred a large amount of cash to him and paid for his plane ticket.

Little did we know going into the operation, however, that the larger crime lay below the surface. By the end of the second week of the operation, while the last of the workers were entering guilty pleas and being sentenced, we three lead prosecutors met with the criminal chief to talk about what was now bubbling up from the evidence we had seized. I remember the meeting well because I was sick as a dog; the sleep deprivation the prior week had taken its toll on me. But what I recall at that time was that it was just becoming apparent that the company was operating through a massive financial fraud.

In the months that followed, through countless grand jury subpoenas, upon reviewing reams of bank and financial documents, and after questioning scores of witnesses, here is what we learned in a nutshell. The company's operations were financed by a revolving line of credit of approximately $30 million. The line of credit was secured, as usual, by accounts receivable and inventory. The company would provide monthly reports to the bank setting out its accounts. The accounts, though, were largely falsified. The CEO, with the help of the chief financial officer, the chief accountant, and another three or four people in the accounting department, had falsified the company's records. They engaged in wholesale fabrication of accounts receivable documents by altering documents for companies with whom they actually did business, by claiming to do business with real companies with whom they didn't do business, or by simply fabricating the existence of companies altogether. One of the most extreme examples was that the company claimed to have sold tens of thousands of dollars' worth of meat to a New York City business entity that turned out to be a clothing store. The CEO was the primary fraudster. To get his employees to go along with the fraud, he bribed them. He literally paid them cash in envelopes.

When the raid shut down the plant, because the plant had no lawful workers, the cash flow stopped. When the cash flow stopped, the bank came calling, looking for its collateral. It was at that point that the fraud was discovered. While the plant was operating, the fraud was difficult to discover. Once the music stopped, the bankers learned there wasn't a seat for them. The company's entire operation was founded upon a massive financial fraud. Meanwhile, the CEO lived in a palatial home and tons of money flowed into his accounts and others'.

On top of everything else, we discovered they committed another crime, albeit one that had literally never been charged before and likely hasn't been since. At the turn of the century, there were only a few meat processing companies who together controlled the market. The meat processors, recognizing their power, developed a practice whereby they basically used the farmers as bankers. The processors would take delivery of the cattle, slaughter them, process them for meat, send the meat to market, and only after selling the meat and paying their other expenses would the meat processors pay the farmers for the cattle, sometimes many months after the farmers had parted with their cattle. This essentially made the farmers lenders of their cattle to the processors, allowing the processors to reap the financial gain and avoid the risk of loss. Congress put an end to this by passing a law that required meat processing plants to pay farmers for their cattle within a week of purchase. Congress made it a criminal offense to intentionally delay these payments.

The CEO of this company was such a cheat that he even broke this law. He intentionally paid the farmers late, many weeks after he took delivery of their cattle. He covered up the fraud by having his staff cut timely checks for the farmers and process the checks through a postage meter so they'd show a timely payment. But instead of mailing the checks, he had his staff hold the checks for a while before sending them out. Whenever farmers complained, and they often complained to the company and to the USDA, the CEO was able to show that the checks had been written and postmarked on time. He'd essentially blame the United States mail for any delay. We ended up charging the CEO with this little known and never-before-used crime.

The special agent with the USDA who discovered this crime was an earnest young man in his twenties, who looked about 16. When he asked to meet with us to tell us what he uncovered, we were at first skeptical. But the more we investigated, the better the evidence got. The big break came when the secretary in charge of sending out the mail each day finally confessed to us what the CEO did. The young USDA special agent ultimately received an award from his agency for his work. I suspect to this day that case was a highlight of his career.

Charges, Pleas and Trial Prep

After many months of investigation, grand jury sessions, and negotiations, we ultimately charged about a dozen corporate personnel with immigration-related offenses. All of them pled guilty in the end, except for the CEO. The charges encompassed criminal conduct such as falsifying immigration documents submitted to the government, lying to government officials, and aiding undocumented workers in obtaining fraudulent documents. As for the financial fraud, we charged half a dozen corporate employees with the various forms of fraud. The employees included the chief financial officer, the head accountant, and accounts payable and receivable clerks, among others. All pled guilty, except for the CEO, who claimed he wasn't the CEO.

The CEO had an endless supply of money from his father and other backers, and he was determined to fight the charges to the end. He hired a team of lawyers and they fought hard, filing many pretrial motions challenging various aspects of the investigation, seeking to suppress evidence, and seeking dismissal of the charges, among other legal maneuvers. The motions were all unsuccessful, except for two.

The CEO filed a motion to change venue. The defense alleged that there was too much pretrial publicity, and that publicity was very negative about the CEO, such that there was no way he could receive a fair trial in Iowa. After a long evidentiary hearing, the judge agreed and decided to try the case in Sioux Falls, South Dakota.

The CEO also filed a motion to sever the charges so that there would be two trials, the first on the many financial fraud charges and a second on the immigration-related charges. He pointed out that there were more than 100 counts charged against him and that a trial encompassing all the charges would take months and be too difficult and complicated. He also argued that he'd not receive a fair trial on either set of charges if tried together. He argued that a jury might acquit him of the financial charges, but not if the jurors thought he was complicit in employing hundreds of illegal immigrants. Similarly, he argued that a jury might acquit him of the immigration-related charges, but not if they heard that he was accused of defrauding a bank and others of tens of millions of dollars. The judge agreed and decided there would be two trials. The first would encompass the bank fraud related charges, and also the fraud against farmer charges related to intentionally delaying their payments. The second trial would include all the immigration-related charges.

The first trial was scheduled for October and was estimated to last at least a month. We had several months of trial prep, which involved identifying the evidence we wanted as exhibits at trial, marking the exhibits, and preparing charts, diagrams and any other demonstrative aids we'd use to help educate and persuade the jury. We also had to prepare witnesses. Many of the witnesses were located in Iowa, but many more were spread all over the United States. Trial prep involved trips to Los Angeles and New York, and many places in between. One particular witness prep session stands out in my memory.

An FBI special agent I had worked with many times before was the case agent on the financial fraud portion of the trial. He and I traveled to Saint Paul, Minnesota, to prepare a couple of witnesses who ran a tannery. As part of the fraud, the CEO and his co-conspirators falsified invoices from the tannery to make it look like the tannery was buying many more cow hides on a monthly basis than they actually were. To prove this, we needed one of the members of management to testify.

The tannery was located in an industrial park on the south side of Saint Paul. The minute we got out of the car, the stench assaulted our nostrils. After a while we got somewhat used to the smell, but it stayed on our clothes like paint until we threw them in the laundry days later. The owner met us outside in the parking lot and offered to give us a tour. I have found that people are very proud of where they work and what they do. Often, they want to show visitors everything. We agreed to a tour, even though it had nothing to do with the purpose of our visit. The owner explained that he'd walk us through the tannery in the order of how they processed raw hides into leather goods.

The tour began next to a large vat holding thousands of gallons of boiling water and some chemicals. After a meat processing plant slaughtered a cow, the hide was removed from the carcass and thrown into a long semi-truck trailer that looked like a large trough. The truck would back up to the vat and the trailer would lift up like a dump truck and dump the pile of bloody cow hides into the vat. Large paddles moved and stirred the hides in the vat, somewhat like a washing machine. One worker stood at the side of the vat and, using a long pole with a hook on it, he'd snag a hide and then lift it up a foot or so to set it onto another hook that passed by on a conveyor belt just above the vat. This took both strength (the hides were heavy to begin with, but now they were wet as well) and skill because he had to hook the hide the right way so that the top of the hide, the portion near the missing head, was placed on the conveyor belt hook.

From there the conveyor belt would lift the hide out of the vat and raise it above a long drain and down to the next station along the line. That station was occupied by a man who sat on a stool such that his head was at about the height of the bottom of the hides as they passed by him fairly quickly on the conveyor belt. In his right hand was a curved and very sharp knife. His job was to watch the hides and if he saw a bull hide pass by, identified by the testicles hanging down beneath the hide, to castrate the lifeless hide. I can only imagine the typical conversation he had at night with his wife when he got home.

"How was your day, honey?"

"Great!," he might say, "I cut off a hundred pairs of balls today."

Past the castrator were other workers who fed the hides into machines that pressed and scraped the hides clean of any remaining biological matter and fur. These machines were massive and operated somewhat like an old-fashioned washing machine where the damp clothes were fed between rollers to squeeze the water out. From there, the hides were sorted by an expert based on quality of the hides. Some were rejected because of blemishes on the hides or other imperfections. These were made into dog food or other byproducts. The very best hides were sorted to be processed into fine leather goods, like hats, boots, belts and purses. Other hides were processed into any number of other leather goods. This particular plant didn't make the final goods; rather, it processed, cured, and dried the hides into leather and then shipped the leather to other companies that turned the leather into goods for the marketplace. It was an interesting tour, but at the end I was very glad I made my living as a prosecutor and not as a tannery employee.

Trial

The case finally came on for trial. The trial team occupied a wing of a long-term hotel in Sioux Falls, a city I came to like very much. It had excellent restaurants and a thriving downtown. The courthouse was located in the heart of the downtown and dated to the mid–1800s; it was the oldest federal courthouse west of the Mississippi. Unfortunately, it wasn't made for large trials. The courtroom was very small for this very large trial. We had three prosecutors on our side, two case agents, a paralegal, and a witness coordinator. The CEO had five attorneys and two paralegals, along with one or two other staff members. It was a very crowded courtroom.

The trial lasted four full weeks from start to finish, with the jury out a few more days before returning a verdict. I recall many long nights and little sleep, but also recall some pleasant dinners with the trial team and agents. One weekend the lead ICE agent took us three prosecutors pheasant hunting in the tundra of South Dakota. It was brave of him; none of us were experienced hunters and the idea of three lawyers with lethal weapons is frightening. But he was a brave special agent, so he did it anyway. We shot nothing. We did come upon some pheasants, but we missed them all.

I have a few distinct memories of the trial itself. I was responsible for presenting the opening statement for the government, questioning about a third of the witnesses, and cross-examining a third of the defense witnesses, including the CEO if he testified. The lead prosecutor was responsible for closing argument, about a third of the witnesses, and crossing a third of the defense witnesses. The last of the three prosecutors took the last third of witnesses on direct and cross.

One of the witnesses I questioned on direct examination was the owner of a company from New York. The CEO and his co-conspirators had fabricated documents related to this company as part of the fraud. The witness had his own lawyer because the witness had knowingly assisted the CEO by lying to regulators to cover for the CEO. The witness's lawyer had been a pain in the back from the beginning. We had agreed not to prosecute the witness, but only if he fully cooperated and told the truth. His lawyer, though, was an impediment to working with this witness by interfering during trial prep and, it appeared, trying to get his client to say things that might have been more favorable for his client, but weren't true. Anyway, at trial when the witness was on the stand, I was asking questions, methodically going through direct examination when there was an objection.

"Objection, your honor," a defense attorney roared indignantly, "he's coaching the witness!"

I was nonplussed and then angry about this objection. To accuse me of coaching a witness is a serious allegation of wrongdoing. It was patently false and I wouldn't take it lightly.

"Your honor, I was doing nothing of the sort!" I nearly screamed.

"You weren't, Mr. Williams," the judge responded, "but he was," she said, pointing behind me.

I turned to see the judge pointing at the witness's attorney sitting in the back of the courtroom, attempting to portray his best "who, me?" look.

Addressing that attorney, the judge dressed him down and told him that he was no longer to shake or nod his head, use hand gestures, or do anything else to communicate with the witness or she'd have him removed from the courtroom.

The other witness I recall specifically was the CEO himself. As we anticipated, he testified. The defense theory was that this CEO wasn't really a CEO. They claimed he was an absentee, hands-off manager for his father, and knew really nothing about what his employees were doing and was shocked and offended when he found out what awful things they had done without his knowledge or permission. On direct examination he came across as a meek, mild-mannered man who was unable to understand or explain much of anything that had happened, try though he might, because he was just out of the loop on things. This was a defense that he had seemingly planned for years in advance because he made a point of claiming only the title of vice president and made his underlings sign almost everything so as to keep his own signature off as many documents as possible. This, despite the fact that he had the largest office in the plant with a window looking down upon the accounting department.

When I trained prosecutors I often emphasized that defendants are the hardest witnesses to cross-examine. This is because, if we're doing our jobs correctly, they are criminals (otherwise, we shouldn't have charged them) and thus aren't truthful people to begin with. They are also on trial for their liberty (or life) and have every motivation to lie. Thus, unlike other witnesses whom you can sometimes box in so that they have to tell the truth, criminal defendants evade almost every attempt to pin them down.

So I found this criminal defendant. He was one of the slickest witnesses I questioned. He was very intelligent, anticipated where I was going with many questions, and felt no need to be hemmed in by the truth. What I did accomplish, though, was to crack the veneer of the mild-mannered, meek persona he presented on direct examination. The longer my cross examination went, the angrier and more confrontational he became. By the end of my cross I think the jury saw that his direct examination presentation was a false act and this was the type of guy who very much was capable of bribing and intimidating his employees and orchestrating a massive fraud, as we alleged.

The only fun part of the cross I remember was my effort to get into evidence one of the key bank documents that bore his signature. Below his signature was the title "chief executive officer." On cross I got him to assert that he never, not one time, claimed to be the CEO of the company. I pressed him several times, but he was adamant that he had never claimed that title. He claimed that some of his employees may have used that title for him, but it was part of their criminal scheme to make him responsible. But I had one of the very first loan documents in my hands that had his signature above the title "chief executive officer." There were so many documents in this case—tens of thousands of pages—that even though the defense had a copy of this document they had seemingly missed the significance of the signature. The document itself was of no great importance in proving the fraud, but it was important to prove the defendant's command of the company's operation.

The rub was how to get him to admit that it was his signature. If I just showed him the document he'd claim someone else signed his name. There was no way he'd admit signing a document that showed him to be the CEO. We didn't conduct handwriting analysis on the document and so wouldn't be able to refute that. Thus, I needed him to admit it was his signature without him seeing the CEO title below his signature. I decided I'd use my thumb to cover his title.

I asked the CEO some preliminary questions so as to act like this was just a mundane matter and I'd get to the point soon, but just needed him to confirm this was his signature on some routine document. The judge had a rule that when a lawyer approached a witness with an exhibit, the lawyer was to hand the exhibit to the witness and then step back away from the witness so as not to intimidate the witness. When the witness was done examining the exhibit, the lawyer could approach again to retrieve the document. But I couldn't comply with that rule here or else he would see the title and deny it was his signature. I had to stay at the witness box with my thumb over the title long enough to get him to admit it was his signature.

I approached the witness box holding the document in such a way that my thumb was over the title. I showed the CEO the document and asked him to confirm that he signed this document.

"Mr. Williams," the judge said, "please step back from the witness."

"Yes, your honor," I said, nodding to her, then "now, sir, you signed this document, didn't you?"

"Mr. Williams," the judge said more firmly and a little annoyed, "hand him the exhibit and step away from the witness."

"Yes, your honor," I replied very agreeably, then continued without stepping back or letting go of the document: "This is your signature, isn't it?"

"Yes," he answered, just nanoseconds before the judge ordered me in no uncertain terms that I was immediately to step back from the witness.

"Gladly, your honor," I said.

And I was glad. After I moved the document into evidence I went straight to a projector and placed the document on the projector, showing the jury, and the CEO, the signature he just admitted was his prominently above the title "chief executive officer." The defendant was irate and claimed I tricked him and then claimed someone signed his name to the document. I moved to strike his testimony because I hadn't asked him a question. The judge sustained my motion. I could detect just the slightest sign of a smile on her face; she knew what I had done.

The case was submitted to the jury on a Friday afternoon. The jury didn't reach a verdict that day and would return on Monday to continue deliberations. Many of the trial team members returned to Cedar Rapids that weekend, but the lead prosecutor and I remained. That Saturday we went on a long hike along South Dakota's mini–grand canyon; I guess it was a petite canyon. It was about an hour's drive from Sioux Falls and was very pretty. We hiked the canyon all morning and around 2:00 found a small café in a small town where we enjoyed a pleasant meal.

On Sunday I learned that my father-in-law, who had been in the hospital, wasn't doing well and was likely to pass, so I, too, left the lead prosecutor to take the verdict alone while I headed to a hospital back in Iowa.

The jury convicted the CEO on almost every count. The jury acquitted him on a couple of counts, which to me meant that they performed a careful job reviewing the evidence. It made sense why they acquitted him on those counts; the evidence we had on those particular counts was weaker than it was on the rest of the counts.

Disposition and Commutation

Sentencing followed many months later and was its own minitrial. The CEO had fired his trial attorneys and had a whole new bevy of defense attorneys. The United States Sentencing Guidelines scored the CEO such that it recommended a sentence of 30 years to life in prison without parole.

We decided to dismiss the immigration-related charges against the CEO, concluding he'd do enough time without the additional convictions. We also considered the sentence carefully and decided the advisory guideline sentence was too harsh and that a lesser sentence was appropriate. So, at the sentencing hearing we recommended a sentence of 25 years. The defendant asked for probation. The judge sentenced him to 27 years in prison.

There was an uproar by the CEO's supporters after the sentencing hearing. This case brought national news coverage and the defense attorneys took to the cameras to declare the whole trial and sentence was a miscarriage of justice and a witch hunt. They swore the case would be overturned on appeal.

It wasn't. The Eighth Circuit Court of Appeals affirmed the conviction and the United States Supreme Court declined to review it. The CEO filed a post-conviction petition claiming that the prosecutors and judge engaged in misconduct in various ways. The CEO lost before the district court judge and again before the Eighth Circuit Court of Appeals. Again, the United States Supreme Court declined to hear the case.

We assumed that was the end of the case and that the CEO would do his time like other defendants. In 2019, the president of the United States commuted the CEO's sentence. Importantly, it wasn't a pardon; the president didn't declare the CEO innocent or pardon him for his crime, but did commute the sentence to time served—about eight years.

Chapter 20

Child Prostitution in Iowa

Iowa does not evoke images of child prostitution, thankfully. Unfortunately, Iowa, is no more immune to the crime than any other state as I found out when, on several occasions, I prosecuted cases of child prostitution. The pattern was always the same. The child victims came from troubled backgrounds, typically from lower-income and single-parent households. They often used drugs and alcohol, and at some point left home and found themselves on the street. There, they got connected somehow to an exploitive man (often with the aid of women) who played to the child's insecurities to gain trust. The pimp would ultimately ply them with drugs and alcohol, sexually abuse the children himself, and then, using manipulation, violence, and drugs, force the girls into prostitution. And then, of course, there is the final step in the process; all too many men willing to pay a pimp to have sex with girls they either knew, or should have known, are children.

Two of these types of cases stand out in my memory, each following this same pattern. In the first a young girl of 15 ran away from home in a suburb of Milwaukee and soon found herself walking around downtown looking for a place to sleep and for something to eat. An adult female prostitute walking the streets saw the child. She befriended her and persuaded the child to stay with the prostitute for the night. At the prostitute's apartment, she provided the child with some food and made a call to her pimp. Soon, the pimp, a man in his late thirties, came over to the prostitute's apartment.

The pimp presented himself as the prostitute's friend and the three of them sat around the prostitute's apartment for several hours drinking, smoking weed, and doing a little cocaine while both the prostitute and pimp sympathized with the girl's complaints about her overbearing mother. The prostitute and pimp assured the girl that she was misunderstood and was smart to leave home. They assured her they'd help her and take care of her. That night the girl slept on the prostitute's couch.

The following morning the prostitute took the girl to the pimp's apartment, saying they were going to go visit him. Once there, they sat around in his living room using more drugs for a couple hours before the prostitute got up to leave. As she left, the pimp paid her with an ounce of cocaine; he had just purchased the child. As soon as the prostitute left, the pimp began trying to get close to the child, caress her arm, kiss her. The girl resisted. Then the pimp hit her, for the first time. He told her that she belonged to him, that he's providing for her, and that she'd do what he told her to do. Using his fists and ultimately a belt, he forced her to strip and then took her into his bedroom where he forced her to have sex with him. When he was done he called up a couple of his friends to come over and then ordered her to have sex with them, too. When she resisted, there were more blows.

For several days the pimp continued to ply the girl with drugs and alcohol while he and his friends used her sexually until the pimp determined she was broken in. Then he took her to the streets. One evening, around 7:00 p.m., he drove her to a portion of Milwaukee where prostitutes walked the streets. There, he met up with one of his prostitutes. He instructed the girl that she'd be working under the prostitute's direction and that he'd be back to pick her up later. That night the girl had sex for money for the first time, with the prostitute collecting the cash from the customer, or john. Around 2:00 a.m., the pimp was back and ordered both the prostitute and the girl into the back seat of his car. He drove to a secluded parking lot to collect the cash. When he was told that the girl only turned one trick, he was angry. First, he hit the prostitute. He yelled at her for not drumming up more business. He emphasized that this was a new product that should be making him a lot of money and she was a lazy slut. He hit her so hard the second time it split her lip and she started bleeding from her mouth. He told her to get out of the car. Then he hit the child several times, told her that she was worthless and if she wanted to be taken care of she had to do better.

The next day, the pimp had one of his other prostitutes take the girl out and buy her some new, more provocative clothes. He provided the girl with a cellular phone with his number pre-programmed in it and let her make a phone call to her mother, which he monitored. At the pimp's instructions, the girl told her mother she was fine and staying with friends. Then the pimp took the girl out. He bought her a fine dinner and a necklace and treated her like a queen. That is, until about 7:00 p.m., when he drove her back to the strip and dropped her off with the prostitute to work the streets again.

About a week later the pimp had the girl pose for photographs. She was clothed, but provocatively, and he had her pose seductively. He then used these photos to advertise her on the Backpage, a website pimps used to advertise their prostitutes. The ad listed the number for the phone he gave her and she very quickly began receiving calls. Over the course of the next several weeks, the pimp took her on trips to Chicago and several other cities in Illinois, as well as to hotels in the Milwaukee area, so that she could turn tricks for him. Often he took along another prostitute and one of the men who worked for him as enforcers. Of course, the pimp and his enforcers used the girl and prostitutes themselves whenever they wanted as fringe benefits of the job.

Then the girl got a call from a john in Iowa. The caller wanted to have sex with two girls, he said. She quoted the price for two girls and the man agreed and gave her the address of a hotel in eastern Iowa. They arranged for a meeting in two days. When the day came, the pimp drove the girl and another prostitute to Iowa, and brought along an enforcer. They checked into a hotel the night before the tryst and they all partied in the room with alcohol and drugs. The next afternoon they drove to the hotel to meet the john. The pimp and his enforcer sat out in the car while the girl and prostitute went into the hotel. The prostitute and the girl knocked on the hotel room door and a man answered and invited them in. They exchanged pleasantries briefly, but the older prostitute quickly got down to business and asked what he wanted to do with them and told him how much it would cost. The man reached into his back pocket and pulled out a badge.

At that point two more officers came into the room, while six more descended on the car in the parking lot, arresting the pimp and his enforcer. The prostitute and girl both quickly cooperated and informed on the pimp and the enforcer. The girl told the officer how old she was and what had happened to her. The prostitute confirmed what part of the girl's story she could, then related a similar story. Though she was then 22 years old, she started out as a prostitute for the pimp at the age of 17.

In the end, the pimp and his enforcer were sent to federal prison for more than a decade and a half. The prostitute was released and provided transportation back to Milwaukee. The girl was returned to her mother. We provided all the information we could to authorities in Milwaukee, but I never heard whether they were able to prosecute anyone else who had been working with the pimp, or any of the johns who had paid for having sex with the child.

The second case that stands out in my memory follows a similar pattern, but was more egregious in many ways. A 13-year-old girl from a troubled background ran away from home in Minneapolis and found herself on the street. She was befriended by a woman who, it turned out, worked for a pimp. The child soon found herself in the clutches of the pimp through manipulation, drugs, and violence much like the girl in the prior story. This pimp, however, had a girlfriend as well. She knew what her boyfriend did for a living and saw it, and the sex he had with his girls, as the cost of being his girlfriend. The pimp was also involved in the distribution of drugs in Minneapolis and when the police nabbed one of his dealers, he thought it best to get out of town for a while. Both the pimp and his girlfriend were originally from Iowa, so they decided to return there.

Their van, however, was experiencing mechanical problems. They took it, and the girl, to a repair garage. The mechanic said they could fix the van in a couple hours and told the pimp how much it would cost. Then the pimp negotiated with the mechanic. The next thing the girl knew, she was instructed to go into the garage where the mechanic and two of his workers had sex with her in the shop's office. Then the mechanic fixed the van and the three of them were on their way to Iowa.

On the way out of town they picked up one of the pimp's friends. The pimp's girlfriend drove. The girl said she didn't want to leave Minneapolis. The pimp smacked her across the face in response. The pimp's friend decided that he wanted to have sex with the girl on the way down, but she resisted. After the pimp hit her a few more times, and took $40 from his friend, she found herself being raped in the back of the van as they crossed the border into Iowa.

The group ended up at the home of the pimp's father, in a small town in Northern Iowa. The father was himself a pimp, and a small-time criminal with convictions for various things including drug distribution. The pimp's adult brother also lived in the same home and had a criminal history. The father also had a girlfriend living with him. After a few days, the pimp, his girlfriend, and his friend left after the father got into a fight with his son. The pimp left the girl with his father.

The father, who was in his mid–50s, and his other son, sexually abused the child and also physically exploited her. She lived in the basement and was ordered to clean the house and perform other chores. The other son left after a few days, but not before he helped his father take provocative photos of the girl and post them on the Backpage, since the father didn't know how to do it. Soon, the father had one of his adult prostitutes taking the girl on many calls all over eastern Iowa. Although the father bought the girl clothes and some presents, the money from the prostitution all went to the father.

At some point, the girl decided to trust the father's girlfriend and confided in the woman that she was only 13 years old. The woman knew she was young, and figured she was underage, but 13 was too young even for this woman. So, one day when the father was gone, the woman took her to the bus station, bought her a ticket for Minneapolis, and put her on the bus. When the father found out, he beat his girlfriend mercilessly. The girlfriend was able to call 911. When police arrived and found her bleeding from a gash in her head, they arrested the father.

Then the girlfriend told the police about the girl. The authorities brought me into the case a short time later. There were several federal offenses involved, including interstate kidnapping and child trafficking. I ended up prosecuting the pimp, his girlfriend, his father and his brother for their involvement. The pimp was sentenced to 25 years in prison and the others received lesser sentences. Then we worked with state authorities in Iowa and Minnesota. With the help of the adult prostitute and a thorough investigation of phone records and the like, we were able to identify about 20 of the johns who had paid the father for sex with the girl. The johns were all prosecuted in state court. In

Minnesota, authorities were able to prosecute the mechanic and one of his workers.

These two cases are just the tip of the iceberg. Unfortunately, the sexual exploitation didn't end with these two successful prosecutions. It's a sad fact of life that wherever there are vulnerable children, there are adults who will exploit them.

CHAPTER 21

Bankruptcy Fraud on the Beach

I mentioned previously that among the dog assignments I received when I first joined the United States Attorney's Office was responsibility for handling bankruptcy fraud cases. I knew nothing about bankruptcy law, and had no desire to learn. Apparently I wasn't alone, hence the reason it was quickly assigned to me when I joined as the most junior member of the office. As it turned out, I had much fun handling bankruptcy fraud cases and it led to me spending a week in a hotel on the Gulf of Mexico.

Bankruptcy is a unique area of the law and can be very complicated. I'm going to try to tell this story with the least amount of discussion of bankruptcy law as possible. But to understand the story, and appreciate the nature of the fraud, some explanation is necessary.

The basics of bankruptcy law are rather simple. In the times of Charles Dickens, people who fell into debt were imprisoned if they couldn't repay their creditors. Because they were in prison and couldn't work, it seldom helped either debtor or creditor. Failure to pay debts was then seen as a moral failing, however, meriting punishment. In time, views changed and in the United States the federal government created bankruptcy protection. The quid pro quo arrangement is straightforward. If a debtor declares all assets, income, debts and liabilities, the bankruptcy court will allow the debtor to walk away from the debts with the basic property necessary for continuation of life (a reasonably priced home, clothing, tools of any trade, etc.). Any assets above and beyond these basic necessities are seized and liquidated with the creditors being paid from the proceeds. Creditors may not be made whole—indeed, they almost never are—but they at least walk away with a portion of the debt owed them, albeit sometimes only a few pennies on the dollar. After bankruptcy, though, creditors are barred from trying to collect on the former debt. The debtor's debts are erased.

Whenever a system depends on honesty, especially honesty about money, fraud is never far away. Debtors can commit fraud by failing to disclose assets, hiding assets, or diverting assets in such a way as to avoid collection. Creditors can commit fraud by submitting false or inflated claims of debts allegedly owed. Indeed, trustees, lawyers, accountants and anyone else involved in the bankruptcy process may be tempted to defraud the system.

The case that took me to Florida involved an Iowa couple who declared bankruptcy. The couple were relatively wealthy people with a net worth of around $5 million. They had become involved investing in a chain of businesses, however, that became upside down financially. The company that owned the chain of businesses was itself going into bankruptcy and its owners, including the couple, were going to be on the hook for tens of millions of dollars. The impending failure of the business apparent early enough that the couple hired an attorney to help them plan for the bankruptcy more than a year in advance.

Now, there are many things that a person can legally do to come out of a bankruptcy with the most possible assets. The assets that are considered exempt from seizure in a bankruptcy varies from state to state. Some states, like Florida, grant far more and different exemptions than other states, like Iowa. In Iowa, for example, life insurance purchased more than two years in advance of a bankruptcy is exempt up to $50,000 in face value, while in Florida at the time of this case there was no upper limit and no time restraints. Thus, a careful debtor in Florida could, before the bankruptcy was filed, sell off all the assets that weren't exempt and use the proceeds to purchase life insurance.

The problem for our couple, though, was that they lived in Iowa. To solve this problem, their bankruptcy attorney told them to move to Florida. He told them to purchase a house in Florida, and live there for a year to establish residency. One year and one day after they lived in Florida, they could file for bankruptcy in Florida. The bankruptcy attorney identified all the debtors' assets that weren't exempt from seizure in bankruptcy and told them to sell the assets and convert the proceeds to life insurance.

The couple followed their lawyer's advice. To a degree. They did purchase an inexpensive condominium in Pensacola, Florida, visited it a couple times, registered a car in Florida and took other steps to create the appearance they moved to Florida. But medical bills, credit card statements, and other records we later recovered showed that they were seldom in Florida.

Once the couple purported to establish Florida residency, they then proceeded to sell off almost all their assets. They sold millions of dollars of assets, including investments, stocks, and bonds, and used the proceeds to purchase millions of dollars in life insurance. After about ten months, the couple were in a very good position to weather the failure of the business and their own bankruptcy. They could come out of bankruptcy multi-millionaires and then cash in their life insurance and reinvest the proceeds in stocks, bonds, other investments and whatever toys they wanted to buy.

There were some non-exempt assets, however, that they didn't want to sell because they had personal or sentimental value to them. This included some heirloom furniture, jewelry worth tens of thousands of dollars, a boat, a collector car, and similar assets. In total, these assets were valued at approximately $400,000. The couple contacted their bankruptcy lawyer and posited the question: "Can we 'sell' these items to family members and then get them back after the bankruptcy?" The lawyer responded in a three-page letter that said, essentially, no. Although it was likely not intended, the letter provided a bit of a roadmap to the couple, however, on how they could "pretend" to sell the assets to family members. For example, the letter told the couple that such assets could be sold to a family member only if the assets were sold at a public auction and a family member happened to be the highest bidder.

It followed, then, that debtors engaged in transactions that resulted in close family members coming into nominal possession of these assets. For example, for the heirloom furniture worth tens of thousands of dollars, the husband's father paid a visit to a local auctioneer with whom the father had done business over the years. He laid out a business proposition for the auctioneer. If the auctioneer filled out some paperwork that said that the couple consigned him to sell off their heirloom furniture, and if the auctioneer filled out paperwork saying that the father was the highest bidder, then the auctioneer could earn a sizable commission of several thousand dollars without having to actually do anything. The auctioneer agreed, generated the paperwork, pocketed the commission, and the furniture never left the couple's house.

As for the tens of thousands of dollars in jewelry, the couple went to a local well-known jeweler. They presented all the jewelry to the jeweler and asked him to appraise it. They then took the appraisal to the husband's mother and asked her to give them a check in that amount. She did, and a few weeks later they gave her a check back in the same amount (later claiming it was repayment for an old debt they owed her). The jewelry never left the wife's jewelry box.

As for the boat, it was "sold" to their son under similarly fraudulent means. Funds flowed into and out of the couple's and their son's accounts showing that the transaction was a sham. The boat was titled in the son's name, but his father completed the paperwork and the boat never left the father's possession. It was an added twist to the case that their son was a deputy sheriff. The son later testified that he didn't know why his father wanted him to have the boat in the son's name because he used the boat both before and after it was titled in his name just as often and in the same manner. Once the couple got through the bankruptcy, the boat was retitled in the father's name and the son continued to use the boat whenever he wanted.

The most unique asset the couple had, though, was stock in a former religious-based corporation. In the early 1800s, various religious sects from Europe settled in the United States. One such community in Iowa was founded on a commune system, meaning that assets were owned by the community and each member contributed to the community what they could. In the middle of the last century, this particular commune dissolved and the community assets were transferred to a corporation. Each member of the community received shares in the corporation. The shares could be inherited, bought, and sold. The corporation then funded and ran many businesses located in the bucolic little community that drew in flocks of tourists year around. The corporation generated a nice profit but very, very rarely issued any dividends and when it did, they were paltry. That's because the corporation used the profits to pay for a significant expense for its stockholders. The truly priceless value of owning this stock was that it entitled the owner to full health care coverage of all expenses, without limit, copay or deductible, for life. Thus, the profits generated by the corporation went to pay tens of thousands of dollars a month in health care expenses for its stockholders. The twist was that this one, almost priceless, benefit of owning this stock was available only to the original members of the commune or their direct descendants. Any outsider could certainly purchase the stock, but to outsiders the stock would have almost no value.

The husband had inherited stock in the corporation. If it was seized by the bankruptcy court it would fetch almost nothing on the open market because the only value it had to anyone outside the community was the rarely issued and paltry dividends it paid. Almost all members of the community already owned stock themselves, so they didn't need more to enjoy the benefits of the medical coverage. Because the corporation almost never issued any dividends, the free market value of the stock was virtually zilch. Yet, it was invaluable to the couple.

To resolve the conundrum of retaining this priceless stock through bankruptcy, the couple decided to "sell" the husband's stock to his aunt, who already owned stock in the company and therefore already had the benefit of free medical care. They filled out the paperwork showing that the aunt purchased the stock. They gave her a check for a few hundred dollars and in return she gave them a check back in the same amount a few days later. The aunt was quite elderly and when later questioned about the transaction didn't have a clue what was going on. She simply did what was asked of her.

We conducted much of the investigation in Iowa, but when we had completed the investigation I needed to decide what charges to bring and where to bring them. Because the couple committed part of the crime in Iowa (concealing and fraudulently transferring assets) and part of the crime in Florida (filing false bankruptcy documents claiming they disclosed all their assets), I could bring charges in either district. In Iowa, though, I could only bring the fraud charges related to the concealment of assets, while in Florida I could bring both the concealment fraud changes and false statements in the bankruptcy pleadings. Thus, I decided to bring the charges in Florida.

It is true that I wasn't a prosecutor in Florida, but that wasn't difficult to overcome. A federal prosecutor in one district can be easily appointed by the United States Attorney in another district to become a Special Assistant United States Attorney (a "SAUSA"), appointed either to handle a single case or for a limited period of time. I contacted the United States Attorney's Office in the Northern District of Florida and spoke with the criminal chief. I describe my case and desire to bring charges in her district. The Florida office was extremely cooperative. I was appointed a SAUSA and a short time later flew to Florida with the case agent where we presented evidence to a grand jury. The grand jury returned an indictment against the couple, charging them with mail fraud (using the United States Postal Service in part to commit the fraudulent concealment and transfer of assets in Iowa), and with bankruptcy fraud.

The couple hired an Iowa criminal defense attorney to represent them both. That is generally a very bad idea. There is an inherent conflict of interest for a lawyer to represent two people in the same case, even when the two people are husband and wife. An attorney has an ethical obligation to represent each client zealously and to do what is in the client's best interest. Here, for example, it might have been in the wife's best interest to cooperate with us and testify against her husband. Although the evidence showed that she knew what was happening and willfully signed bankruptcy documents knowing they were false (for example, she knew all of her jewelry that had allegedly been sold to her mother-in-law was still in her jewelry box), it was the husband who appeared to be orchestrating everything and conducting all the transactions. Had she cooperated and testified against her husband it may have ended their marriage, but she might not have gone to prison.

The Florida judge ordered a hearing on the issue of the lawyer's joint representation of both defendants. I was excluded from the hearing because it required the judge to talk with the lawyer and his clients about their communication and my presence might have invaded the attorney/client privilege. During hearings like this one, though, the judge points out to both parties the inherent conflict, explains exactly why they may want to have their own lawyers, and makes sure the lawyer has also explained all of this to the parties. People can waive such an inherent conflict and insist on the same lawyer, and that's what they did here.

The case came on for trial about six months later, in mid–November, not a bad time of the year to get out of Iowa and head to warmer climes. The trial was estimated to take a week and a half or two weeks to complete. The case agent and I drove to Pensacola in a government van, carrying with us all the files, exhibits, and other materials, along with enough suits to last us two weeks. I also had a witness coordinator who cajoled me into insisting to management that I needed her to help me with the case (I'm sure the Florida United States Attorney would have lent me their witness coordinator). In any event, the case agent and I arrived on a Sunday and moved into our hotel rooms, a few miles inland from the federal courthouse in Pensacola. My witness coordinator flew in that evening and so we picked her up at the airport.

She had taken care of her own hotel reservations so when she gave us directions I found out she was staying at a high-rise hotel on the gulf coast. The beach was literally outside the back of the hotel. She had a room with a view of the ocean. The case agent and I were envious, but when we checked with the front desk we were told that they had rooms for us, too, and within the government per diem rate. We were already booked into our other hotel for Sunday night, but we changed our reservations right then and after trial on Monday moved into new accommodations. I was located on the eighth floor with large windows looking out onto the beach and Gulf of Mexico, with a small balcony I could access through sliding glass doors. It was a vast improvement over the other hotel's view of the neighboring gas station.

The trial was hard fought. The defense attorney didn't have a sophisticated or subtle style, but he was a street fighter of sorts. He made many objections in which he accused me of doing something wrong, but we got along professionally very well and left the fighting in the courtroom where it belonged.

The husband's parents were key witnesses because they had "purchased" most of the property. The Friday before trial, an attorney representing them filed a last-minute motion to quash their subpoenas, claiming they were too old and frail and making them come to Florida was too much to ask. The judge promptly denied the motion. When the father testified, he pretended to be unable to hear my questions and acted as if he were about to expire right on the stand. Fortunately, we had him locked down in grand jury testimony and through documents so tightly that he was forced to admit facts showing the transactions were fraudulent.

The defense theory was an advice of counsel defense; the couple claimed that they only did what their lawyer told them to do. That put their bankruptcy lawyer right in the thick of it. He had his own lawyer for this trial and he wasn't the least bit happy having to testify. But he also wasn't happy at being accused of advising his clients to commit fraud. He had written the three-page letter I think precisely so that if he was put in this position he could bring it out in defense. It is true that his clients used the detailed explanations he provided as a roadmap on how to commit the fraud, but they didn't follow his advice.

I rested the government's case on Friday morning and the defense started calling its witnesses. With our case over, there was no need for my witness coordinator to stick around so she was going to fly out Saturday morning. The case agent, my witness coordinator and I happened upon a local art festival that evening and then had a nice dinner at a restaurant on the beach. My witness coordinator took a taxi to the airport the next morning.

Over the weekend I had much work to do. I had to prepare for cross-examining the defense witnesses and had to write and revise my closing argument. There was also some legal research I had to conduct to deal with a last-minute defense motion as I recall. Suffice it to say, I spent my entire weekend in my hotel room. I did move my desk to the window and spent time once in a while glancing out the window. But other than a couple of walks on the beach in the mornings, that was the extent of my enjoyment of the seashore that weekend. My agent, though, had both days off and had a great time enjoying the ocean.

I did have the benefit of dinner with my father, his wife, and my older brother and his family. My mother had died a half-dozen years before this trial and my father had remarried. My brother has two children who were then in their late high school careers. They all lived in Destin, Florida, about an hour and fifteen-minute drive from Pensacola. I invited the agent along and we had a fine dinner at my brother's house.

Trial continued the next week and we presented closing arguments early on a Thursday morning. After the jury left the courtroom to deliberate, the defense attorney and I shook hands in a customary show of professionalism. It's much like Little League baseball players who at the end of the game pass by each other saying "good game" over and over again.

I said, "Well done."

He replied, "You're a tough motherfucker!"

I was taken aback at his wording, but I guess that's close to saying "good game."

While the jury was out, the agent and I had a relaxing lunch at a sidewalk café and then strolled through the historic district a few blocks from the courthouse. The jury was out a few hours, but then returned a verdict of guilty on both counts for both defendants. Afterwards, the judge invited the defense attorney and me back to her chambers to express her appreciation for our professional performance; she said she didn't know what to expect from a couple of Iowa lawyers, but one of her current law clerks came from Iowa, so she had high hopes and was pleased with us.

The agent and I spent one last night in our hotel on the ocean and had a nice celebratory dinner out at an Italian restaurant. The next morning I got up before the dawn and walked along the beach as the sun rose over the horizon. I walked out on a pier and looked down at the Gulf of Mexico as waves gently washed the shore. I spied a school of stingrays frolicking in the shallows near the shore and watched sandpipers skitter along the empty beach. It was beautiful and warm and peaceful. In an hour the agent and I were back in the government van driving north. We ran into a snowstorm outside St. Louis and spent the night in a hotel there. As we drove into the snow-covered Iowan expanse the next morning I rued my decision to become an Assistant United States Attorney in the Northern District of Iowa instead of in the Northern District of Florida.

Chapter 22

Prosecution of a Pyromaniac

There is an obscure legal theory called the Doctrine of Chances. First employed in England in the late 1800s, it stands for the proposition that the existence of a series of unusual events may be admissible to prove on a given occasion that the events weren't accidents. The doctrine arose in a case involving a man whose wife apparently drowned while taking a bath. It was a horrible tragedy to befall this new husband. The trouble was that his first two wives had died in the same manner. The prosecution was permitted to present evidence of the deaths of his first two wives at the trial of the husband for murdering his third wife. The logical, legal argument posited that no man could be so unlucky to have three wives just happen to accidentally die in the same very unusual manner. The jury convicted him.

I had attempted to employ the doctrine in a case I prosecuted involving a serial arsonist. Alas, few American courts have adopted the Doctrine of Chances and at first blush it might appear in violation of the Federal Rules of Evidence. It isn't, and I published a law review article fully explaining its application in a serial arsonist case, citing a renowned evidence professor from Arizona who has published extensively on the Doctrine of Chances. Nevertheless, the judge I was in front of was understandably hesitant to serve as one of the first federal judges to adopt the doctrine and in her order denying my request told me in so many words that I didn't need it to win my case. She was right.

One day an ATF agent and fire marshal came to visit me in my office to talk to me about a possible arson case. In fact, it was a series of possible arson cases they wanted my help on. Arson is typically a crime prosecuted at the state level, but it can be a federal offense if it affects interstate commerce. Thus, the arson of any business, apartment building, or even a rental house may constitute a federal offense because each has some effect on interstate commerce.

The agent and fire marshal laid out the evidence they had so far. They were focused on one fire in particular in a city of about 8,000 people in northeast Iowa. A brick building in the downtown business district had caught on fire one evening. A business occupied the ground floor, but the upper two floors were comprised of a half-dozen apartments. A woman in her late 70s occupied one, a family of four occupied another, and a few single people, men and women, occupied the rest. On the night of the fire most of the occupants were home. The only smoke alarm in the upper floor of the building was either not working or had been disabled. One of the renters smelled smoke, though, and raised the alarm. All the renters escaped, but not easily. By the time the fire department arrived, the entire building was engulfed in flames. The fire spread to the adjoining building which also had an apartment on the second floor. Firefighters had to rescue occupants of that apartment through an apartment window.

The fire marshal determined the fire started in the apartment of a man in his 30s who was, at the time of the fire, in a nearby bar. The fire marshals said that the cause of the fire was indeterminate, meaning that he couldn't declare it to be arson because there were no obvious signs, such as the use of accelerants. But there was also no other explanation for the fire such as a short in wiring or someone falling asleep with a lit cigarette or such. It was the man who rented the apartment where the fire started, however, that made the agent and the fire marshal convinced it was arson. We'll call the renter Firebug.

It turns out that Firebug was previously convicted of reckless use of fire a few years back when an apartment he was renting in a different town in northeast Iowa caught on fire under similarly suspicious circumstances. That time a friend of Firebug had been asleep on the couch in the second-floor apartment in an old house when the fire erupted. Firefighters rescued him from the burning apartment, but not before he had suffered serious burns. Firebug later admitted that he had been on the sun porch of the house and claimed he had lit a match to see in the dark and must have accidentally dropped it among some discarded trash on the porch.

Firebug had also been investigated for a car fire and another apartment fire in yet a third city in northeast Iowa. Although authorities ultimately didn't charge him with any criminal offenses, both fires were highly suspicious and with no apparent innocent causes. But Firebug was charged for a third fire that broke out in a business after hours. Firebug had been the last person in the building late at night as part of a janitorial crew. The fire started near a coffee maker in the break room, but the coffee maker wasn't plugged in and a fire marshal determined that it wasn't the source of the fire; instead, someone had lit some napkins and plates on fire. In that case a dogged and skillful police chief had questioned Firebug who reluctantly admitted to starting the fire and conceded that he enjoyed seeing things burn. Convicted of arson, he received a suspended sentence.

Given Firebug's history, and the fact the fire started once again in his apartment, the agents were sure it was arson. This case intrigued me and I immediately agreed to work on it. We would, of course, focus part of the investigation on the building fire itself, questioning everyone in the building and at the bar where Firebug was drinking at the time of the fire. But I wanted to expand the investigation. I reasoned that if this guy was already tied to four other fires in two other cities, he was likely tied to other fires. I directed the agents to research Firebug's history. I wanted to know everywhere he had lived or worked since he was in high school. He was, at this time, in his late thirties. I also asked the fire marshal to get information on every suspicious fire in the last 20 years in northeast Iowa, even if the fire hadn't been declared an arson.

The investigation took months and we questioned scores of witnesses. We learned that Firebug was tied to at least 23 fires in the prior 17 years. The first fires connected to Firebug started when he was still in high school. We learned that Firebug grew up in a very small town in northeast Iowa where his father served as a volunteer firefighter on a one-engine force. When Firebug was a junior in high school, he, too, joined the force. The fire department received very few calls in their small town. That is, they received few calls until about the time Firebug joined the force. Then the fire department received a surprising number of false alarm calls. They also responded to a fire in front of

Firebug's house when his car caught on fire. The fire was determined to have started somewhere under the dash and was chalked up to faulty wiring. Another fire was reported in a field outside town when a group of hay bales were found on fire. Firebug was reported to have been seen nearby shortly before the fire, but claimed it was mere coincidence. No natural cause for that fire was discovered. The chief of the volunteer fire department grew suspicious and retrieved all the false alarm calls. Although the caller had attempted to conceal his voice, the chief could tell it was Firebug. He called in Firebug's father and played the tapes for the father. Firebug's father stated that a few of them sounded somewhat like Firebug, but he adamantly denied that Firebug had made the calls. Nevertheless, the chief removed Firebug from the force.

Soon thereafter, Firebug graduated from high school and moved away from home. Over the course of the next 15 or so years Firebug flitted from town to town, and job to job, never staying very long in any one place, and never staying employed in the same job for more than a year or two. He was briefly married for a few years and had fathered two children, but the marriage had ended a few years before our investigation began.

Through researching the towns where the Firebug lived at the times he lived there, we found more and more fires linked to Firebug. None of them had resulted in criminal charges. Indeed, almost all of them were determined to be unexplained or accidental or caused by faulty wiring or something else. The pattern told a different story.

We discovered that Firebug had been the apparent victim of car fires on five occasions, in addition to when he was in high school. We also discovered that either his apartment, or the apartments or houses of friends, had caught fire on more than a dozen occasions. Fortunately, no one was hurt in any of these fires, but in some cases they caused significant damage. In one town an entire building had burned to the ground in the middle of the business district, very much like the fire that had started our investigation. In that case, the fire had started in his friend's apartment. Firebug had been over to visit a friend when they and the friend's girlfriend decided to go out for dinner. They all went downstairs to the friend's car when Firebug claimed he forgot something in the friend's apartment. He ran back up to the apartment and returned after only a few minutes. While they were all at dinner, a fire erupted, starting in the friend's apartment.

We looked very closely at each of the fires that occurred less than five years before. There is a five-year statute of limitations on most federal offenses. Thus, I couldn't charge him with fires more than five years old, even if I had solid evidence of arson. We finally focused on two other fires that were within the statute of limitations. One occurred at the rental house of another friend, while the other burned down his ex-wife's rental house.

The fire at the friend's rental house occurred one hot summer night. Firebug was between jobs and residences, and had just recently separated from his wife. His friend let Firebug camp out in a back room that the friend used as a computer room. On the fourth of July the friend had some extended family come over to join his wife and kids to swim in a backyard pool and enjoy some food off the grill. The witnesses later told a jury that Firebug was moody and wasn't socializing much with others. As the evening wore on, it was time for the youngest children to go to bed. Shortly before the friend picked up his sleepy young daughter to take her to bed, a few of the people had seen Firebug go inside the house for a few minutes. When he came out he announced he was going to visit a coworker and would be back shortly. Firebug was the last person in the house. When the friend entered his house about ten minutes later to take his daughter to bed, he walked into his kitchen to see it engulfed in flames. He quickly ran out and raised the alarm. Someone called 911 while the friend attempted to douse the flames with a garden hose and others attempted to scoop water out of the above-ground pool with any container they could find to form a make-shift bucket brigade. By the time the fire department arrived, though, the house was fully engulfed in flames.

A later forensic examination of the room where Firebug was staying showed that fire started near the outlet where the friend had all of his computer equipment plugged in. We had a forensic expert examine the scene more closely and the expert determined the outlet had nothing to do with the origin of the fire. I won't get into the technicalities here, but the burn pattern was inconsistent with the fire starting in or near the outlet and the wiring didn't have any of the telltale signs that would have been present had it caused the fire.

The fire at Firebug's ex-wife's house was the most difficult of all to tie to Firebug. First, it took place in a town that was at least 30 miles from where Firebug lived. Second, we had no evidence Firebug had ever been in the town. He didn't visit his children there or have any business in the town. We did discover he once called the college where his ex-wife worked to find out her schedule, but that was as close as we came tying him to the town. Third, the insurance company's investigator had ruled the fire accidental. That investigator concluded that the fire began in a toaster, and that the ex-wife's purse, found next to the toaster, must have been on the toaster when the fire started. The ex-wife was certain that when she came in the back door earlier that day she had placed her purse on the counter and not on the toaster. But her mind was muddled and she finally conceded that perhaps it was possible that she had placed her purse on the toaster. How the toaster handle got pushed down was never explained.

When the fire started she was upstairs in the two-story rental house sorting clothes with her and Firebug's children. She and the children may owe their lives to the purely chance decision her father made to stop by that day to see his daughter. When he came through the back door that led into the kitchen he encountered an inferno. The entire kitchen was aflame. He yelled and yelled for his daughter, but got no answer. He ran around to the front of the house and came in through the front door. By now the fire had moved beyond the kitchen and was encroaching on the rest of the first floor. He ran upstairs and found his daughter and grandchildren and ushered them all to safety. The house was soon completely engulfed in flames and by the time the fire department arrived, it was a total loss.

Despite the insurance investigator's conclusion that the fire was accidental, we had our expert conduct his own examination. He concluded that the fire had started on top of the toaster, but was certain the purse wasn't on top of the toaster at the time. Photos taken by the fire department and photos taken by the insurance investigator were taken at different times. When compared, it showed an area of the counter the size of the purse hadn't burned, suggesting it had been sitting on the counter the whole time. It appeared the purse was moved after the fire. When we followed up, the ex-wife recalled that she went into the kitchen after the fire to retrieve her keys and wallet from inside her burned purse and must have left it near the toaster.

We still had the problem that we couldn't place Firebug at the scene. We did establish that he had called in sick to work that day and didn't have an alibi. And we had a motive. Beyond his admitted fondness for fires, he and his ex-wife had gone through a bitter divorce and she had won full custody of their children after persuading the judge that Firebug was abusive.

We also thoroughly investigated the fire that had brought the agents to my office in the first instance. We established that, though Firebug had attempted to establish an alibi by being at a local bar when the fire erupted, witnesses noted that he left briefly about a half hour before the fire was reported. The bar was only a few blocks from the apartment building. It was also noteworthy that several bar patrons testified that they thought it odd that when the firetrucks rushed to the scene and the bar emptied because everyone ran to see the fire, Firebug stayed in the bar nursing a beer despite people telling him that his apartment building was on fire. Unsolicited, he said to the barmaid that it was a good thing he had an alibi. A neighbor later testified that he thought he heard Firebug's apartment door open and shut twice about fifteen minutes before the neighbor smelled the smoke, though he didn't see Firebug.

Our expert determined that this fire started in a wastebasket next to the stove. He found the remains of a cigarette and matchbook together in the debris. Firebug didn't smoke. Our expert explained how one can start a delayed fire using a cigarette and a matchbook. The way it works is to light the cigarette and then place the base of the cigarette in the matchbook and close the matchbook over the cigarette. The cigarette will slowly burn down to the matchbook and when it reaches the matches, the whole thing will erupt in flames. Our expert opined that Firebug made this timer and set it on the edge of the stove, right next to the waste basket that he stuffed with paper. The weight of the cigarette would keep it on the stove until it burned down so far that the weight shifted, causing it to fall into the wastebasket.

In the end, the grand jury charged Firebug with three arson fires; the apartment building, the friend's rental house, and his ex-wife's rental house. After his arrest, the court ordered him detained pending trial at my request when I argued that he was a danger to the community. Then we got lucky. While in jail waiting for trial, Firebug befriended another inmate. They got to chatting and Firebug soon started talking about fires. He commented on how easy it is to make it look like fires started near outlets and appliances, specifically mentioning toasters. He also made comments about the fire at his ex-wife's home that suggested he knew more about it than he could have learned from the government's evidence. None of the statements by themselves were explicit; he never admitted to the other inmate that he started any of the fires. But there were enough comments that it tipped the scales on connecting him with the fire at his ex-wife's house.

After a two-week-long trial, a jury convicted Firebug of all three fires. The judge would only let me put on evidence of the one arson and one reckless use of fire convictions, and wouldn't let me introduce evidence on all the other fires. In the books called a *Series of Unfortunate Events*, by the author using the nom de plume Lemony Snicket, two orphaned children are seemingly the victims of a series of seemingly accidental unfortunate events, but they turn out to be part of a plot against them by an evil uncle. Here, I would have asked the jury, "what are the odds of this one man being so unfortunate that five of his cars have caught on fire, a half-dozen of his apartments have gone up in flames, and fires seemly erupt in the homes and apartments of his friends and in places where he works?" Common sense would tell you, like it did in the case of the man who lost three wives in accidental bathtub drownings, that something evil is afoot.

Alas, I wasn't allowed to put on the evidence or pose the questions or argue the conclusion I would have the jury reach. But the judge was correct. In the end, we didn't need the additional evidence.

Chapter 23

The Tale of the Marijuana-Laced Brownies

In the federal system, after a defendant serves a prison sentence the offender is placed on supervised release for a period of years. Supervised release is like probation in the sense that offenders are subject to certain conditions and restrictions, and a probation officer supervises the offender to ensure compliance. The goal of supervised release is to assist offenders in re-integrating into society and to help them with any drug addiction or mental health issues they may have. If an offender violates the terms of supervised release, the court can revoke the supervised release and send the offender back to prison.

One day an email was circulated among the prosecutors asking for someone to cover a hearing on an offender's supervised release revocation because the prosecutor had a conflict with another hearing. This was routine in the office and we often helped each other out when we could. I volunteered to take the case. It happened that it was the criminal chief's case. It involved an offender convicted of drug dealing. While on supervised release he had to provide urine samples to test for drug use. He had provided a urine sample that tested positive for marijuana. This was after he had missed a half-dozen other times when he was supposed to provide urine samples and had provided dilute (or watered down) samples on a couple occasions such that the urine couldn't be tested. This was a rather routine set of facts that often led to revocation hearings. Typically, the judge would verbally reprimand a defendant for these relatively minor violations, or impose some minor sanction like a couple of weekends in jail. So, I had no reason to believe this hearing would turn out as interesting as it did.

There are two things about revocation hearings that are important to know to appreciate this story. First, there is little advanced notice. The court set revocation hearings within only a week or two of the probation office filed a petition with the court requesting them. Second, as a prosecutor you are largely on your own in these hearings. The probation officer cannot investigate the case; the probation officer only reports on the known facts about the offender. Further, there is no law enforcement agency to help the prosecutor investigate violations. It is possible, perhaps, to ask the agency originally involved in the underlying case to lend a hand, but you're unlikely to get assistance. Agents have a lot more important cases to work on and little time to help out on a mere revocation hearing. Thus, I was on my own here.

When I reviewed the file, I saw that the offender had denied knowingly using marijuana. He claimed that a co-worker at the restaurant where he was employed had brought in a pan of brownies for everyone to eat and, unbeknownst to him, the brownies were laced with marijuana. Further, the defense attorney had filed an exhibit for the revocation hearing. It was a letter from the manager of the restaurant attesting to the laced brownies incident and stating that the employee who had brought them in was fired. The letter identified that employee by name, Mary Jane Baker, and was signed Mike Marshall, Manager.* Given this evidence it certainly didn't look like this defendant did anything wrong at least as for the use of marijuana.

But, just to make sure, I called the restaurant. A woman answered.

"Hello," I said, "I'd like to speak with the manager, Mike Marshall, please."

There was a long pause.

"Well, Mike is here," the woman said, "but he's no manager."

"What is he?"

"The fry cook," she said.

"Well, I will certainly be wanting to talk with Mr. Marshall before I'm done, but is there a manager there?"

The manager was there and I ended up speaking with her. I identified who I was and why I was calling. She confirmed that the offender had worked at the restaurant as a dishwasher and busboy,

*The names above are fictional.

but she had fired him last week because of repeatedly being tardy. She confirmed that Mike Marshall was the fry chef. She said the offender and Marshall were kind of friends. I asked about the brownie incident.

"What?!" she replied. "If that happened, I certainly wasn't told about it."

"I have a letter signed by Mr. Marshall purporting to be the manager and he said that he fired the woman who brought in the brownies, a Mary Jane Baker"

"Mary Jane wasn't fired," she replied. "In fact, she's here right now. Do you want to talk with her?"

Of course, I did. Ms. Baker told me she had no idea what I was talking about, had never made marijuana-laced brownies, and had never brought any brownies into work, laced with marijuana or otherwise. Nor had she ever possessed or used marijuana. Moreover, she added, her father was a police officer.

I also ended up speaking with Mr. Marshall. At first he equivocated about the letter, claiming not to know what I was talking about. When I reminded him I was a federal prosecutor and lying to me was a felony offense, he came around. Yes, he admitted, he typed out the letter. He had pilfered the restaurant's stationery from the manager's desk and during a break he and the offender had written it. Marshall typed what the offender dictated. Marshall explained he was just trying to help the offender who told him that he had innocently eaten marijuana-laced brownies his sister had prepared, but he didn't want to get his sister into trouble and figured his probation officer wouldn't believe his sister.

Now this was getting fun, I thought. The manager, Ms. Baker, and Mr. Marshall agreed to accept service of subpoenas by fax, requiring them to appear at the revocation hearing that was to take place the following day. I spoke with my witness coordinator and asked her to intercept my witnesses when they appeared at the courthouse and keep them away from the courtroom until the hearing started. I didn't want the offender to know that I knew he had lied and fabricated evidence.

On the day of the hearing, however, it turned out that the offender saw Ms. Baker at the courthouse when they arrived at about the same time. When I entered the courtroom, the defense attorney approached me. He told me that his client would now admit the violations.

The hearing started. The judge asked the defense attorney if the offender contested the violations. The defense attorney said no. The judge asked the offender if he admitted the violations. The offender said yes.

"Mr. Williams," the judge addressed me, "in light of the offender's admission, does the government wish to present any evidence," fully expecting me to say no.

"Yes, your honor," I replied, "I do wish to present evidence."

The judge looked at me quizzically, but suspected something was up.

"Very good, then," she said. "You may proceed."

"Your honor, first I'd like to move into evidence Exhibit 1, the letter the defendant filed in advance of the hearing, a letter from the manager of his employer, Mike Marshall."

"Any objection?" the judge asked, addressing the defense attorney.

"Um, no, your honor," the defense attorney said, dreading what was coming next.

"Exhibit 1 is received," the judge ruled. "Do you have any other evidence you wish to present, Mr. Williams?"

"Yes, your honor. The United States calls Mike Marshall."

At this an audible gasp came from the offender.

I proceeded to have Mr. Marshall testify, admit he was a fry cook and not the manager, and explain his role in the creation of the false and fabricated letter. Then I called Ms. Mary Jane Baker to have her deny bringing in marijuana-laced brownies, that she was still employed at the restaurant, and to explain that her father, the police officer, with whom she lived, would never allow marijuana in their house. Finally, I called the manager who corroborated the testimony of the other two employees.

The judge found the offender violated his supervised release conditions based on his own admission and the evidence I presented, revoked his supervised release, and sentenced him to prison for six months. Unfortunately for the offender, his misfortunes didn't end there. The criminal chief, never one to let a crime go unpunished if he could help it, took the file back over after the hearing and then charged the offender with obstruction of justice for submitting a false document to the court. The offender received two more years in prison for that.

As a prosecutor, I learned that one never quite knew when a case might turn out to be very interesting.

Chapter 24

Flimflam Artist

There is a lot of fraud in this world and most of the federal fraud cases I prosecuted were all too common and routine. Embezzlements, lying to banks to obtain loans, hiding assets from banks when the banks try to foreclose, and so on. But a few of my fraud cases stand out from the rest as uniquely aggravating or because they involved particularly reprehensible people. One in particular involved both.

An investment broker lost his license because of some unethical transactions and other failures. But he persuaded a handful of his former clients to retain him as their investment advisor, even though he couldn't retain control of their investments. This guy was a slick wheeler-dealer, who dressed in fine clothes, drove an expensive car, and appeared as the ultimately successful financial guru. He was so slimy, though, that the court reporter later shared with me her own nickname for him: "Mr. Suave." I'll borrow the moniker for purposes of this story.

Looking for a new money-making venture after losing his job, Mr. Suave hit upon a couple options. First, he found some land for sale outside an Iowa city, near a state park, and along a major highway. It was, and remains, an ideal location for a housing development. It constituted about 80 acres of gently rolling hills, backed by a forest, and largely buffeted from the highway noise and view by a low ridge. Mr. Suave persuaded a bank to loan him money to build a housing development. We later discovered he lied to the bank in several ways to obtain the loan, including claiming he was still employed as an investment broker and by falsely inflating his income and assets and omitting liabilities.

Unfortunately for Mr. Suave, and ultimately for others, he had never been a property developer before and didn't know what he was doing. As a result, there were significant cost overruns and unforeseen expenses, poor marketing, and few sales. About two years into the project, he had only one-third of the property developed with utilities and roads, and a single house had been built. He was far behind in his loan payments, vendors were unpaid, and the property wasn't generating a positive cash flow. In short, he was losing money hand over fist in what could and should have been a very successful endeavor.

At about the same time that he started the housing development, Mr. Suave also tried to purchase some fast-food franchises. He approached the owner and operator of one of them and proposed a partnership to snap up several others that were for sale. The man agreed and together they applied to the fast-food company to become owners of three other restaurants in the area. This company performed better due diligence than the bank, however, and having discovered Mr. Suave's firing as an investment broker and his heavy debt connected to the housing development, rejected him as a potential franchise owner, but accepted the other man's offer to purchase another restaurant. Mr. Suave persuaded the other man to let him ride along on the deal as a silent partner. Mr. Suave promised to provide half the purchase price of the first restaurant. When the time for the closing occurred, however, Mr. Suave showed up without any money. The partner was able to scrounge together some additional funds at the last minute and purchase the restaurant in his own name, cutting Mr. Suave out of the deal.

Stymied at his attempt to own restaurants, and hemorrhaging money in his housing development, Mr. Suave turned to the few former clients he had persuaded to keep him on as a financial advisor. He approached one couple and asked them to invest in his housing development. They agreed and provided him with $10,000. They were unsophisticated investors, unfortunately, even though both worked for an aerospace company and were educated. Thus, they got nothing for the $10,000. Not a promissory note, not stock in his corporation, not a lien on the land. Nothing. He gave them just an empty promise that they were partners in the development. He approached them a few months later and proposed they invest another $20,000. They said no. So did two other former clients.

Unable to persuade his clients to invest in his failing housing development, he decided to lie to them. He next proposed they invest in his chain of fast-food restaurants. He showed them some of the paperwork from the restaurant company he had obtained when he applied to become, but was rejected as, a franchise owner. He told his clients that he owned several restaurants and even told them which ones in town he owned. This restaurant chain was very successful and he had the financials from the restaurants that he and his former partner had obtained through the application process that he shared with his clients to show how much money they could make. Unlike his housing development, this business looked like a good investment. The aerospace couple and several other clients agreed to invest in the restaurants. From some of the clients, he solicited investments on multiple occasions. Unfortunately, once again these investors were unsophisticated and only a couple insisted on promissory notes or any other indicia of ownership in the restaurants; most simply took Mr. Suave's word for it that they were now partners with him and would be making money. As for the promissory notes he did provide, they weren't worth the paper they were written on because a careful reading of them showed they contained language that would allow Mr. Suave to extend the due dates of the notes indefinitely and without notice.

One of his clients was an elderly widow who was beginning to suffer from the early stages of dementia. She was also rather poor and physically infirm. Mr. Suave visited her tiny home in an attempt to persuade her to invest in the restaurant business. He convinced her to do so, but while sitting in her living room chatting he noticed she had a Social Security check sitting on her table that was a month old. He offered to deposit it in her bank account as a favor to her. She thanked him and mentioned she also had a death benefits check from her late husband's insurance company that she had been unable to deposit since he passed several months before. Mr. Suave happily offered to get that check deposited in her account as well. She signed the back of both checks. Mr. Suave then took the checks to his bank, where he still had an investment brokerage account that he hadn't closed since he was fired, and deposited the checks into that account. He then transferred the funds to his other corporate account for the housing development and used the funds to make payments on his outstanding loan and to pay personal debts.

One last and final fraud occurred in connection with the sale of lots in his housing development. Mr. Suave finally sold a second lot in the development and the prospective buyer provided Mr. Suave with a down payment in advance of the closing on the lot. Instead of retaining the funds for that purpose, though, Mr. Suave comingled the money with the rest of his ill-gotten gains and used it for other purposes, putting off the buyer month after month, promising they'd get the deal closed soon after he got through some red tape.

Mr. Suave used the funds from his fraudulent scheme to make some payments on the loan and other outstanding bills connected to his housing development, but he also used some of the funds for his own personal living expenses. Not surprisingly, Mr. Suave didn't disclose this income on his tax returns.

The case ultimately came to the attention of law enforcement officers when the bank went to foreclose on the housing development loan and discovered some of the financial shenanigans having to do with his financial disclosures made to secure the loan. When we got involved and the outstanding IRS agent I had working with me on the case followed the money trail, we unraveled the rest of his scheme over the course of a year-long investigation. The grand jury ultimately returned a 16-count indictment against Mr. Suave, charging him with bank fraud, wire fraud, money laundering, aggravated identity theft, and tax fraud. The indictment also sought forfeiture of property, including the housing development. In the course of the investigation we had discovered that Mr. Suave had engaged in another fraudulent scheme years before, while acting as an investment broker, that caused a loss of more than $120,000, but it occurred outside the statute of limitations so we couldn't charge him with that offense. The investors had sued him and won a judgment against him, but had been unable to collect.

Mr. Suave pled guilty to our charges and signed a plea agreement with the government. Between the bank victims and fraud victims, Mr. Suave owed hundreds of thousands of dollars in restitution. A key provision of the plea agreement involved his agreement to forfeit the property so that we could sell the development property and use the proceeds to make the victims whole. In negotiating the plea agreement, I sat down with my agent, Mr. Suave, and his attorney in our conference room. We explained that the land was valued in the millions and if he cooperated with us in an orderly forfeiture of the property it could be sold at a significant profit that would fully restore his victims and wipe out his restitution debt. Alternatively, if the forfeiture was subjected to prolonged litigation, it would likely decrease its value, increase expenses, and might very well not leave enough proceeds to pay off the restitution. That would leave Mr. Suave not only with no land, but also a debt to pay when he got out of prison. Mr. Suave and his attorney saw the wisdom of working with us and agreed to forfeit the land.

At the sentencing hearing the court granted my motion to sentence Mr. Suave to more time than the advisory guideline range called for, given his history of fraudulent conduct and the nature of the fraud. In sentencing Mr. Suave to about nine years in prison, the judge called him an "unrepentant, flimflam artist" who used his claims of being a Christian to get money and lull victims.

Mr. Suave appealed the sentence. And, in a surprise to us, appealed the forfeiture. His new appellate attorney asserted that the court didn't have a factual basis to establish a linkage between his crimes of conviction and the development property we forfeited. We argued that he signed a plea agreement consenting to forfeiture. The court of appeals said that Mr. Suave's plea agreement wasn't sufficient and remanded the case for an evidentiary hearing on the issue. Following a multi-day evidentiary hearing, the district court judge once again ordered forfeiture after we proved the connection between his crimes and the property.

One might think this is the end of Mr. Suave's story. But it goes on. After his sentencing, and as the IRS started the process of seizing the forfeited property, it discovered that there was a lien on one lot because a buyer had made a down payment, and that Mr. Suave had sold another lot. This was news to us because it had never come up when we researched the property before we indicted Mr. Suave. Mr. Suave and his attorney never mentioned any of this when we sat down with them to negotiate the plea agreement and forfeiture of the property. When we looked into the matter, we discovered why it hadn't arisen earlier.

After we indicted Mr. Suave and filed notice of intent to forfeit the land, Mr. Suave engaged in additional transactions in an attempt to thwart our ability to forfeit the land. He sold one lot, pocketing $90,000, without disclosing that it was subject to forfeiture. Unfortunately, the title company didn't do its job and failed to find the notice of forfeiture that was on file. When we looked deeper into the financial transaction we learned that Mr. Suave had used a power of attorney for his mother to open a bank account in her name and funneled the proceeds from the sale through that account so that we'd not discover it. He used the same account to deposit the $4,000 down payment on another lot.

It is a federal offense to intentionally engage in acts designed to interfere with the federal government's attempt to forfeit property. You can fight the forfeiture in court, of course, but you can't attempt to sell or dispose of the property once the government has put you on notice of its intent to forfeit the property.

For this reason, the grand jury indicted Mr. Suave a second time for this conduct. The court imposed an additional sentence of two years and ordered it to run consecutive—or back-to-back—to the nine-year sentence the court previously imposed. Because of his interference with the forfeiture of the land, and because of other bureaucratic roadblocks in forfeiting land, as of this writing the land still hasn't been fully forfeited and sold, and the victims remain unpaid. The widow passed away.

Chapter 25

Wiretapping with a Baby Monitor

Even seemingly routine cases can involve interesting facts and interesting people. One bank fraud case involved a rather complex fraud scheme and creative criminal conduct. It also involved the only case in which I prosecuted someone for illegal wiretapping, a rare charge indeed.

My job as a prosecutor required me to travel often between two federal courthouses in Iowa, one located in Cedar Rapids and the other in Sioux City. I recall in the mid–2000s as I repeatedly made that trek, that a farm implement dealership had sprung up along the interstate. In a very short period of time the implement dealership lot grew to cover acres and had seemingly scores of large machines, such as combines and tractors, each selling for hundreds of thousands of dollars. This dealership was located just outside a very small town and the largest city of any size was an hour's drive away. It seemed an unusual location for such a large implement dealership. Then suddenly a few years after it arose from the prairie, the dealership was closed and the equipment disappeared, seemingly overnight. During the next few trips across Iowa, as I passed by the former dealership, its dramatic rise and fall barely registered on my consciousness.

Then an FBI agent I knew well came to visit me. He was the same agent I worked with early in my career with the bumbling bank robbers. This time he came to me with a case that was much more attuned to his skill set and specialty. The FBI agent was an accountant by education and certification before he became an FBI agent. His focus as an agent was on white collar cases. The agent laid out before me that day the outline of a bank fraud scheme involving the disappearing dealership. The investigation had just begun, but he provided me with enough evidence of what he had uncovered so far to warrant my opening a case and pursuing the investigation with him.

The agent and I worked the case, issuing subpoenas, interviewing witnesses, and reviewing reams of documents and financial records over the course of the next year or so. As often happens in financial fraud cases, the feds don't learn of the crimes until months and sometimes years after the crimes have been committed, and then the crimes are so complex that it takes years to unravel them and uncover the evidence to find out who committed what crime, and how. That is one reason, probably the main reason, that although most federal offenses have five-year statutes of limitations, financial crimes have a ten-year statutes of limitations. After we completed the investigation, here is what we learned.

The owner started his own implement dealership after working in the industry for a couple decades. As is inevitably the case, he funded the start-up with a bank loan and a revolving line of credit. The bank's collateral for the loan and line of credit was the dealership's assets, including its accounts receivable. The amount of money the bank would extend the dealership in its line of credit depended on the net value of the assets (the tractors, combines, etc., tools for making repairs, supplies) and the net value of the accounts receivable. The accounts receivable's value was equal to the amount of money that customers owed the dealer, discounted to whatever degree the bank thought it might not be collectable. The implement manufacturers would also extend the dealership a form of credit, letting the dealership take possession of and title to a combine, for example, in exchange for a minimal down payment, with the understanding that the dealer would pay the manufacturer the rest of the purchase price when the dealer sold the implement.

Each month the bank would determine how much money it would extend the dealer in its line of credit, based on its valuation of its collateral. The dealership sent the bank regular reports of its purchases and sales, reporting how much it owed its vendors (like the implement manufacturer) and how much its customers had paid and owed the dealership. Periodically, and somewhat on a regular schedule, the bank would also send examiners to the dealership to conduct a physical inventory of the collateral backing the loan, and to examine the books. The examiners would meet in the dealership's conference room to review the documents and identify the collateral they needed to locate and confirm was on the dealership lot or at a farm. There was too much collateral to locate every single piece, especially when the equipment was spread far and wide at many farms. So, the examiners would randomly choose the serial numbers of a dozen or so pieces of recently purchased or sold equipment so as to conduct a representative confirmatory search. The examiners would then proceed, clipboards in hand, to walk down the lines of equipment to find their collateral, confirmed by serial number, and would drive to the various farms in the area to do the same.

In understanding this fraud, it is also important to understand two additional facts. First, each implement had a unique identification number, like an automobile's VIN (vehicle identification number). The number was stamped into a piece of metal, then riveted to the machine. Second, title to the implement remained in the name of the dealership until the customer fully paid for it.

The dealership's owner was larger than life. He was literally a large man, who had swagger to his gait, and who talked loud and boisterously. He considered himself a brilliant businessman who could do no wrong. He was heavy-handed and domineering both physically and emotionally with his employees. He had a short temper and was quick to verbally accost anyone who didn't do precisely as he said. To customers, however, he put on a different face. He was a back-slapping, joke-telling, smiling and laughing salesman who quickly earned his customers' trust.

At first, the dealership started off at a normal pace. It built a reasonable-sized office and showroom, and acquired an inventory of implements that was consistent with other dealerships in similar-sized communities. As the owner began to sell some equipment, though, he wanted to grow in size. He wanted to become the largest implement dealership in the Midwest. To do this, he needed more money from the bank. He assured the bank that if the bank extended his line of credit, it would pay off for them both. The bank was reluctant, keeping a sharp eye on its debt to collateral ratio. Frustrated with the bank's unwillingness to trust his business acumen, the owner decided to start fudging things to give the bank more confidence.

To do this, he needed help. He couldn't cook the books alone because he had employees who handled the bookkeeping. Most importantly, he had a chief financial officer (CFO) and an accounts receivable clerk. He needed their cooperation to make it work. The accounts receivable clerk was a middle-aged woman in her 40s and this was the best job she ever had, lacking a college degree. She was also a small and timid woman, easily intimidated by the owner. He used his size, domineering demeanor, and veiled threats that if she didn't help the business would fail and she'd lose her job, to get her to falsify records.

As for the CFO, a man in his 50s, the owner used effective bribery and bluffing. The owner persuaded the CFO that he knew more than the bankers on how to make things work and convinced the CFO that they needed to fudge things a little for the bank's own good. If the bank extended the line of credit like he asked and knew was best, they'd all make a bundle of money. And because he was so confident on how things should work, he'd increase the CFO's salary.

With these two key employees on board, he began having them generate paperwork and alter the books to show that they had sold more inventory and had greater accounts receivables than they really had. This required creating false invoices and records reflecting the purchase of inventory they didn't have for sale. They did this by modifying records for the machinery they had bought and the sales they made. For example, let's say they bought combine number 978937 from the manufacturer and sold it to Farmer Jones. They'd make copies of the paperwork, doctoring the dates and such, so that it showed Farmer Smith had purchased combine 978937. In short, they created false paperwork claiming that two or three different farmers had bought and paid for a single piece of equipment with the same serial number. Had the bank thoroughly examined not just the recent sales, but historic sales, the examiners would have seen the re-use of serial numbers. But they didn't.

A complication soon arose, though, the first time the bank examiners came to the dealership to conduct an inspection. When they went to find some of the equipment with the reported serial numbers either on the dealership lot or at the home of a farmer to whom the dealership claimed to have sold the equipment, they couldn't find some. The owner backpedaled a little, suggested there might be some typographical errors on the dealership's part and suggested they come back the following week and he could show them the equipment. With the owner's smiles and jokes and jovial reassurances, the bank examiners' concerns were allayed temporarily and they left.

The owner and his employees then scrambled. He went to his repair shop on the premises and spoke with the foreman and one of the other workers about the problem. First, he had his shop employees create and stamp their own identification tags. They had the equipment and ability to do this because sometimes in normal farming operations a tag might be damaged or torn off a piece of equipment and needed replacement. The owner provided the shop workers with the serial numbers he needed and then told them to go out on the lot and replace the tags on existing equipment of the same make and model with the new tags so when the examiners returned he could take them to the machines.

As for the equipment he had sold to one farmer—but then used the same serial number to claim he sold the equipment to another farmer—it would be a bit more complicated. For example, the combine he actually sold to farmer Jones was sitting at his farm. But the owner had fabricated paperwork claiming he sold the same combine with the same serial number to Farmer Smith. If the examiners wanted to find the machine sold to Farmer Smith, that meant that somehow the owner had to get the combine moved from Jones' farm to Smith's farm. He couldn't simply create a new duplicate tag because Smith wouldn't have a combine of that same make and model on his farm to attach it to. Thus, the owner had other workers take the large flatbed they used for delivering equipment and move the equipment from one farm to another to make it correspond with the false documents. This also required the owner to talk to the farmers to come up with a story about what he was doing and why. On this first occasion he just came up with a story that was plausible enough to convince the farmers that the bank was trying to screw him and this was just a temporary fix. In the future, though, the owner found it helpful to motivate the farmers by awarding them with rebates from the manufacturer for the sale of new equipment. The owner had his loyal workers fabricate paperwork for fictitious sales and submit it for manufacturer rebates. The manufacturer didn't do a good job cross checking the paperwork submitted for rebates against the paperwork for actual sales, such that the manufacturer ended up sending out multiple rebates for the same piece of equipment.

To avoid being surprised like this again in the future, the owner decided that he needed to have advance notice of which pieces of equipment the bank examiners were going to check on. The owner accomplished this in a very low-tech but effective way. He bought a baby monitor and hid the speaker portion of it in an artificial potted plant in the corner of the conference room where the examiners' met. Because these devices have a very short range, he couldn't listen to it in his own office because it was too far away. But the repair shop was located immediately below the conference room. Thus, when the examiners came he had one of his shop workers listen in on the examiners' conversations and jot down the serial numbers of the equipment they intended to find and confirm were present either on the lot or at a farm. This gave the dealership enough advance notice to quickly stamp out new identification tags and affix them onto the equipment on the lot before the examiners conducted their inspection.

Because the trips to the farms to check on equipment required calling the farms and arranging a visit, and because of the distance of the farms, these inspections were typically carried out in the following week or two. Because of the advanced notice again, this gave the owner time to call the farmers at issue and have them come up with an excuse to delay the visit by the examiners until the owner could get the equipment moved to the right location. Even then, some employees later testified that they were sometimes moving equipment in the middle of the night and getting it to the correct farm only shortly in advance of the examiners' visits.

This fraud eventually failed. The owner truly believed, I think, that his scheme was only a temporary fix, that he was smarter than the bankers and with the extra money from the expanded line of credit he'd soon be making so much money that he could stop having to fabricate anything and all would be well in the end. It was my experience that this was the mindset of most white-collar criminals. They believe their conduct is just temporary, no one will get hurt, and all will be well. But it rarely works out that way. Here, the bank eventually conducted a more thorough examination and realized the owner was using the same serial numbers over and over again. This sparked a deep dive into his books and inventory, the fraud was discovered, and the bank quickly called the loan, seized their collateral, and foreclosed on the dealership.

We eventually prosecuted a number of people connected to the fraud, including some of the line workers and shop workers, some of the complicit farmers, some of the accounting staff, and, of course, the owner. Among the charges I brought against the owner was criminal wiretapping by using the baby monitor. At the time, my research suggested that it was the first case to ever bring such a charge when the electronic device used to eavesdrop was a baby monitor. It may remain the only such case.

Chapter 26

A Woody Fraud

Even seemingly mundane criminal cases can have an unseemly side to them.

Shortly after World War II, a returning veteran from Iowa started a logging and lumber company in the hilly woodlands of northeast Iowa. Part of the vast driftless area covering southeast Minnesota, southwest Wisconsin, and northwest Illinois, this portion of Iowa bypassed by the glaciers of the last ice age remains rugged terrain with steep hills and deep valleys. Not conducive to farming, it has remained heavily forested with hickory, oak and some walnut trees. The veteran built a sawmill and began harvesting the valuable wood, logging some himself on lands he slowly acquired over the years and processing wood he purchased from other landowners in the area. He sold the wood to furniture and cabinet makers and other craftsmen. It was a successful and profitable business that he passed on to his son, who likewise operated the business successfully for decades after the veteran passed away.

The vet's son died of a heart attack in his late fifties. His son, of the third generation, I'll call him Woody, had grown up in the family business but had grown restless and bristled at his father's oversight. Woody was a strong-willed and undisciplined man who had little time for his father's strict ways and exacting expectations. Their personalities clashed, leading to many unpleasant disputes. In his mid-twenties, Woody left the lumber company and moved away from his hometown. College-educated, he worked in various positions for various Midwest furniture and cabinet manufacturers in sales and marketing, not staying with any one employer very long. When his father died, Woody was in his late thirties, married, with two children.

His mother begged Woody, her only child, to return home and take over the family business after his father's untimely death. Woody quickly agreed. Free of his father's ruling hand, Woody realized he could run the operation as he saw fit. His father's will left half ownership of the company to Woody, on the condition that he take over its operation; his mother remained co-owner.

Though highly profitable, the company had a modest office and a small staff. Woody's father and grandfather were good businessmen, who carefully watched the bottom line and didn't indulge in extravagance. Neither were versed in financial matters and from the beginning hired an outside accounting firm to keep the company's books. Daily, the office secretary would deposit checks in the company bank account. On a weekly basis, the office secretary would provide the accountant with copies of invoices and bills, along with deposit slips showing the daily deposits of revenue. The accountant relied on these source documents to maintain running accounts receivable and payable balances and the general ledger. The accountant also provided the company with a list of payments to be made to creditors. The office secretary wrote the checks and then provided them to the owner to sign. Every six months, the company would conduct a "wood" inventory inspection of logs and boards, its primary assets, along with an update on any changes in equipment and tools. Taking wood inventory was a tricky business. Some of the logs on the company's storage lot were owned by others; they paid the company to cut them into boards, but ownership of the raw logs and processed boards remained with the original owner. The company harvested and purchased many logs of its own as well however, processing and selling them. The logs and finished boards were all marked in various ways with paint, markings, or tags to keep track of their ownership from raw product to finished boards. These six-month inventory reports of equipment and product were passed on to the accountant.

In turn, the accountant provided the financial records to a local bank providing funding to the company. The company had several loans on equipment purchases (trucks and trailers, along with tractors and other equipment used for moving the massive logs from piles and feeding them into the sawmill, and for stacking and hauling the finished boards). The company also had a revolving line of credit. The pieces of equipment served as collateral for the individual loans, while the accounts receivable and company-owned inventory of logs and boards served as collateral for the revolving line of credit.

Woody made his presence felt soon after taking over operations. First, he found his desk and other office furniture beneath his dignity and purchased nicer, more expensive furnishings. He also disrupted the flow of paperwork and financial documents. He instructed the office secretary that all mail must be brought to him unopened. He'd then go through the bills and payments and provide her with the daily checks for deposit and the weekly bills to be sent to the accountant.

For about three years the company continued to operate under its new leadership. Not long after Woody took over, though, the company's revenue began to slip and its expenses increased. The bank pulled back a little, reducing the line of credit, straining the company's increasingly difficult cash flow position. A year in, however, it appeared that matters had stabilized. The revenue stream continued to appear weaker than before, but accounts payable decreased and the wood inventory was also increasing a little. Although the bank continued to encourage the company to collect on its increasing accounts receivable to bring in more revenue, it maintained the line of credit and even brought it back up a little closer to where it was when Woody took over from his deceased father.

As is often the case, a thorough audit uncovers fraud, and that's what happened in this case. It started with the bank sending out its own auditor to conduct a wood inventory. Woody was given only a day's advance notice of the audit, which gave him little time to adjust. We later learned that he did consult with one of the workers about the feasibility of altering some of the identification markings. The worker prevaricated to avoid answering his boss's questions, finding the questions themselves suspect and likely reflecting some scheme to cheat someone out of something. The worker assumed that Woody was simply trying to steal logs belonging to others by altering the identification markers. The truth was more complicated. It turned out that Woody had been altering the wood inventory records submitted to the bank by inflating the numbers owned by the company by claiming logs and boards owned by others. The auditor soon discovered that the numbers were way off from his inventory versus the inventory the company gave him. Woody acknowledged there might be some slight discrepancies in the inventories, but suggested it was due to some wood inventory being improperly marked as belonging to others when it really belonged to the company, and perhaps some honest miscounting by his employees which he assured would be corrected in the future. When the auditor then requested copies of invoices and bills for the last 30 days from the company's files to compare against what the bank had received from the company's accountant, Woody became evasive. He explained that they were in the process of moving filing cabinets and furniture while remodeling the office and it might take a couple days to get the requested documents.

The bank shut off the line of credit when it received the auditor's report. Further investigation led the bank to conclude that it had been defrauded and that the information the company had been providing it had been falsified and inflated. The bank quickly contacted the FBI and an investigation ensued. The FBI agent, an IRS agent, and I worked to follow the money and paper trails, and questioned a number of employees and others to unravel the fraud. We discovered Woody had done more than falsify the inventory.

Shortly after taking over the business, Woody opened an account in a different bank, under the company's name. He then began taking a few checks the company got from its customers from the mail the secretary brought him each day. At first, he took just one or two a week, but after a few months he took more and larger checks. He then deposited these checks into his secret business bank account. Although the company's customers had actually made payments, the company books showed they hadn't, so that's what resulted in the accounts receivables increasingly slowing on the company's books over time. To falsely increase the company's net profits, Woody also diverted some of the invoices and bills the company received, sticking them in one of the desk drawers. Thus, the company's accounts payable failed to reflect these bills. When creditors complained to him about not getting paid, he'd pull their invoices out of the drawer and send them along in the weekly submissions to the accountant, and then sideline some other creditors' bills in their place. Thus, he kept a running and slowly increasing but revolving pile of bills from getting paid on a timely basis. We learned of his secret bank account by tracing the tracking numbers on the deposit information found on copies of the customers' checks.

The obvious question we needed to answer next was what he was doing with the thousands of dollars he was diverting on a monthly basis into his secret business account. We weren't surprised by much of it. Like many fraudsters, ill-gotten gains are spent on luxuries and self-indulgent pleasures. We found records of payments for trips and hotel rooms, dinners at nice restaurants, and purchases of a new vehicle, golf clubs, flowers, lingerie, and payments to spas and European wax centers. There were many cash withdrawals from the account (which we would never be able to trace to purchases), but he made several purchases by way of a company credit card and by writing checks.

Among the checks he wrote on that secret account were some rather curious ones. There were two dozen or more checks made payable to women, and two made payable to a woman's business: something like "Suzie Smith's Services." We hadn't at first bothered to run these checks down because they were for relatively little money, most only a few hundred dollars at a time. But after we charged Woody with bank fraud and tax evasion, his attorney said that Woody wouldn't plead guilty and the case would go to trial. So, in preparation for trial we started tracking down even the smallest of the checks. From the back of these checks we were able to find where they were deposited and cashed, and through those records identify the recipients of the checks. Interviews with these women proved rather revealing.

It turns out they were high-priced call girls. Unbeknownst to his wife, Woody, the grandson of a World War II veteran who started the lumber company from scratch, was leading a secret second life. The purchases for flowers and lingerie, spas and wax jobs we assumed were for his wife were really for these women. One of the call girls was also attending college and turned tricks on the side to pay her college tuition. My exchange with her during an interview revealed more details than I really wanted or needed to know. The conversation went something like this, as I remember it:

> ME: What would you charge him?
> CALL GIRL: Typically $150.
> ME: For how many? (in my mind, I said "For how many hours?")

CALL GIRL: For one. When he wanted another man involved, the price went up to $200 an hour.

That helped explain the few times he wrote her checks for $700 or $800, when most of the others were for only $300 or $400.

When we revealed this new evidence of his secret payments to his defense attorney, the defendant decided discretion was the better part of valor and pled guilty.

Chapter 27

On a D.C. Detail

In 2010, I was recruited to serve a one-year detail in Washington, D.C., in the Capital Case Section. The federal government rarely seeks the death penalty, and even more rarely do federal prosecutors try death penalty cases. I had tried two during my career. When I went through my two capital cases, the Capital Case Section at Main Justice was to be a resource to help me. In reality, it was not of much assistance. At that time, the Section's priorities were to help process possible death penalty cases through the approval process, to assist on post-conviction litigation, and to provide some limited training once in a while to prosecutors in the field, like me, who had the responsibility to try capital cases. It had not been set up or equipped to provide much practical assistance to prosecutors trying death penalty cases.

In 2009, the Department of Justice realized that there was a need to have more expertise in trying death penalty cases at the national level and, as with other sections such as the Environmental Crimes Section, have prosecutors specially trained in handling death penalty cases travel to various districts to take the lead in prosecuting the cases or to at least provide hands-on, substantive assistance to prosecutors in the field working the cases. The Department named a new chief of the Capital Crimes Section and charged him with setting up a litigation unit within the section to carry out such a mission. It would take some years to recruit prosecutors with capital crime experience, or train new ones who lacked such experience, to have a fully-functioning litigation unit. In the short term, the chief's solution was to recruit people like me, who had tried death penalty cases, to come on board for one or two-year details to help get the unit started and to train other attorneys.

My home office didn't want to part with me for two years, or even one year. After some back and forth, my United States Attorney reluctantly negotiated a deal with the chief of the Capital Crimes Section. My office would loan me to the Section for one year, with nine months on the ground in Washington, and the last three months with me back in Iowa. During the three months I was back in Iowa, I was to devote at least 50 percent of my time to the Capital Crimes Section. As it ended up, I spent almost eleven months living in D.C., and three years continuing to do work for the Capital Crimes Section from my home office.

To say that I lived for eleven months in D.C. is a little inaccurate because I traveled a lot during that period. I started November 1, 2010, and left at the end of September 2011. During that time I spent a total of three weeks in Puerto Rico, three to four weeks in Tucson, four or five weeks in Williamsport, Pennsylvania, a week in northeast Arizona, and had a couple other small trips added in. In all, I spent about half my time on detail away from D.C. This was good because I like to travel and I got to go to new places, meet new people, and work on interesting cases. It was also good because my personal office space in D.C. was terrible. It was a very small, windowless, featureless office. Although I liked my co-workers in D.C., the less time I spent there, the better.

Work in Puerto Rico

One of my first assignments with the Capital Case Section was to aid prosecutors in Puerto Rico. A United States territory, there is a United States Attorney's Office on the island and federal prosecutors with responsibility to prosecute violations of federal law. As it turns out, there were many such violations, many of which were violent and bloody. Puerto Rico had become a way station in the narcotics trade between South America and Florida. Large quantities of drugs flowed north through the island. Connected to the drug trade was a firearms trade. Firearms are tools of the drug trade, so they were in high demand, but there are no firearms manufacturers in Puerto Rico, so the firearms supply is limited to what can be imported, legally or illegally. Drug dealers and gangs therefore sometimes stole firearms from law enforcement and security services. There was also an inordinate number of violent carjackings, which is a federal offense.

With all of this crime came a large number of murders. Each one of them was a potential death penalty case. Federal prosecutors must evaluate each such potential case and submit paperwork up the chain, ultimately to the Attorney General of the United States, for a decision about whether to seek the death penalty. If approved, the prosecutors then must prepare the case for a capital trial, which also required them to deal with an avalanche of defense motions. Death penalty cases are extremely difficult to prosecute and very resource-intensive. The United States Attorney's Office in Puerto Rico is relatively small, but had a large volume of criminal cases and, in particular, potential death penalty cases. It was also a very young office, meaning that the vast majority of the prosecutors were relatively new and had no capital case experience.

My section chief asked me to fly to Puerto Rico to help them. There were too many cases for me to actually enter an appearance and help prosecute them. Rather, my job was to meet with each of the prosecutors working on death penalty eligible cases, especially on cases for which the Attorney General had instructed the United States Attorney to seek the death penalty. I was to help them evaluate the case, give guidance on how to work up the case and develop the evidence, assist in responding to various defense motions, and just generally to aid the prosecutors any way I could short of actually prosecuting the cases myself. In addition, on one of my trips I provided training to all the prosecutors on how to prepare, litigate, and try death penalty cases.

There were many cases there, but a few of them stand out in my memory. In one case, a young man driving a relatively new BMW was traveling in tandem with his mother and sister in a car behind him down a highway on the island. A van full of young men got in between the two cars and then forced the young man off the road. Several men from the van jumped out, dragged the young man out of the BMW, and shot him, then drove off in his car. The whole thing took a manner of minutes and was brutally cold blooded. They murdered the young man for his car.

In another case, three armed young men scaled the fence of a National Oceanic and Atmospheric Administration facility. Their object was to steal the security guards' firearms. They confronted the first guard they came upon and shot him, then took his gun. Another guard heard the gunshot and, when he came running, a firefight ensued. He was wounded, but kept firing until he ran out of bullets. As he lay bleeding on the ground with serious wounds, one of the men walked up to him and shot him again.

In yet another case, there was a turf war between two gangs, each of which controlled a high-rise housing project on opposite sides of a freeway. The gang from one side conducted a retaliatory raid on the opposing housing project, driving there, jumping out, shooting, and then driving back to their own housing project. This prompted a fire-fight between the two housing projects using high powered rifles across the freeway. Hundreds of rounds of ammunition were expended between the two sides. Not one of the bad guys from either side was hit. But their reckless firing struck and killed an off-duty police officer on her way home from work, and a librarian who was driving to her mother's house, as they innocently drove down the freeway.

Still another involved the murder of an undercover police officer. The police have so many cases on the island that they don't have the luxury of staffing cases like we do on the mainland. On this instance the undercover officer was making a controlled buy of narcotics on his own, without backup. Apparently, this wasn't uncommon, although I found it shocking. He had a recording device. It recorded his death. The drug dealer either knew he was a cop because some corrupt officer tipped him off, or perhaps the drug dealer just correctly suspected it. Either way, the drug dealer walked up to the undercover officer's car and when the officer rolled down the window to do the deal, the drug dealer just shot him multiple times at point blank range. The officer didn't have a chance to pull out his own weapon. He left a wife and two small daughters behind.

I could go on and on. There were so many of these cases, each one exceedingly violent, each tragic. I tried to help each prosecutor with their cases, but I quite honestly don't know if I was of any help at all. I came away from that assignment with the greatest respect and awe for the United States Attorney's Office in Puerto Rico, and for the law enforcement officers working those cases. They were overwhelmed and understaffed. I can only hope that things have gotten better since I was on the island. It's a shame. It's such a beautiful island and the average Puerto Rican is so very kind and generous. It could be a paradise and perhaps in places it is. Unfortunately, in my job I saw much more of the underbelly of society than most people ever see. I'm glad most people don't have to see the purgatory side of paradise.

Tragedy in Tucson

Early one day in January, my chief and I were headed from our office (on F Street, a few blocks from the White House) for a meeting at the Main Justice building. While we walked, we talked. The previous day United States Representative Gabby Gifford was shot in Tucson, Arizona, while meeting with constituents at a strip mall. The gunman shot her in the head at point-blank range. She was the gunman's target and was severely wounded, but survived. After shooting Gifford, though, the gunman also shot 17 others, killing six. Among the dead was one of Gifford's staffers, a federal judge who just happened to have stopped by to thank Gifford for her efforts in securing funding for more judicial resources and a 9-year-old girl. When the shooter stopped to reload his handgun, brave bystanders tackled him and disarmed him until police arrived. It's fortunate he was stopped; he had expended one extended magazine of bullets, but had three more magazines on him, along with a long knife.

My chief said that the department asked him to send a prosecutor to Tucson because this would certainly be a potential death penalty case. He asked me to go. I said yes (I don't think I really had a choice) and as soon as we finished our meeting at Main Justice, I went home and packed. The earliest flight I could get left late that evening. By the time we landed in Tucson, after a delay, it was 2:00 a.m. I was expected in the United States Attorney's Office by 8:00 a.m. The Attorney General of the United States was flying in later in the day and we'd be meeting with him and his staff mid-afternoon.

With a few hours' sleep, I took a taxi to the United States Attorney's Office, located in the federal courthouse, and met with the criminal chief and the prosecutors assigned to the case. I was briefed on what they knew thus far and we discussed the next steps. We met with the Attorney General and his staff a few hours later. I had met the Attorney General years before at a birthday party for my friend, who was his former law clerk and was now his chief of staff. My friend was traveling with the A.G. and it was good to see him again.

I stayed a little over a week on that first trip, working long hours with the rest of the prosecution team. I remember eating dinner in a restaurant later that week while watching President Obama on the television as he spoke at a memorial service in Tucson. It was a great speech, but what I remember is how tired I was. I fell asleep sitting at my table in the restaurant.

I made at least two other trips to Tucson to work on the case over the following six months. We charged the shooter with multiple counts, including the killing of a federal judge. Several of the counts could carry the death penalty. The court initially found the defendant incompetent to stand trial and he was treated at a Bureau of Prisons medical facility for paranoid schizophrenia. Eventually, after treatment, he was declared competent and pled guilty to 19 counts, agreeing to a sentence of life in prison on the condition that the death penalty was dropped. Much of the resolution of the case happened long after I went back to my home district, though I continued to assist to a limited degree from afar.

The case was very tragic, including for the shooter. He suffered from a very severe mental illness. His crime was horrific and he was legally sane at the time he committed it, if deluded in his motivations. But he suffered from paranoid schizophrenia, a debilitating mental illness.

My role in the whole case was minimal and I doubt I contributed much. I was impressed, though, by the prosecutors in the Tucson United States Attorney's Office. They were all bright, focused, and calm in the midst of one of the most sensational and important cases in the United States. The criminal chief and his wife were very kind to me as well, inviting me to dinners in their home on several occasions while I was there, sending me back to D.C. with grapefruit picked from the tree in their backyard. I regret the circumstances that took me to Tucson, but I will always have fond memories of the people I had the privilege to work with there.

Murder in Prison

One of the other cases I worked on directly, and on which I appeared as co-counsel, involved the murder of an inmate in a federal prison by two other inmates. The federal prison was located in a small district in Pennsylvania, in a small city where the United States Attorney's Office had only a half-dozen prosecutors in a branch office. They already had another death penalty case they were handling as well. Helping out in this type of situation was exactly what the new chief of the Capital Crimes Section was hoping to provide by standing up a litigation unit.

I was assigned to assist on the case and enter my appearance, essentially taking over all the capital-related motions and practice while letting the resident Assistant United States Attorney focus on just proving the murder part of the case. The AUSA I worked with was very experienced and had been a federal prosecutor for more than three decades (at least a decade longer than I had at that point). He was fully capable of handling the death penalty work if he hadn't been so busy with other work.

I made many trips and spent weeks at a time in central Pennsylvania. Because of its proximity to Washington, D.C., and because it was in a very small town, it was easier for me to drive there than to fly. I enjoyed the driving trips, although several were during inclement weather. It is pretty country.

The murder itself was ugly. The motive was revenge. The victim was in his 40s. The two murderers were in their 30s and were both already serving life sentences for murder. Apparently, the victim had refused to join a prison gang. The gang became angry about that, and then worried that perhaps he'd inform against them. So, in cold blood they plotted his murder. It was all caught on film from the prison's security cameras.

The victim is seen walking down a hallway with other inmates headed to the mess hall for lunch. The two murderers were waiting for him. One, who was leaning against a wall, stepped out and walked alongside the victim for a short distance. The other was seen coming up from behind and falling in step with the victim, a pace behind.

Suddenly, the man behind the victim grabbed him and pinned his arms behind him, while the man who had been walking alongside the victim pulled out a homemade shiv and started stabbing him in the chest again and again. The victim dropped to the floor. The one attacker continued to stab the victim a few more times in the face and neck, while the other attacker kicked the victim brutally and repeatedly in the chest and head. Remarkably, other inmates continued to file past the melee, barely pausing, some not even glancing that way.

The attack was over in only a few minutes. An unarmed jail staffer was seen arriving. The video had no sound, but it is apparent that he commanded the attackers to stop. The man with the shiv dropped it and stepped back; the other assailant kicked the victim in the face with brutal force one more time, then stepped back as well. The attackers moved apart from each other and faced the wall, apparently in response to more commands. The lone staff member stood there, holding the attackers in their position by force until a minute or two later when armed guards arrived and took the attackers into custody and other personnel arrived and rushed to the victim's aid. It was too late. He was dead.

When an inmate already serving a sentence of life in prison for murder murders again, the death penalty begins to seem like the only option. There is apparently nothing left to deter such men from murdering again and again; further life sentences wouldn't prevent it. The alternative is a harsher and more restrictive life sentence. By that I mean that an inmate may be sent to the United States Penitentiary in Florence, Colorado, the so-called Supermax. There, an inmate doing a life term is kept isolated in his cell for 23 out of 24 hours a day. When allowed outside, he is permitted to enter, alone, a wire cage of about 100 square feet in a concrete yard, for an hour. These inmates aren't allowed to participate in any group activities, no prison jobs, no educational programs—nothing that would put them in contact with other inmates or staff on a regular basis. Personally, I'd rather be dead than serve a life sentence under those conditions. In this case, though, the defendants chose the life option. The Department of Justice agreed to allow the attackers to plead guilty and serve life sentences, and we withdrew the death penalty.

One side note on this case was the opportunity it presented me to travel to an Indian Reservation in Northeast Arizona. One of the defendant's mother was dying of cancer and the defense attorney wanted to preserve her testimony for trial by taking her deposition. She wasn't in a position to travel, so we all traveled to her. This portion of Arizona is rugged and barren, though also beautiful in a way. The reservation itself was sad. The poverty was palpable. The reservation was located in a relatively barren and unproductive portion of Arizona where there were few natural resources and little chance of farming. We took the deposition of the old woman in the only building of any size on the reservation—a one-story cinderblock rectangle that served as church, city hall, and convention center.

The people of the reservation, though, were kind and friendly. I could see they still had pride and neatly maintained their very modest homes as best they could. The elderly woman we deposed was gentle and reflective as she spoke of her son, and of his struggles growing up on this remote reservation. It was an important trip to provide us with perspective that we couldn't have gained from the evidence, even if she had testified at a trial.

Incompetency in Idaho

The last case I'll mention in relation to my work for the Capital Case Section began before I left D.C., but continued for two years after I left. It was one of the most horrific and procedurally unusual cases I worked on. It took me to Boise, Idaho, with a side trip to West Virginia.

Decades ago, in a small mid-western state, a fifteen-year-old boy sexually abused a younger boy. The state prosecuted him as an adult because this wasn't the first time he had sexually abused other children. He spent ten years in a state penitentiary. When at last he was paroled, he almost immediately violated parole by committing yet another sexual abuse crime on a minor. When he was sent back to prison for another fifteen years, he vowed revenge against society for what he believed was the theft of his youth. For years while sitting in prison he plotted and contrived the form of his vengeance. He finally settled on the plan to sexually abuse, torture, and kill children as a way to make society pay for what he believed were the wrongs it committed against him. As he later explained, he felt victimizing innocent children fit the crime of what he believed was the victimization of his own youth.

When released from prison a second time, the predator skipped out on his parole and headed to the West Coast where he began his killing spree. His first victim was a ten-year-old boy in a small town in central California. It was a random victim. He drove around the town for a while looking for children who were vulnerable to being kidnapped: children on their own, no adults present, in an isolated area. He found several boys playing in an alley. He drove his car down the alley, got out, and grabbed one of the small boys. His older brother came to his defense and pulled his little brother away, so the man took the older brother instead. The predator drove away with the victim. In an isolated spot near a rock quarry, over the course of several hours, the man sexually assaulted, sexually tortured, and eventually beat the child to death, burying his body beneath a pile of rocks.

The predator traveled north, eventually to a small town in Washington State. There, he again drove around looking for potential child victims. He spotted two little girls, ages 11 and 9, park their bikes near an abandoned house on the outskirts of town. He parked his car and approached the girls in the backyard where they were exploring. He told them he owned the house and they were trespassing and made them come with him, claiming he was going to take them to their parents where they'd get in trouble. The girls got in his car. He took them out into the country instead and, over the course of several hours, sexually assaulted, tortured, and killed them, burying their bodies beneath some debris.

A week later the predator was exploring small towns in Idaho. There he spotted a house with three children. The oldest, a boy, was 13; another boy was 9, and the youngest, a girl, was 8. The predator somehow obtained a shotgun, sawed it off, and purchased a hammer and zip ties. He also bought a tent and camping equipment. This time he waited outside the house until nightfall. Late in the night he forced entry into the house, holding the parents and children at gunpoint. He had them lie down on the floor of the living room, face down, and zip-tied their hands behind their backs. He gathered up the two youngest children and herded them outside and put them in his stolen car. On the way back into the house, he decided it was too risky to take the oldest boy, so he killed him with a blow to his head with the hammer. He then killed the parents by smashing their skulls with the hammer. He later told investigators he was being humane, believing killing the victims in that way led to the least suffering.

The predator then took the children and drove into the remote wilds of northwest Montana. It was summer. He pitched the tent in a forest, off a dirt road, miles and miles from civilization. Over the course of the next several weeks he systematically sexually assaulted and tortured the two small children every day, filming some of it. On what appears to be a somewhat spur of the moment decision, he shot the boy in the stomach with the sawed-off shotgun, in front of the boy's little sister. Then he continued to sexually assault and torture the little girl for another week or so before he decided to kill her, too. He had her lying naked on the ground, on her back, while he kneeled over her. He lifted a large rock to bash in her head when she said, "I forgive you."

He paused, then put the rock down. As he later explained to FBI agents and to a jury, he had a sudden epiphany. He said he suddenly realized that wreaking vengeance upon children was wrong and couldn't right the wrong society inflicted on him as a child. After some thought, he had the girl dress and they loaded up his car and drove into the nearest town. He asked her where she wanted to eat and she said Denny's. So, they went to a Denny's, sat down, and ordered a meal. There was a missing person's poster with the girl's and boy's photos on the front door of the restaurant. He said that he knew it was only a matter of time before someone would recognize the girl, and he was right. The police arrived at the restaurant shortly and within minutes he confessed to kidnapping the girl and was arrested.

Charged with capital murder, he was tried in federal court in Idaho. He waived representation by an attorney and represented himself at trial. He presented no real defense; rather, he used his opportunity to speak to the jury to pontificate on his enlightenment, his theory that pedophilia wasn't wrong, and to explain that society had wronged him by imprisoning him for decades beginning when he was still a child, and that his acts were therefore justified in the greater scheme of his view of enlightened justice. The jury returned guilty and death penalty verdicts in very short order.

Then the case went up on appeal where it languished for years. There, lawyers appointed to represent him asserted that the trial judge hadn't held an adequate evidentiary hearing to determine if the predator was competent to waive representation by an attorney in his trial. I won't get into the legal technicalities except to say there are many technicalities in this area. Although the judge did make some findings, he didn't strictly adhere to the procedure or apply the precise legal test. Thus, the court of appeals sent the matter back down for the court to hold a retrospective competency hearing. This meant that, seven years after he was tried, there would need to be an evidentiary hearing to determine whether, seven years before, he had been competent to waive representation by a lawyer.

That's when I got involved. By chance, over the years I had encountered a number of cases involving legal disputes and defenses tied to psychological issues. While with the Capital Crimes Section I had authored a primer for the Department of Justice on the matter. The United States Attorney for Idaho had requested assistance from the Capital Crimes Section and my chief assigned me to the case. The problem was it arose only a few weeks before I was scheduled to return to my district to resume my usual duties. Thus, my United States Attorney, the chief of the Capital Crimes Section, and the United States Attorney in Idaho all had to negotiate and agree about whether I could help and under what terms. In the end, I was approved to work on the case and given leave to spend whatever time was necessary.

The case in Idaho was headed by the United States Attorney herself, which is unusual; heads of such offices rarely perform trial work because their other responsibilities are overwhelming. But this United States Attorney had been the lead prosecutor of the case seven years before and although she had since been promoted to the U.S. level she was determined to see the case through. Two other Assistant United States Attorneys from her office were also assigned to the case. All three of the Idaho attorneys were amazingly good and it was an honor to serve with them.

I made several trips to Boise as we prepared for the very difficult and lengthy hearing. We divided up the work. We'd be presenting multiple fact witnesses and experts, all focused on trying to determine if the defendant was mentally competent to waive counsel and represent himself at trial. On the other side were three of the most prominent capital defense attorneys in the nation; I had encountered two of them in my prior work and they were formidable opponents. They also had scores of witnesses, including eight or ten experts. In preparing for the hearing, I traveled to West Virginia to meet with and prepare a prison psychiatrist who evaluated the defendant before he was tried years before. I had never really been to West Virginia before, except for Harpers Ferry in the very northeast tip. I found the state beautiful.

The retrospective competency hearing took place in February, in Boise, and lasted three weeks, or perhaps a little longer. It was largely a battle of experts. The hearing was complex, dealing with the science of psychology and tricky legal tests. The defense tried to persuade the judge that the defendant was psychotic; that his claim of having an epiphany and his claim of having a special enlightenment of understanding superior to every other human showed he was delusional. We tried to persuade the judge that the only psychological problems the predator suffered was an antisocial personality disorder and narcissism, and that his claim of enlightenment wasn't a belief that he was somehow divine or a god, but rather a sincerely held belief in having a superior intellect. In short, his belief about the righteousness of pedophilia and his sense of justice justifying the slaughter of children wasn't delusional; it was just wrong based on the legal and moral precepts of modern civilization.

The judge eventually found that the predator was competent to waive his right to be represented by an attorney, a ruling eventually upheld on appeal. Again, I'm not sure I contributed much to the effort, but it was a pleasure to serve with the attorneys and agents who worked on the case in Idaho. They treated me as an equal member of the team and I valued their friendship. I recall, in particular, the two lead FBI agents, a married couple, who had worked on the case from the beginning. After his original conviction, they sat down for more than 14 hours of recorded interviews with the predator in an effort to investigate his other murders. Listening to this egomaniac go on and on bragging about the gruesome ways in which he sexually abused, tortured, and killed children must have been grueling. Uncovering and viewing the evidence of the predator's crimes inflicted a form of torture on the agents. Some images simply cannot be erased from the mind.

These were outstanding agents who served their country well. I'm happy to know that they have since retired and live in a home in the beautiful mountains of Idaho where they raise horses and have several giant Newfoundland dogs. For a while after the hearing I got Christmas cards from them featuring their horses and dogs. I hope they have found peace.

In 2021, the predator died in prison from brain cancer.

My Continued Service on Capital Cases

My service with the Capital Crimes Section continued until I became a judge, serving for years on the Attorney General's Capital Case Review Committee. I won't delve into the particulars, but the Department of Justice has a very robust review process for deciding whether to seek the death penalty in a particular case. It includes the committee made up of members of various sections of the department along with several AUSAs who have handled death penalty cases. The committee's job is to vote on whether to recommend that the Attorney General seek the death penalty after hearing from both the prosecutors and defense counsel.

I believe the Department's protocol is as close to perfect as humans can achieve in ensuring fairness and decisions made on facts and not race or any other inappropriate factors. Regardless of the protocols adopted for the process, though, the death penalty is the most extreme punishment possible. When I became an Assistant United States Attorney, however, I took an oath to enforce the laws of the United States. That oath wasn't qualified such that I could choose to enforce the laws I thought appropriate but not enforce ones I didn't, or only take easy cases but not the hard ones. By chance of assignment to a death penalty case in my district, I became one of the few federal prosecutors at the time who tried more than one death penalty case and that led me to deeper involvement with death penalty cases on behalf of the Department of Justice.

In my capacity as a member of the Capital Case Review Committee, serving on the detail, and in my own cases, I was unfortunately exposed to scores of grizzly murder cases. They haunt my memories. To this day I still think of them, sometimes have nightmares about them. I'm glad my service has come to an end. I hope, with time, the facts and images of those cases, and the other horrific cases I worked on as a prosecutor, fade from my memory. I doubt they will. Perhaps they shouldn't.

Chapter 28

Not Everything Is Too Good to Be True

After years prosecuting criminal cases, I got to the point where I felt I had a pretty good sense of when someone was lying to me and when they were telling me the truth. I dealt with many defendants who sought to cooperate in an effort to evade charges or get their sentences reduced. Almost all of them tried to lie to some degree, fudging the facts to favor them or to get someone else in trouble. In one fascinating case, I worked with a cooperating defendant who told me a story that I thought was too good to be true, but wasn't. Because of that, her husband was held accountable for murder.

A 70-year-old man owned and operated a modest grocery store in a small town in Northern Iowa for his entire career. Eventually, he retired and sold his store. He had divorced years before and lived alone in a humble but nice house on an acreage outside town. His house was located off a gravel road, down a long tree-lined, winding driveway, backed up to a wooded ravine. His house wasn't visible from the road. He had built the house about ten years before and it included a special feature. There was a concrete enclosure in the garage large enough to hold a large steel safe. The man had grown up during the depression and had a healthy distrust of banks. So, in his safe he kept around $60,000 in cash, along with some valuable collectable coins and a small amount of gold and silver; in all, there was about $150,000 in valuables.

Unfortunately for him, word got out in the community that he had this hoard of treasure in his house. At one point, a shirt-tail relative visiting his home stole $30,000 of the cash. He discovered the theft, sued, and got the money back. But he came to realize he was vulnerable to theft even with his elaborate precautions. Unbeknownst to the community, he moved his safe to his insurance agent's office. The safe also held the man's important paperwork, a collection of photographs he took of his many power tools, and a sheet of paper listing his firearms with their serial numbers, and the description and serial numbers of electronic appliances he owned, such as his flatscreen television.

In the fall of 2012, the man visited his ex-wife where she worked at a convenience store, which was captured on the store's video. That was the last time he was seen alive. When his mail started piling up in his mailbox and he hadn't been in contact with his ex-wife or other family members for several days, the police were asked to conduct a welfare check. When officers inspected the exterior of the house, they found the doors locked. But when they peered into the house through windows they saw that the house was in complete disarray. When no one responded to repeated knocking, the officers gained entry through an unlatched rear window. The first thing they noticed was an overpowering stench. They soon found the source; the man was dead, in his heated waterbed, and had been dead for about ten days.

A forensic examination would later reveal that he was shot in the left temple with a .410 shotgun. He was lying in bed in a manner consistent with him being asleep, the covers pulled over most of his body. He lay under an overturned bookcase, however, and his bedroom, like the rest of the house, had been ransacked. It was difficult for officers to determine what, if anything, was missing. With the help of family members and the man's insurance agent, officers assembled a list of stolen property, which included one handgun and two long guns, many power tools, a flatscreen television, a dummy surveillance camera that had been ripped off the side of the man's home, and a few other items.

Interviews with neighbors (the closest lived about a mile away), family, and friends provided no leads. The victim was a generally well-liked man with no enemies, no vices, and no known dangerous or questionable associates. His only real pastime was birdwatching, he volunteered at an animal shelter, and he liked cats. Although agents distributed a list of the stolen property to area pawn shops and the like, they received no calls of anyone pawning or selling the stolen items. After almost a year passed without leads, the case went cold and it seemed like perhaps it would never be solved.

A little less than a year later, in a nearby city, officers responded to several 911 calls reporting an apparent burglary. Neighbors saw a man they recognized taking things from his stepmother's home while she was gone. We'll call him Badson. Officers executed a search warrant at Badson's home which he shared with his wife. They quickly found items Badson stole from his mother's house. They also saw a handgun and a few long guns; knowing Badson was a convicted felon, they seized them as well. When, a few days later, the local officers ran the serial numbers of the firearms through a database, they discovered the handgun was one of the three firearms stolen from the murder victim's home. The local officers contacted the state agents and five days later state agents executed a second search warrant at Badson's home looking for other property belonging to the murder victim.

The agents found more than they expected. Of the items stolen from the murder victim's home, agents recovered the flatscreen television (mounted on the living room wall), several power tools that matched those shown in the murder victim's photos of his tools, the dummy surveillance camera, a chainsaw, and a night vision scope. Between the two searches of Badson's house, agents recovered 32 firearms. When agents ran the firearms' serial numbers through databases, they were able to trace all but two. Three had been purchased by Badson's wife (then girlfriend) about three years before the murder. Three of the firearms (the handgun and two long guns) were stolen from the murder victim. Two more long guns were stolen from the murder victim's neighbor about a month before the murder during a burglary of the neighbor's house. Twenty-two firearms (an assortment of handguns and long guns) had been stolen from an auction house about 60 miles away during a burglary that occurred a few months before the search of Badson's house. Two firearms were untraceable because they had no serial numbers. Both of these were sawed-off shotguns. One was a ten-gauge shotgun, the other a .410-gauge shotgun.

The DCI special agent in charge of the investigation interviewed Badson in his home after the search. The agent told Badson that he wasn't under arrest, but he wanted to ask Badson some questions. Badson admitted burglarizing his stepmother's house, and admitted stealing the 22 firearms from the auction house. He claimed not to recall where he obtained the long guns stolen from the murder victim and his neighbor. As for the murder victim's handgun, Badson claimed he had purchased it from a friend months before, but claimed he couldn't remember the friend's name.

Then the agent shifted the discussion to the murder victim. Badson claimed he knew the murder victim. He claimed to have met him one time when working for the murder victim's neighbor (it later turned out that that Badson had worked for the murder victim's neighbor once, which explains why Badson knew the neighbor had firearms and burglarized his house). Badson said that he had sort of become friends with the murder victim, but Badson called him Carl, which wasn't the victim's name. Badson did, however, provide a fairly accurate description of the murder victim's appearance. Badson claimed he didn't know where the murder victim lived and denied ever being at his house. When the agent asked if there was any reason agents would find his fingerprints in the murder victim's house, Badson confidently exclaimed that no one would find his fingerprints inside.

The DCI agent kept pressing Badson about what he knew of the murder and where he was on the night of the murder. Badson's behavior changed. He became fixated on a blemish on his hand, became evasive in his answers, and asked to get a drink of water. Badson evaded further questions and the agent ended the interview.

It was at about this point in the investigation that I got involved. The state agents had presented the evidence to an excellent Assistant Iowa Attorney General for prosecution, but they and the prosecutor recognized that they had a weak murder case. A ballistics expert I knew well had conducted a forensic examination of the .410 shotgun. The best he could say is that the number of pellets in the victim's head and the shotgun shell wad found in the victim's bed were consistent with being expelled by a .410-gauge shotgun. He also noted there were some mars on the wad that could be consistent with it coming from a sawed-off .410-gauge shotgun. But he couldn't say definitively that the sawed-off .410 shotgun recovered from Badson's home was the murder weapon. No witness placed Badson at the crime scene or could even establish that Badson knew where the victim lived, let alone that he had been there. Without knowing exactly when the murder occurred (the medical examiner could only give an estimate within a 24-hour range) there was no way to determine if Badson lacked an alibi. Agents hadn't recovered any forensic evidence like fingerprints or DNA from the scene linking Badson to the crime scene. And, Badson had a criminal history that involved possession of stolen property where he had purchased stolen property from others.

The DCI agent came to the United States Attorney's Office to see if we could help, given that firearms were involved and Badson could be charged with federal firearms offenses. At the time, and probably even to this day, the agent looked like he was just a few years out of high school, though he had two or more decades of experience as a law enforcement agent by the time he was ushered into my office by the criminal chief who asked me to talk to him about the case. This was the first time, but wouldn't be the last time, I worked with this agent. He was one of the best agents I worked with. He was bright, calm, thoughtful, skillful, and diligent, and his work was impeccable.

I spoke with him that day for a bit, and then a week or so later met with him, the state prosecutor, and all the other agents (I recall about three others) who were working on the case. The team provided me with a complete briefing of what they knew and what they didn't know, showed me the evidence, and answered all of my questions. Then we talked about strategy and possibilities.

The plan we developed was this. First, we'd charge Badson with some firearms charges. He was a felon and couldn't lawfully possess firearms, so that charge was easy. We could also charge him with theft of firearms from the auction house, which was a federally licensed firearms dealer; it is a federal offense to steal firearms from a licensed dealer. And we could charge Badson with possession of sawed-off guns which is also a felony. Given Badson's criminal record, I was confident he'd be held in custody pending trial. I explained that if convicted, and I was certain a jury would convict him of these offenses based on the evidence, then at the time of sentencing we could attempt to prove that he committed the murder. In a sentencing hearing, the burden of proof is only by a preponderance of the evidence. Though he wouldn't be convicted of murder, the judge could sentence him as if he had been if I could prove that the murder was part of his crime of unlawful possession of firearms.

Second, once Badson was detained pending trial, we'd focus on his wife. She was evasive during prior interviews and the agents had a hunch she knew a lot more than she was saying. Police records showed that officers had been called to the house on several occasions for domestic abuse, although no charges were brought. The agents were also certain that she had acted as a straw purchaser of three firearms, which is also a federal offense. In other words, when people purchase firearms from licensed dealers, they must fill out paperwork under oath that requires, among other things, a statement that they are purchasing the firearm for themselves or else identify the person for whom they are purchasing the firearms. This is because, under federal law, some people, like felons, cannot lawfully purchase or possess firearms. A straw purchase occurs when someone lies on the form, typically to purchase firearms for someone who is prohibited from possessing them. If we could charge her with making straw purchases, then it might create sufficient pressure on her to cooperate. With her husband in custody, perhaps she'd finally feel safe enough to talk.

I asked why the agents believed the wife didn't purchase the firearms for herself. They explained the firearms were high powered rifles, they were found with all the rest of Badson's firearms, and a records check showed that she had never before and never again purchased firearms. Hardly enough to prove a straw purchase, clearly, but it was some indication of one.

The grand jury soon returned an indictment against Badson, the agents arrested him, and the court ordered him detained pending trial. Now the race was on to try to develop a case against the wife and persuade her to cooperate. I asked the agents to do a few things. First, visit the dealer who sold her the guns and see if the salesclerk recalled anything about the sales. Second, check all hunting license records to eliminate the possibility that she was a hunter. Last, approach her again and this time question her about her purchase of the guns.

The first task proved somewhat helpful. The salesclerk had a vague memory of the sales; they took place on two occasions, about a week apart. He said the wife came in with a man. The man identified the firearms he wanted to look at, he's the one who handled them, and he appeared to be the one who chose which firearms to purchase. The salesclerk didn't recall the woman touching the firearms. He also recalled that the man gave her the money to purchase the firearms. The salesclerk said he wouldn't be able to identify the man, however, and the store had long-since recorded over the surveillance tape.

The second task was successful. The state had no records of the wife applying for a hunting license.

When the agents interviewed the wife, she admitted that Badson was with her both times she purchased the firearms, and that he provided the money, but insisted that she purchased them for herself. She acknowledged that she knew Badson was a felon and couldn't lawfully possess firearms. When asked why she purchased the firearms, she said personal protection. This made little sense because all three were long guns; typically people purchase handguns for person protection and she was unable to explain why she needed three rifles for personal protection. But then she shifted gears and said she sometimes hunted with them. When pressed, though, she couldn't say when or where or what she hunted. The agents confronted her with the absence of records showing she had ever obtained a hunting license. Finally, when asked to describe the firearms she claimed she purchased for herself, she couldn't provide make, model, caliber or any other description other than they were long.

When the agents reported on the results of their investigation, I concluded we had sufficient evidence to charge her with making straw purchases for her husband. The grand jury returned an indictment, she was arrested, and the court appointed her an attorney. She had only two prior misdemeanor convictions, so I didn't ask the court to detain her pending trial.

The day after her arraignment I was on the phone with her attorney. I was frank. I told her attorney that although the wife needed to answer for her own criminal conduct, we believed she knew more about the murder and were looking for her cooperation. I wouldn't dismiss the charges against her, but if she cooperated I'd make the judge aware of her cooperation and it might affect her sentence. I emphasized that time was of the essence, however, because Badson's trial was only about a month away.

A couple weeks later, the wife's defense attorney called. The wife wanted to cooperate, the defense attorney said, and "she knows a lot more" about the murder. A few days later, we sat down with the wife in the defense attorney's office and she told us what she knew.

First, she admitted that the firearm purchases were straw purchases for her husband. Then she told us what she knew about the murders. About two or three weeks before she heard about the murder on the news, she recalled being upstairs in her house when Badson's uncle stopped by. She was walking down the stairs when she overheard Badson ask the uncle something about whether the uncle would be interested in helping him burglarize a house. She said she stopped on the stairs and listened without them being aware of her presence. She remembered they mentioned the murder victim's last name. She also heard the uncle say that he wasn't up for it, but would help show Badson where the guy lived. She stated a few days later the three of them were riding together in Badson's truck, driving out in the countryside, when the uncle pointed out the victim's home. It wasn't visible from the road, but the uncle explained it was down the wooded lane.

The next thing the wife remembered is that she woke up one night at 2:00 a.m. to get a drink of water. She found that her husband, who said he was going to stay up late watching television, wasn't home. She looked out to the driveway and saw that his car was gone. She thought this odd because her husband's shift at the factory started at 7:00 a.m. She went back to bed and got up early the next morning to take her daughter (from a prior relationship) to school. As they were pulling out of the driveway at about 8:00 a.m., Badson was pulling in. She stopped long enough to ask him what he was doing and why he wasn't at work. He explained that he had gone to work, but felt sick, so left.

The next thing she recalled was that when she got back from taking her daughter to school and before she left for her shift at a fast-food restaurant, she saw Badson moving boxes from his truck to a storage shed in the backyard. Some of the boxes were long, she said, and all appeared to be heavy. And her husband didn't appear to be sick. A few days later, he installed a new flatscreen television set in their living room, saying he had purchased it on sale, though she never saw a box for it or any receipt.

A week or so later, she recalled that she and her husband were sitting on the couch watching the television news when they announced the murder. She said that Badson turned white and swallowed hard, then promptly turned the channel. The next day his uncle came over and she once again overheard their conversation. The uncle asked Badson if he had anything to with the murder. Badson laughed, but then denied having anything to do with it.

I thought the wife's story sounded too good to be true. It seemed unlikely that she just happened to overhear these conversations and also be present when the uncle showed Badson the location of the murder victim's home. It occurred to me that there might be an easy way to test it, though. If she was telling the truth, perhaps she could make a recorded call to the uncle, tell him that the police were asking many questions, and solicit his advice about what she should say about the trip when he pointed out the murder victim's home. If the uncle really had shown Badson the location of the home, perhaps he'd make some statements during the recorded call that would affirm her story. If she was lying to us, though, she'd prevaricate and avoid making the call, or if she made the call it would become apparent that the uncle didn't know what she was talking about.

When I proposed the plan, I half expected the wife to backtrack to avoid making a call that could show her to be a liar. But she didn't hesitate. The agents made the recorded call with her the next day. Not only did the uncle confirm the trip, he ended up telling more and, when the agents approached him later that same day, quickly and fully cooperated with them.

The uncle stated that about a month before the murder, Badson had told him that he had heard that the murder victim had a huge amount of cash in his house. The uncle confirmed that he had heard the same rumor. Badson asked if the uncle knew where the man lived, and the uncle admitted he did. Badson asked if the man had dogs, but the uncle didn't know the answer to that question.

Then a few weeks before the murder, the uncle said he was at Badson's house when Badson asked if the uncle would be interested in burglarizing the house with him. The uncle admitted that he had a prior burglary conviction, but denied burglarizing anyplace with Badson (which may or may not have been true). In any event, the uncle told Badson on this occasion that he wasn't interested. His version of the conversation matched the wife's version, and there had been no opportunity for the two of them to get together to coordinate stories. He also readily admitted, but said he now regretted, driving in the country with Badson and his wife and pointing out where the murder victim lived.

But that wasn't all. The uncle also stated that approximately a week before the murder, Badson had bragged about how he was able to get into the house to case it to make sure the victim didn't have a dog. Badson said he stopped his car on the gravel road in front of the house and then walked up to the house, claiming his car broke down. The victim opened the door and Badson asked if he could use his phone to call for a friend to come help him.* The victim invited Badson inside and let him use the phone. Badson confirmed the victim didn't have a dog.

After the uncle learned about the murder, he went to Badson's house again. He confronted Badson and asked him if he had anything to do with. The uncle said that Badson laughed, but then denied it. The uncle said that Badson's tone and expression told him that Badson was lying.

Our operation not only confirmed the truthfulness of the wife's testimony, it also developed new evidence showing how Badson was able to accurately describe the victim and knew where he lived. Our case was stronger than ever. We were also able to get Badson's work records and confirmed that he had called in sick before he went to work on the day of the murder, so he lied to his wife when he claimed he went to work and then left because he felt ill.

Then Badson made our case stronger when his attorney passed along the names of two men Badson told his attorney had sold him the murder victim's guns. Badson claimed that he was certain these men committed the murders and Badson was, at worst, guilty of buying stolen property. Both men had multiple burglary and theft convictions. The problem with Badson's claim is that we discovered that one of the men was attending in-patient drug treatment at the time of the murders and the other one was in custody from the time of the murder until after we arrested Badson, making it impossible that the two men sold Badson the firearms as he claimed.

We laid out all the evidence before Badson's attorney. A few days later, Badson agreed to plead guilty to several counts, but wanted to contest the sentencing. Two primary matters were at issue in the

*He claimed he didn't have his cell phone with him.

sentencing. First, we believed Badson would qualify as an armed career criminal (ACC). A person qualifies as an ACC if they unlawfully possess a firearm after three or more convictions for felony crimes of violence or drug trafficking. Badson had one prior felony drug trafficking conviction and four or five felony burglary convictions. Based on the then-prevailing case law, burglary qualified as a crime of violence. If a person doesn't qualify as an ACC, the maximum sentence for being a felon in possession of a firearm is ten years. If a person qualifies as an ACC, then being a felon in possession of a firearm is punishable by a mandatory minimum sentence of 15 years and a maximum penalty of life in prison. Badson's attorney said he wanted to contest whether Badson qualified as an ACC. Second, Badson's attorney would contest any attempt to have the judge sentence him for the murder, claiming he didn't commit the murder. As long as Badson could contest both of those things at sentencing, he'd plead guilty. I agreed to the terms.

Badson pled guilty. Then a few months later the court presided over a day-long sentencing hearing during which we presented all the evidence we had showing the defendant killed the victim. The judge took the matter under advisement and a week or so later issued a written opinion finding that Badson committed the murder. The judge also found under the caselaw he qualified as an ACC. A few days later, the judge reconvened the sentencing hearing and sentenced Badson to life in prison without the possibility of parole.

Badson appealed his sentence. The Eighth Circuit Court of Appeals affirmed the district court, finding that the evidence was more than sufficient to prove Badson committed the murder and also agreeing that he qualified as an ACC. Badson then filed a petition for writ of certiorari with the United States Supreme Court. To our surprise, the Supreme Court granted the writ, which means that the Supreme Court would hear the appeal. In the meantime, though, the Supreme Court granted a writ on a similar case out of the Southern District of Iowa and consolidated the case with others on the same issue. I won't get into the legal complexities here, but the U.S. Supreme Court found that the Iowa burglary statute couldn't be used as a predicate offense to establish a crime of violence for purposes of ACC status. The Court then remanded Badson's case back to the district court for resentencing in light of its decision in the other cases. On remand, the district court had no choice but to follow the Supreme Court's decision, so Badson's sentence was reduced from life in prison to 20 years.

The State of Iowa has since charged Badson with murder.

CHAPTER 29

Murder on the Reservation

One snowy February night, a Native American man in his late twenties slaughtered his parents with a three-foot long machete in their home on an Indian reservation. This gruesome murder was one of the last cases I prosecuted. Under statutes unique to Native American land and using archaic language, the federal government has jurisdiction over crimes committed on "Indian" land committed by "Indians." Thus, it was that, as a federal prosecutor, I found myself trying a murder case that was otherwise unconnected to any federal crime.

A man in his late twenties lived at home with his parents. His father was unemployed and had a drinking problem. When intoxicated, the father was allegedly verbally abusive, but apparently never physically so. For some unknown reason, this man's father had a three-foot long machete which was missing a handle. He sometimes held the machete while watching television and often left it lying about the living room. The man's mother was by all accounts a kind and gentle soul who worked part time.

The tribe benefited from a casino that generated significant revenue that was shared with each member, even minors. The funds are held in trust for minors until they turn 18. This young man, like all other members of his tribe, received a lump sum payment of about $200,000 when he turned 18. Within three years, he had spent it all and had nothing to show for it but a used car. Hence he was back living in the basement of his parents' house on the reservation. He worked episodically, and mostly part time. He sometimes attended a community college, part time as well. The annual funds from the casino were enough for him to get by, but not get ahead.

The man had a girlfriend and they had three children. She had her own apartment in town and the children mostly stayed with her. He appeared to love his children, but was distant and seldom took primary care of them.

The man had a significant criminal history with 26 prior convictions, mostly involving driving offenses, one domestic abuse assault incident with the mother of his children, and one incident of assaulting a man at a bar in what appeared to be a largely unprovoked attack. He had no history of mental illness and none ran in his family. He had several siblings, all of whom appeared to lead normal lives; one was a tribal counselor and lived nearby with his wife and children.

One snowy and very cold night in February, the man's girlfriend came to his parents' house with their children. She brought some food and they ate in one of the basement rooms. Then, while the children played in one room, the man and his girlfriend smoked some marijuana in another room and listened to music. Around 9:30 the girlfriend decided it was time to go home. The oldest girl, who was around 8, however, wasn't feeling well. The girlfriend decided the girl should stay home from school the following day and asked her boyfriend to let their daughter stay overnight with him because the girlfriend had to work the next day. The man agreed and the woman soon left with the youngest two children. The girlfriend later testified that her boyfriend seemed normal and happy that evening.

What happened next isn't clear and we were left to piece it together from the crime scene and the man's comments to others.

A short time after his girlfriend left, the man came upstairs, leaving his daughter sleeping on a bed in the basement. We eventually concluded that the man's father, who had been drinking, must have said something obnoxious or mean to the man as was the father's habit when drinking. In response, the son picked up his father's machete which had been sitting on the arm of the sofa. While the father sat watching television, the man walked behind the couch where his father sat, raised the machete, and brought it down in a stabbing motion. The blade pierced the father's left shoulder and plunged about a foot or so into his body.

The man withdrew the blade and swung it again as his father tried to evade the attack. The next contact sliced into father's scalp and down to his neck. It appears the father crashed into the coffee table, got to his feet, and ran around the other end of the couch as his son pursued him. When police later found the father, he was lying on his back between the couch and the coffee table. He had several other stab wounds and one slice on the underside of his left arm that went all the way to the bone and nearly severed his arm.

The man later made a passing comment to his brother that their mother just stood there as he butchered their father and didn't say anything. That is, she said nothing until the son attacked her next. She was near the stairs to the basement and screamed "no, no!" according to the man's daughter who awoke when she heard the attack upstairs. The man caught his mother on the stairs with a slicing cut across her neck and shoulder. When she reached the landing halfway to the basement, he brought the blade down in a stabbing motion, piercing her chest and plunging the blade a foot into her. She stumbled down the remaining stairs and was heading to the back door to escape, but the man got in several more blows with the machete. When she fell to the ground he finished the job with more stabbing strikes.

Both parents bled to death.

The little girl later said that it was quiet for a few minutes and then her father came into the bedroom and told her it was time to go. He took her by the hand and led her past her dead grandmother and up the stairs where he had her take a seat at the kitchen table. Her dead grandfather was visible only a few feet away. There was blood everywhere, having sprayed on the walls and ceiling. On her feet the girl was wearing only socks and they became soaked with blood.

The man called his girlfriend. When she answered, he told her that he had killed his parents. He made several rambling statements, saying, among other things: "Are you afraid to die?"; "Just go to the light"; "I killed my mom and dad"; "We're free. We're saved"; and "My mom and dad raised me wrong. The white man's religion is wrong." He also said that when he told his parents there were sexually transmitted diseases on the settlement, his father responded, "It was right here." The man hung up. The girlfriend called a friend of hers to report what had happened and begged the friend to come over; she was afraid her boyfriend was coming to get her next. The friend, who lived in an apartment in the next building, came over immediately. They called 911 to report the crime. Then the man called again. This time both women heard him repeat that he had killed his parents, and make some other statement about his parents putting bad medicine on him, causing him to have sexually-transmitted diseases (he didn't actually have any). The girlfriend asked about their daughter and he said she was fine. Then the man hung up.

A few minutes later he showed up at his brother's house. His sister-in-law answered the door and saw him standing on the porch without a coat. She invited him in. His brother came out of a back room. They saw blood all over the man, and noticed his right hand was cut between his thumb and fingers (the result, we later concluded, of his hand slipping down the metal handle and onto the blade, which would have been easy because the machete had no handle). They asked what happened. He explained that he had killed his parents, and that he was sorry. He made more comments about spirits and said they'd find peace now. At some point he mentioned that his daughter had been downstairs sleeping when it happened. They asked where she was now and he said in the car. His sister-in-law looked out the window and saw that the girl was in the car, and the car wasn't running. She begged him to bring his daughter into the house because it was too cold to leave her outside. The man complied and his sister-in-law quickly took the child aside, intent on protecting her.

The brother tried to ask the man why he had killed their parents and what happened, but the man wouldn't answer the questions. He said he didn't know what to do now. Then he decided to leave. He went out the door, got in his car, and drove away. The man's brother called 911 and reported what he knew.

Soon, the call went out to law enforcement officers in the area to be on the lookout for the man's car. A half-hour later a lone deputy sheriff saw the car driving down a snow-covered gravel road to the northeast of the reservation. The man stopped when the deputy activated his lights and siren. The deputy opened his car door, drew his weapon, and took a protective position behind his car door. He ordered the man to get out of car with his hands in the air. The man complied. The deputy ordered him to the ground, face down, hands to his sides. The man complied. The deputy approached the man and was able to handcuff him without incident. The deputy took the man to the county jail.

When the deputy brought the man into the booking area he saw the wound on the man's hand. It was still bleeding. A female nurse on staff at the county jail administered first aid. All of this was captured on a video of the holding area. The man didn't say a word. He sat quietly and complied with every request. He thanked the nurse after she had bandaged his hand. He was placed in a cell. He was monitored that night and the next for suicidal ideations, but he appeared calm.

Another prosecutor in our office was assigned responsibility for handling crimes on the reservation when they went federal, but I was then the senior litigation counsel and the criminal chief asked me to take the lead on the case. We charged the man with first degree murder and he was appointed counsel. To prove murder in the first degree, the government must prove premeditation and deliberation; that is, he had sufficient time to consider his acts and consequences before he acted. About a month later, the defense attorneys filed a notice that the defendant would assert an insanity defense.

Very few federal cases involve insanity defenses. Indeed, in the Northern District of Iowa there hadn't been a case with an insanity defense for as long as anyone could remember. There may never have been one. So, this was novel territory for me and the office. The defense attorneys had their own expert and we soon hired one ourselves. I chose one that I had worked with before who was a psychiatrist at Rush University, had an impressive background, and was someone I knew I could trust to give me a candid assessment. Although the defense expert said the defendant was insane when he committed the offense, our expert said otherwise. The defense expert didn't have impressive credentials and as I reviewed his report I found many problems with it. For example, the defense expert presumed that the defendant's references to "bad medicine" was a sign he was delusional. Given the defendant's Native American religion, however, there wasn't anything inherently delusional about him believing in the spirit world or believing in bad medicine. Indeed, it was a shared cultural belief that people can put "bad medicine," or a curse, on another person. There were enough other problems with the defense expert's opinion and our expert's opinion was so solid, that we told the defense attorney we wouldn't agree to an insanity plea. We were going to trial.

When I trained younger prosecutors, I consistently advocated that prosecutors must go to crime scenes. There is often no substitute. In one case I discovered that a bank teller couldn't have seen what she claimed she saw because a pillar would have blocked her line of sight. I learned that only by going to the crime scene and standing where she stood. Here, I felt it important that my co-counsel and I go to the crime scene so that we could fully understand how the attack occurred. In particular, I was troubled by the hacking slice across the backside of the father's arm. No one could explain to me how it occurred. It seemed like an odd injury because it seemed as if it would have required the defendant to swing the machete in an upward movement and at an odd angle. I was also bothered by photos of the father from the crime scene. Several photos showed him lying on his back where he was found on the floor of the living room. He was wearing gym shorts and a t-shirt. Blood was everywhere, but the blood on his right leg had a peculiar pattern. Although he was lying on his back, the blood on his right calf appeared to have dried while flowing upward. The agents assured me that no officer had moved the victim's body before it was photographed. Again, no one could explain to me how the blood had defied gravity and flowed upward.

When we visited the house, I was able to arrive at an answer for the slice that nearly severed the father's arm. Once we were in the house, I was able to get a feel for the layout and dimensions of the room. It appeared to me that at one point the father got behind the couch and was near the door, but the door opened inward toward the wall. Because of the location of the couch, the father had to open the door most of the way before there would be room for him to slip by the couch and out the door. The father was right-handed. I concluded he grabbed the door handle with his right hand and was trying to open it when the defendant attacked him in the narrow space between the couch and wall. The father must have raised his left arm up to block the blow that his son was directing toward his head. Hence the deep slice across the back of the father's upper left arm. The defendant hadn't brought the blade upward, after all, but downward. The slice that nearly severed the father's arm was a defensive wound. This would prove important at trial because the defense was also claiming the father had first attacked the son and the son killed his father in self-defense. This evidence suggested just the opposite.

In preparation for trial, I once again called upon the Special Projects Unit of the FBI. This time, I requested they make a replica machete. The machete itself was evidence, and in any event it was heavy and sharp. Yet, I thought it was going to be important for the medical examiner to have a replica of the murder weapon to explain the entry wounds on the victims. It would also be helpful to me in argument to show how the defendant struck his parents. The Special Projects Unit came through, as always. They created an exact replica with the same dimensions and even painted it silver to make it appear the same color as the raw steel of the machete. Only the replica was made out of balsa wood and thus was very lightweight and easily handled and, importantly, not sharp and dangerous.

The case came on for trial and it lasted a couple weeks. The insanity defense is an affirmative defense. In practice, that means the government first puts on evidence showing the defendant committed the crime and had the necessary premeditation to commit murder. The defense next presents its expert and other witnesses to try to prove that the defendant was insane at the time he committed the offense. The government then has an opportunity to present its own expert and other witnesses to rebut the insanity defense.

I took on the defense expert in cross examination and tore him apart in multiple ways, from his lack of qualifications, erroneous assumptions, and selective focus on evidence that supported his conclusion while ignoring evidence that didn't support his opinion. Our expert performed well and we emphasized through him and other witnesses the deficiencies in the defense theory. First, there was absolutely no history of mental illness in the defendant or even his extended family. Second, the defendant made statements, like apologizing to his brother for killing their parents, showing he fully understood the wrongfulness of his conduct. We also pointed out how his behavior immediately after the murders was calm and reasonable; he didn't harm his daughter, he left her with his brother, he obeyed the deputy's commands, and he acted completely normal when he was booked and treated by the nurse for his injury.

The defense closing argument, presented by a very talented and experienced Assistant Federal Public Defender (and an all-around great guy), pushed an attractive theme. That is, anyone who slaughters his parents in cold blood with a machete without provocation must be insane. In other words, he argued that no sane person would commit such a horrendous crime. He suggested alternatively that the father first attacked the defendant and the defendant only killed his father in self-defense. He argued that this act caused something to snap in the defendant's mind and then the defendant attacked his mother in a fit of insanity.

I presented the closing argument for the government. I emphasized our solid rebuttal of the insanity defense for all the reasons I mentioned above, going over the evidence in some detail. At some point I turned to address the defense theory that the attack on the father was made in self-defense. Only a few minutes before closing arguments, as I was going back over the photographs of the crime scene, it suddenly came to me like an epiphany why the blood on the father's leg was defying gravity by flowing upward. During closing argument, I revealed my conclusion.

I first pointed out all the evidence showing that the first wound occurred while the father was sitting on the couch. I pointed out the defensive wound across the back of his arm that occurred while he was trying to flee the home. Finally, I pointed out that he received what was probably the final, fatal stab wound to his chest that entered above his right nipple and the trajectory was downward into his chest cavity. That meant, I pointed out to the jury, that the defendant was somehow above the victim when he struck this blow. "How could that be when the father and son were roughly of the same height?" I asked rhetorically.

Then I got down on my right knee in front of the jury box.

"It's because the defendant's father was down on his knee," I explained. "The defendant stabbed his father while he was down on his knee. And the defendant's father had been on his knee for a minute or two. This means that the defendant had plenty of time to think about what he was about to do, time to deliberate. And how do we know he was down on one knee for a minute or two before the defendant struck him one last time?"

At this point I clicked the remote to show the next photo on my Power Point slides I was using in closing argument. What came up on the screen before the jury was the closeup shot of the father's right leg with the blood flowing upward on his right calf.

"Blood flows downward with gravity, members of the jury. The victim was found on his back, but the blood here on his calf flows upward. This only works with physics if you realize that he was down on one knee. And he was there long enough for the blood to flow in two or three inch drips down the side of his calf and begin to dry."

When I stood up I could tell from the jurors' expressions that they understood and appreciated the significance of that evidence in explaining both that the defendant wasn't acting in self-defense and also that he had time to think about what he was doing.

The jury ultimately returned guilty verdicts of murder in the second degree, however, finding the defendant didn't premeditate the murders. Despite what I thought was compelling evidence through the blood defying gravity that the defendant had plenty of time to premeditate his father's murder, I understood how the jury could find that perhaps the defendant was acting with rage when he attacked his father. I never understood, though, how the jurors concluded that the cold-blooded murder of his mother wasn't premeditated. The defendant had mentioned to family members that his mother saw him kill his father and then he attacked her unprovoked. She was a foot shorter than the defendant and posed no threat to him.

At the sentencing hearing, the judge found that the defendant committed first degree murder and imposed life sentences. In the federal system, a judge can base a sentence on evidence that a jury didn't find beyond a reasonable doubt because the burden of proof at sentencing is by a preponderance of the evidence, a lower standard. Thus, although jury didn't think there was sufficient evidence of premeditation beyond a reasonable doubt, the judge thought there was by a preponderance of the evidence. Because the statutory maximum sentence for second-degree murder is life in prison, the judge was able to sentence the defendant to life even though he was acquitted of first-degree murder.

What, indeed, compels a man to slaughter his parents one cold night in February without provocation? It wasn't insanity; the jury decided that and the science showed he wasn't suffering from any mental disease or defect. I guess in the end it is what I told the jury. Humans can be inhumane and are capable of inexplicable cruelty. Here, we had a man who had failed, was living in the basement of his parents' home, had blown through $200,000, and had children to support, but lacked a full-time job. All it took, perhaps, was one thoughtless, cruel comment from his intoxicated father to light the fuse that resulted in his explosion.

Conclusion

Such are the memories of this former federal prosecutor. Lost in the folds of my mind are hundreds of other vignettes and incidents that surface from time to time when I hear or see or smell something that tugs at a string and releases them to my consciousness. But here I have reduced to writing those tales that I remember most, even when I strive to forget some of them.

As I ponder the stories I have written here, I reflect on what they represent. Certainly, these stories are a partial tale of my career as a federal prosecutor, spanning the two decades I worked in that capacity. But more than that, they reflect the stories of many other people, including those whose human failings led them to commit federal offenses, those dedicated attorneys who defended them, the tragedies of families torn apart and injured, and of the dedication and sacrifices made by scores of law enforcement officers, prosecutors, and support staff to bring offenders to justice.

I can't help but also ponder whether a collection of stories is all I have to show for my career. The cases I worked, some of which I covered in this book, were more than just war stories to pass along. Each involved an effort to enforce the law, to right a wrong, to make the world a little bit better. In some small way I believe I and the many people who helped me investigate and prosecute these cases advanced those goals.

Index